BELLE and SEBASTIAN

BELLE and SEBASTIAN
JUST A MODERN ROCK STORY

PAUL WHITELAW

 ST. MARTIN'S GRIFFIN 🐾 NEW YORK

www.stmartins.com

Book design by Jonathan Bennett

Library of Congress Cataloging-in-Publication Data

Whitelaw, Paul.
    Belle and Sebastian : just a modern rock story / Paul Whitelaw.
      p. cm.
    ISBN-13: 978-0-312-34137-4
    ISBN-10: 0-312-34137-7
      1. Belle and Sebastian (Musical group)   2. Alternative rock musicians—Biography.
I. Title.

ML421.B45W45 2005
782.42166'092—dc22
[B]
                                          2005042783

First Edition: August 2005

10 9 8 7 6 5 4 3 2 1

For the kids

CONTENTS

CONTENTS

ACKNOWLEDGMENTS

The author would like to thank a good many people, without whom this page would be blank: my dad Bob Anderson, Ronnie Black, Mark Bowen, Hermeet Chadha for the Peel sessions, Paul Clunie for that first tape of *Tigermilk*, Neil Cooper, Stef D'Andrea, Karn David, Lady Sarah Dempster who mercifully kick-started the whole thing in the first place—I owe you more than you may know (no you can't have any money)—Tony Doogan, Morin Glimmer, my agent Kim Goldstein, The Bank of Eddie Harrison (for all those therapeutic nights around the kitchen table), my estimable editor Becki Heller (you put me right so many times, much to my chagrin), the ever helpful Katrina House, Ann Laird at Hyndland Parish Church, "The" Rasmus Lomborg and Adeline African Queen, Ciara MacLaverty, my sister Deborah Mia, Hannah McGill, my indescribably splendid friends Bruce and Jane Nicol (and Pickle), the blessed Britt Marie Veronica Nordensson who supported and encouraged me from the very start—your help is beyond praise—the late John Peel for being kind enough to call me up and tell me that he didn't think he had anything of interest to contribute, Monica Queen, Mark Radcliffe, Neil Robertson (see, I did have enough to write about), Brodie Smithers for the computer and the company, Rosie

Smithers for the awkward portrait, Chris Stone, Andrew Symington, Mark Trayner for the pics, Jonathan Trew for the earpiece, Radovan Jo Ward for being a smasher, Rory Weller and all at *Metro*, my brother Liam Whitelaw (I really couldn't have done this without you), Jon Wilkins, Blair Young for the discs fulla pics, and Elle Zober for your more than accommodating help with pictures.

And extra special thanks to my mum, Heather, without whom none of these words would be written. You have encouraged me every single faltering step of the way, and you've always made me believe it was worth it. Thank you so much.

And, of Goddamn course, thank you to Isobel Campbell, Richard Colburn (even though we never met), Mick Cooke, Stuart David (for the unnecessary second interview in particular), Chris Geddes, Stevie Jackson, Bob Kildea (your covers list was indispensable), Sarah Martin, and last but by no means first, Stuart Murdoch for your hours of patience and cooperation. In varying ways I love you all.

PW 2004

BELLE and SEBASTIAN

CHAPTER ONE
STUART MURDOCH

Nobody Writes Them Like They Used To, So It May As Well Be Me

The curious boy stepped up to the mic and sang.

Here he was, finally doing what he'd prayed for ever since the day he found out, after years of showing no previous aptitude in the area whatsoever, that he could write songs. Good songs, too. Beautiful songs, happy songs, sad, sweet 'n' saucy songs with clever rhyming thoughts and melodies like familiar friends a long time gone.

Granted, it wasn't the most action-packed of settings—a half-busy Halt Bar on a sagging weekday evening—but with guitar in hand, an open mic before him, the city's secret poet was ready to either expose his folly or announce his brilliance to an unsuspecting world. And although Glasgow had more than its fair share of budding singer/songwriters, the curious boy knew that he was smarter than yer average. But still he was tired—more so than even the earliest early bird in this room could ever really understand—and God knows he was nervous as hell in front of all these strangers. He hadn't bothered to invite any of his friends for fear of falling on his ass, and in any case, they probably would've laughed, rolled their eyes like exasperated if affectionate teachers, and put it down as just another one of his daft ideas.

But this was different. This time he'd cracked it.

He just needed other people to realize it first, other, like-minded people—

1

sucker punch 'em with his prose and song—who could nurture his ideas and dress them up with the sounds he heard in his head. But first he had to check— really make sure—that he wasn't pissing in the wind, that he really could do this. His insides squirmed with a mix of mirth and angst as he pretended that the indifferent silence which greeted his arrival was actually a hush of antici- pation. "Hello there. This is 'Expectations,'" he said—too late to stop now— and, imagining himself back in the choir, opened up his heart and sang.

"I Was Happy for a Day in 1975"

Scotland's greatest poet was born in Alloway, an otherwise unremark- able town just outside Ayr on the southwest coast of Northern Britain. Renowned for both his way with the words and the ladies (he reportedly fathered a slick of illegitimate children before his death in 1796 at the age of thirty-seven), Robert "Rabbie" Burns etched his legacy in twin- kling curlicues of traditional Scots tongue, a storyteller and wordsmith par excellence as deft at the comical verse as he was at the sonnet. But just as the inhabitants of Liverpool would rather drown their children in the Mersey than ever hear another Beatles song again, the good folks of Ayr are doubtless bored witless with Burns, what with all those Rabbie statues, plaques, gift shops, and commemorative "film-flam."

Most Scottish children gain a crash course in Burns at school, princi- pally because their teachers believe it teaches them the requisite spot of cultural history amidst the algebra and ritual humiliation, but one can only imagine the indoctrination ordained upon the children of his hometown. Although born in the south side of Glasgow, the child chris- tened Stuart Lee Murdoch in 1968 was brought up in Alloway from the age of six, and listened, like most of his classmates, half-intrigued half- bemused by his teacher's attempts to translate the archaic genius of randy Rabbie into something which could capture their imaginations in the same way as the lyrics of Bowie or Bon Scott. "It was compulsory, the learning of Burns poems, and the singing of Burns songs," states Murdoch matter-of-factly. "And my general keenness and swottiness came into play. I'd always come up against another kid in my class called Gill McCallum, and he usually came first in the poetry, but I maybe used to edge him out with the singing." It's a cherishable and telling snapshot: the preteen Belle and Sebastian singer belting out "Tam

O'Shanter" with precocious assurance, quietly determined to make his voice heard above those of his peers. "I'd hit the notes, put it that way," he shrugs. "I was always good with the drama."

A nascent appreciation of the beauty of language must have buried itself deep in the Murdoch subconscious during those interminable afternoons at Alloway Primary. The poor kid didn't know it yet, but one day a great many people would bestow the mantle of poet upon his own slender shoulders, whether he wanted them to or not.

Very few people with an eye on pop stardom have had the temerity or guts to proclaim themselves a poet—Jim Morrison being a notably brazen exception—and years later, when wide-eyed acolytes would push him to acknowledge his lyrical prowess, Murdoch would skirt the issue with understandable circumspection.

"I find poetry a difficult word to throw around. Most poetry is pish," he states emphatically. "But it can be something special beyond everyday expression. Great words almost always reduce me to tears because, compared to what's normally going on, it's a relief to know that beauty can exist."

"Seven to Eight Years Old, Well, That's Pretty Small"

It was, by his own account, a perfectly normal childhood. As Kennedy and King fell to the assassin's bullet, as tanks rolled through riot-torn Paris and a middle-class ex-economics student from London bawled of fighting in the streets, baby Stuart Murdoch plopped out into a distinctly unswinging '60s still groping towards the modern age (the Murdoch home still possessed an outside toilet). Preceded by a sister, Audrey, he was the first son gifted to Robert and Norma Murdoch, eventually followed three years later by a brother, Fraser. Robert Murdoch spent his adult life in the merchant navy, and later worked for West of Scotland ferry firm Caledonian MacBrae. Father Murdoch's salty veins evidently sliced a sluice into those of young Fraser, who followed his father's career path almost to the letter,[1] while mother Murdoch gained employment as

---

[1] This, as you've doubtless gathered, is the brother who came out at his sister's wedding day in the dream which inspired "The State I Am In," but who, as Murdoch was at pains to point out on stage at the Glastonbury festival in 2002, categorically didn't really, no siree, not at all, actually. But one can only wonder what the younger, definitely heterosexual, Murdoch sibling thought when he first heard the song.

a nurse at Glasgow's Victoria Infirmary before going on to deliver half the south side's offspring as a mobile midwife. "She was carried around in what those days seemed like a limousine," Stuart recalls. "I loved the fact that I was actually born at home, in Fereneze Avenue in Clarkston," he says, emphasizing the address with nostalgic pride. "People always say, 'Oh, right, was it a DIY job?'"

The Murdochs' future musical protégé seems to recall nothing but idyllic family flashbacks from his early childhood. Fittingly, his earliest memory revolves around music. And feces. "My dad used to sing excerpts from *Carmen* as he took us up to bed on his shoulders. But before you went to bed, you'd visit the potty, and the song that he sang for some reason was "The Toreador Song" from *Carmen,* but he adapted it to [sings with gusto], 'Tore the potty, To-ore the potty.'" He laughs incredulously, but with evident affection for his father's gleeful operatic daftness.

Baby Stuart with his older sister Audrey. Photo courtesy of the Murdoch family.

Stuart grew into an intelligent, inquisitive child, albeit something of a dreamer, a trait hungrily fed by his voracious appetite for movies, TV, and books. In fact, young master Murdoch spent much of his childhood wrapped up in books, and tellingly two of his favorites—and indeed they remain so to this day—were *The Screwtape Letters* and *Surprised by Joy* by *Chronicles of Narnia* author C. S. Lewis, a one-time atheist turned devout Christian whose lyrical expositions of faith evidently compounded Murdoch's own developing beliefs.

"My Faith Is Like a Bullet, My Belief Is Like a Bolt"

While the Murdoch family of Ayr could hardly be considered devout, they did attend church every Sunday, and their children were taught the teachings of Gentle Jesus from an early age. "My dad was often away, but my mum was always in the choir, and involved in the church music club," he recalls. "I was always in Sunday school, and in the music club and scouts. But I really never thought of our family as being overtly religious, it never occurred to me for a minute. It just seemed to be something that you did—we never sat and talked about it."

The sense of benevolent community prevalent amongst the church cabal obviously struck a chord with the young Murdoch, and years later when he would take on the job of caretaker at Hyndland Parish Church in Glasgow, he would wax lyrical about the sense of belonging that comes with being part of such a community, a feeling, in fact, that Belle and Sebastian fans—or members of any galvanized subculture for that matter—can doubtless empathize with. His faith would become increasingly important to him as the years rolled by, but for now the kid just wanted to rock.

"I'd Rather Be in Tokyo, I'd Rather Listen to Thin Lizzy-o"

One could be forgiven for imagining that li'l Stu grew up on a strict diet of Donovan and The Left Banke, but his earlier musical predilections bore a surprisingly heavier bent. Before he hit his teens he was already a devout fan of such unreconstructed rock titans as Deep Purple, Status Quo, and especially Thin Lizzy and AC/DC. Stuart describes his foray into the hard rock garden as "just a little enclave of music I got into," a badge he chose to wear in order to inveigle himself amongst his peers. "Kids like to affiliate themselves with something, and I affiliated myself with heavy rock. But before that I was always into pop tunes, and the good thing about those three groups [Lizzy, 'DC, Quo] in particular was the tunes, the songs, and that's why I can still listen to them. The lyrics say something to you. Phil Lynott and Bon Scott, and to a lesser extent, maybe the Quo guys, you got this feeling of lads turning into men, and the adventures that they got into. You got a feeling of people who had dropped out, people who had been lost, definitely loners up against the world, and you sort of empathize with these big guys when you're twelve—you wanted to be Lynott, you wanted to be like him, you wanted him to be your big brother. I still do."

Upon the release of their tight and shiny pop LP, *Dear Catastrophe Waitress,* in 2003, by which time the band—and Stuart in particular—had relaxed their notorious aversion to the press to the point where they were almost becoming ubiquitous, many an eyebrow was raised when this supposedly un–rock 'n' roll creature was heard proclaiming a sincere affection for the music of the metal behemoths who initially opened his preteen eyes to the majesty of rock. To fans this may not have come as that much of a surprise—the band had after all covered Lizzy's "The Boys Are Back in Town" in concert on a few occasions—but to the majority it was a revelation akin to Angela Lansbury coming out as a Rammstein fanatic.

Like most impressionable kids, Murdoch followed the cultural fads of the playground. After all, if you don't know that Nick Drake is out there waiting for you, you're not going to risk your neck looking for him when you can happily boogie at home with the 'DC. Displaying solidarity with the record collections of tuned-in friends is, after all, a much safer and more attractive option to someone not wishing to draw undue attention to themselves. This may not correspond with the widely imagined notion of Murdoch as the archetypal outsider, but as he himself recalls: "The only music I ever heard at that time was what other people were listening to. I didn't start listening to the music that I still listen to today until I went to university. At school I ran with the pack, just like most kids."[2] But you never forget your first love, and he would later pay tribute to his formative musical fumbles with the Lizzy-esque "I'm a Cuckoo" on *Dear Catastrophe Waitress* (featuring the brilliantly silly couplet *"I'd rather be in Tokyo/I'd rather listen to Thin Lizzy-o"*), an album produced by Trevor Horn, who by coincidence was briefly linked with another early influence: Yes.[3]

These bathetically ludicrous prog-rockers have become pop shorthand for the very worst excesses of the pre-punk '70s. Post '77, Yes—with their ale, capes, and triple gatefold concept beards—were vilified as obsolete dinosaurs, but without any barometer of cool with which to gauge his listening habits, young Stuart Murdoch unselfconsciously adored what he heard on the band's early records. Once his sister bequeathed him a Yes album on his thirteenth birthday, Stuart was inducted into a much more expansive, seemingly intellectual music club, whose obfuscating lyrics and shimmering sound-scapes must have seemed like transmissions from another galaxy to someone used to the four-square riffology of heavy rock. "I sometimes think, 'Why do I still like that band?'" he muses, not unreasonably, before adding with some significance, "But by that time it was the prettiness of the music and the ambition."

A sensitive soul such as he was never going to be fully satisfied by the macho posturings of AC/DC, and as he entered his teens, Stuart evidently found something to savor in the mysterious peregrinations of Yes, in whose music he claims to have found a purity of vision which eventually came to bear upon his own work with Belle and Sebastian. As unlikely as it might seem, these earnest longhairs taught him that music could be beautiful and enigmatic, and that a distinctive vision could be created through a firmly held commitment to a firmly held aesthetic. Fortunately, he realized before it was too late that a commitment to foolish capes and Tolkien-esque drivel wasn't the kind of aesthetic he wished to embrace, but it's clear that some kind of lesson had been learned.

Even today, he can't resist dragging out his old vinyl playmates. Indeed, since hitting thirty, he claims to have entered a full-blown second

---

2 His nickname at school was the rather unimaginative "Murdy," which somehow morphed into "Merdy," then "Le Merde"—The Shit. Lovely.

3 Horn had a brief and disastrous stint as Yes frontman in the early '80s.

adolescence. "Since maybe being thirty-one/thirty-two, I honestly feel that my personality is more in line with what I felt when I was twelve, which was a golden age for me. I feel the same person I was when I was twelve. I don't know what Freud or my folks would have to say about that, but it's *great*. It's funny, when you reach the grand old age of thirty-two, you realize that you *really* want to play football, you *really* want to listen to AC/DC, and you *really* want to chase girls around, and that's what I did when I was twelve. It's kinda worrying, maybe. But I'm not worried about it."

"We Rule the School"

Stuart looks back on his formative schooling at Alloway Primary with unabashed affection, painting it as a fantasy haven in stark contrast to his secondary school, Belmont Academy. "You were just left to dream. It was a kind of dreamy time. The days seemed to stretch endlessly, during which you never seemed to do very much, you kind of amused yourself with playing and making up games."

It was at primary school that he made his first faltering steps into making music for himself, thanks to piano lessons "enforced" upon him by his unwittingly prophetic parents. "There's a group of things that you got when you were a kid that you maybe resented at the time," he says, "but which seem to have come with you down the years, the memory has grown and grown, while things that you were really into as a kid have faded. The cultured things that you fought against at the time—things like Burns, certain books that your auntie might've put into your mitts at the time, and piano lessons, which I enjoyed fitfully, but I'd much rather have been playing football—you're so thankful for now. The memories are so nice, the catalogue of musical pieces you played when you were young that you played so often, you'll never forget them."

Once suitably confident behind the keys (he eventually reached grade six), Stuart decided that the time had come to propel himself into the pop 'n' roll stratosphere. And where better to start than in the halls of Alloway Primary, Ayrshire? Years before Belle and Sebastian, Stuart Murdoch played a part in another eight-piece mixed-sex pop combo, namely his school band The Kintyre Keynotes, with whom he played piano, alongside his best friend Brian on acoustic guitar, Brian's twin sister Laura on second guitar, Jennie and Linda on violin, Tracy on tenor horn, and Iain and Hazel supplying indispensable maraca backbone. In between stuffing mountains of sugary confectionary down their necks at rehearsals, the Keynotes managed to knock together some instrumental Beatles covers and secure themselves a few bookings at school concerts and parties—as well as in front of residential and mentally handicapped audiences—during which they wore customized shirts designed by the twins' mum. Years later he would candidly recall in his online diary that before each performance, the band regularly "shat ourselves" and as he laughingly admits, the troupe prefigured Belle and Sebastian in an undeniable way. "If you look at a picture of the group now, it pretty much looks like Belle and Sebastian," he smiles. "It's almost the same lineup, only there's more girls. [But] it's the same kind of mixture."

Later, with Stuart's plangent piano to the fore on songs such as "The Fox in the Snow" and "You Made Me Forget My Dreams," Belle and Sebastian would often be compared to the sadly innocent sound of a school band at assembly, and one can only presume that it's exactly this air of long-gone melancholy that the former Kintyre Keynote was attempting to conjure up.

Much has been made of the recurring themes of adolescent angst and school-days innocence in his songs, causing some critics to accuse him of wallowing in a shallow paddling pool of arrested development, and certainly the number of songs he's written concerning confused adolescents might be considered a tad strange coming from a man in his thirties, and yet there is obviously something about these years which he finds endlessly inspirational. "I tend to base quite a lot of these characters on young people, people younger than me or in the school environment," he explains. "And that comes from having these feelings as an adult, but when you put them in a school environment people can relate to them straight away. You know it was something everybody went through, secondary school between the ages of twelve and sixteen, everybody was contained within that world so you can play out these little stories and fantasies. It wasn't conscious, but it felt good to go back there and explore those feelings."

For someone whose own school days ended nearly twenty years ago,

Stuart Murdoch has still managed to maintain an often sublimely affecting understanding of what it means to be young, free, and confused. It may come as no surprise, then, to learn that not only did he fall victim to the standard bouts of adolescent ennui, he claims he was positively "awash with the stuff." Although his preteen life was something of an idyll, his years at Belmont Academy in Ayr coincided with the inevitable erosion of innocence and all the angst-wracked gloom that comes with this momentous and unprepared-for metamorphosis. Table for one, Mr. Puberty?

"Like many people, I had a sullen period when I got to thirteen/fourteen," he says. "But, I tell you, the first couple of years at Belmont were stupendous. It was a city, a kid's city. It was buzzing all over, it was quite an eye-opener. Alloway Primary School is quite safe, and pretty middle-class, but when you go to secondary school and meet the Belmont boot-boys, and you meet kids with knives, and you meet kids with skinheads, and you meet kids with mohicans, it's terrifying and exhilarating. It was a fantastic place, at least for a few years, and then exams and work and puberty come along and it all becomes a bit more drab."

Happily admitting to being a card-carrying member of the swot team, Stuart showed a particular aptitude for maths and science, although—somewhat surprisingly, considering his fancy for literature—he was less keen on English than he was on PE. Indeed, the boy Stuart, although something of a dreamer, had little in common with the social misfits who populate so many of his songs. If one takes a tune such as "Lord Anthony" as autobiography, then it's all too easy to imagine the singer as a sad and bullied youth, a buttoned-down sap in his pristine blazer and tie, bearing the brunt of bigger boys and snickering girls. And yet the reality is that he managed to marry his intellectual aspirations with a proclivity for the more masculine-orientated charms of the playing field. The voice singing "I Don't Want to Play Football" on the *Storytelling* soundtrack might belong to Stuart Murdoch, but the sentiments certainly don't. A lifelong supporter of his local team Ayr United (team colors black and white unite), he's been chancing his shins on the football fields since an early age and continues to play in his local sport center's five-a-side team to this day.[4]

---

4 Alongside B&S keyboardist Chris Geddes and manager Neil Robertson.

Even more remarkably—again, only if we're continuing under the misapprehension that our hero is a sport-loathing milquetoast—Murdoch later took up amateur boxing in university, although he laughingly describes himself as "a much better runner than a boxer."

Ah, yes. The running.

Something of an athlete in his youth, a still-spry Stuart can often be glimpsed today sprinting determinedly around Glasgow, possibly imagining that he's racing urgently towards the airport in a last-reel attempt to stop his one true love leaving on a jet plane forever.[5] "I think I'm just naturally quite good at [running]," he shrugs. "If my thing was knitting, or swimming, which it isn't, I would pursue it. It's just the one particular pursuit that I'm quite good at. So it becomes a kind of meditation. When I run I can pretty much forget everything that has gone before. It's a little gap between the day and the night. I particularly love running around five or six o'clock, you can pass the day out of your system."

Without any prior knowledge of these athletic tendencies, the lyrics of "The Stars of Track and Field" might seem like a waspish putdown of sport-obsessed narcissists. But to this lonely middle-distance runner the stars of track and field really are beautiful people. Truth is, despite the lazy journalistic cliché—prevalent in British papers particularly—the members of Belle and Sebastian have little in common with the exaggeratedly sensitive image which has dogged them since day dot. As the band's principal creative mouthpiece, Stuart has borne the brunt of this stereotype, and while as an adult he enjoys an evening of tea and Scrabble as well as the next indie bookworm (often encased in a suit of neatly pressed pajamas), he's hardly the wan and winsome wimp of lore.

"You Are Working for the Joy of Giving"

There are no color-blind airline pilots. Stuart Murdoch discovered this at the age of twelve, when a lady optometrist informed him that he would never be allowed to man Concorde on account of his hitherto

---

5 The "I'm a Cuckoo" video, codirected by Murdoch, shows him in full athletic flight. It ends with an extended dolly shot of the harried singer bombing through the Glasgow streets, like Woody Allen at the end of *Manhattan*. In Murdoch's mind, the west end of Glasgow is probably just as romantic as Allen's Upper East Side, monochrome glow or no.

undetected color-blindness. Dreams suitably quashed, he banished all thoughts of future employment to the back of his mind, except for the dreamy possibility of one day scoring a goal for Scotland. Not that he was totally alien to the world of work; by the age of seventeen, he had already—at his father's insistence—spent summers working in various local shops, including a stint as a dairy delivery boy. "We were the cream boys," he says, with as much insinuation as he cares to muster. "We delivered dairy produce to your door on a Friday night/Saturday morning. So you were like a little salesman, with your patter worked out. I can't believe I never got mugged, because at the end of the round you had quite a lot of cash. But at that time I think I'd built up quite a lot of muscles from carrying all these crates of cream around. . . ." Another year his father marched him to a local farm, where he spent the summer as a hay-shifting farmhand. And with every increase in responsibility, his boyhood slipped ever further into the distance. "Whenever you have a job you feel like your adolescence is being stretched," he says. "You feel like you're being pulled towards manhood at a quick rate."

"A Choice Is Facing You, but I Choose to Refrain for Today"

Stuart Murdoch had evolved into a veritable flea market of contradictions. Here he was, academic yet athletic, sensitive yet robust, a piano-playing boxer with a predilection for prog and metal, and by nature a child of grand ambition but little real direction, who had realized early on that life was for the living boy, not the working man. His healthy imagination, coupled with his voracious reading habits, meant that by his mid-teens Murdoch's tousled head was full of fantastical ideas and dreams. The problem was, he hadn't yet managed to whittle these fantasies down to a solid plan of action. All he knew was that there was a whole world of unusual and exciting possibilities waiting to be explored out there, and that the last thing he wanted to do when he left school was to succumb to the concrete mundanities of the real world. He certainly wasn't lazy—you should've seen the kid sweep a pig sty, hose a tractor, hump a crate of cream—but he knew that there must be more to life than commerce.

So seeing as he hadn't exactly decided what he wanted to do with his life yet—his spirit of adventure hadn't quite piqued enough to follow his father and brother into the navy—he decided that he should probably go to university in order to give himself more time to think. As much as it was home, he couldn't wait to wave Ayr goodbye and set up stall in the big city whence he originally sprang.

The big city, Glasgow.

Fortunately—and despite the fact that he'd basically lost interest in school in his steadily evolving adolescent mope years—he'd still managed to score a bunch of fairly respectable qualifications in his final year at school, and in the late spring of 1986 he received a letter informing him that his application to study physics at Glasgow University had been successful.

Now, he thought, was the time for life to really begin.

Images of glorious bohemian excess flooded his mind: bicycle rides through leafy campus gardens, coffee and Camus on summer café afternoons. And the girls! Oh, the beautiful, bookish, mysterious university girls with their sleek vinyl bobs and suede satchels bulging with books. . . .

Books were fine, but it was the girls our budding boho was looking forward to studying most of all.

"It Was a Party, It Was Going Fine"

Before he could vacate to the halls of academe, however, there was another summer job to take, this time at Butlins holiday camp in Ayr. By the mid-'80s, Butlins was already considered archaic, a tacky relic from a simpler time, at which predominately working class families would spend a cheap 'n' cheerful week in a blur of poolside games, shoddy cabaret, and more enforced fun than you could shake a stick of rock at. But despite constant predictions of their demise, they continued to flourish (after a fashion), and as the only Butlins in Scotland, the camp which employed the seventeen-year-old Stuart Murdoch continued to do a roaring summer trade. Initially part of the cashier team, he quickly worked his way up to supervisor (the competitive streak he'd been sporting since his primary school Burns recitations still blazed bright, by God). Camp society was one which nurtured him in more ways than one.

"It was sort of like the feeling you get when you go to secondary school," he explains, "this huge place teeming with life, and an edge of danger, and an edge of sexuality about it, with all these women walking around."

On a darker note, it was at Butlins that Stuart befriended the girl who would later inspire one of his most bleakly affecting songs, "Chalet Lines." Following an after-hours night out on the camp, his cashier teammate was raped in the shadows of the maze-like chalet quarter. The song he later wrote was hardly sensationalistic, but one wonders whether he had any reservations about turning such a devastating incident into, for all intents and purposes, a commercial product. "No, I didn't, or else I wouldn't have written it," he answers, somewhat crisply. "It just felt like the thing to do. We never really play it much live . . . ," he adds, trailing off into nothing.

"You Will Be Known As the Boy Who's Always Dancing"

After a long summer counting holiday-makers' money, Murdoch was ready to embark on the biggest adventure of his young life. Leaving his family home behind, he bundled up his books and Yes LPs, and set up home in Glasgow University's halls of residence. Student life, he quickly ascertained, suited him like a faded Lizzy T-shirt. Perhaps a little *too* snugly. Continuing the trend shown in his last years of school, all thoughts of study steadily succumbed under the weight of the seemingly endless distractions on offer. Ever energetic, Murdoch became a familiar figure around the campus in his industrious role as entertainment and charity convenor. Understandably, a physics degree seems a lot less important when you've got a disco to organize. "I think you can do that sort of thing when you're doing an art degree," he says, years later. "It almost accompanies your art degree, but it demolishes your science degree. I had marched through school and been quite conscientious, and suddenly came up to the big city, just turned seventeen, and I don't think my mind was mature enough to take the leap of independence that university demanded. You had to work and work and work, and there was no way you could get by on drinking and reading the odd sonnet. This was serious shit, and after a while it became clear that I was just too distracted by this new environment."

Describing himself as "an unreconstructed, young, daft student discovering drinking and everything that goes with it," Murdoch was also more interested in working on his biology than his physics. Constantly in the gym, lifting weights and boxing, or running around the athletics track, he had built himself into an enviable specimen of health. The boy was having a ball, frankly, and although he was missing out on his degree, well, at least he had his friends, at least he had his fun, at least he had his health.

"Tenderly You Turn the Light Off in Your Room"

It was in his third year of university that Stuart Murdoch was diagnosed as suffering from chronic fatigue syndrome, more commonly known as M.E. (myalgic encephalomyelitis/encephalopathy). A severely debilitating illness, M.E. causes severe fatigue amongst its sufferers, as well as muscle pain and problems with concentration and memory. It's a devastating thing to happen to anyone, but for someone as active as Stuart, it proved particularly soul-destroying. Although by this time he'd effectively become a part-time student (he failed his second year exam, forcing him to re-sit the semester), he was forced to drop out completely as the illness took its toll, having no choice but to leave Glasgow and return home to Ayr. Entirely housebound, he compares his life at this point to that of old-aged

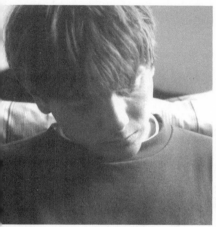

was an amazing time in all respects. Just amazingly
ing. Amazingly *dreadful.*" Photo by Isobel Campbell.

pensioners barely able to look after themselves. From the boxing ring to the same four walls in less than a year, Stuart wondered if his brief flurry of adult life was the only chance he was to get. "It was quite definitely the biggest thing that's happened to me in my life, in practical, physical terms," he says. "It came along and took seven years out of my life. I actually look back on that time and I think about happy spots. I think about the spots I came through and made progress and grew up. It was an amazing time in all respects. Just amazingly boring," he shrugs with a rueful laugh: "Amazingly *dreadful.*"

It was while ensconced in his parents' house that, out of insane boredom more than anything else, Murdoch decided, in his all-too-brief moments of lucidity, to start tinkering with the family piano. Lying alone in his bed, locked helplessly within his own thoughts, he'd been increasingly visited by snatches of melody that he didn't recognize. Keen to record these visitations, he would struggle to the living room piano whenever he could, and mustering all his grade six energy, attempt to find chords to fit them. "I was a completely changed person," he says. "I'd dropped out of life, dropped out of jobs, the city where I lived, and friends. It was full stop, new page—but there were things I wanted to say. This might sound overdramatic, but at the time I had been ill for three years, and the first seeds of energy that came back, I used to enjoy sitting at my mum's piano, and it was a case of having enough energy to sit at the piano for half an hour before I got so exhausted I'd have to rest again. But my energy grew and I spent more and more time there, and I found rudimentary stages of putting very simple tunes to very simple things I'd just played. And when you do something like that it's almost like the first time they made a television picture, the first time they made a flicker on the screen—all right, it's fucked up, but it's something, and you know you'll spend your life refining it. And it was like a picture flickering—'Hey, I can do this, I can write the words, I can change the pitch.'" The songs, it seems, were a necessity. "I started writing songs because I *had* to." Desperation, as he would later note, is the folly of a boy's empty mind. "I had to communicate with the void because there wasn't anyone else around."

After three years, Stuart decided with his family that he

A young Stuart and Ciara. Photo by Michael Mair.

was at least fit enough to return to Glasgow, to the halls of residence, and his studies. Re-enrolling at the university, this time he decided that he was perhaps better suited to an English degree, and returned with a view to making a proper go of it this time. And yet he still wasn't healthy enough to devote enough practical and mental energy to his studies, and he soon fell into a trough of despondency. Feeling utterly helpless and without direction, he started to doubt whether his health would ever fully recover and whether he would ever discover the sense of purpose he so desperately craved. Sharing a room with an old friend, Michael (by curious coincidence, a fellow M.E. sufferer), he continued to immerse himself in music, wondering more and more whether this was the road he should travel. Those afternoons at his mother's piano had proved to him that he at least had some aptitude for songwriting. In fact, he'd already written his first fully formed song, "There's No Holding Her Back," for his best friend Ciara McLaverty (daughter of renowned author Bernard and the cover star of *If You're Feeling Sinister*), herself—by an almost unimaginable coincidence—also an M.E. sufferer. The song was good, he thought, indeed he still thinks so, although he's yet to officially release it, and the ascension of sensitive troubadours such as his newfound heroes Morrissey and Lawrence from Felt convinced him that there might well be a place for a soul such as he on planet pop.

It was during his initial tenure at university that he first discovered what he calls "The New Music," prophesied by underground '80s delicates such as The Cocteau Twins and Glasgow's own Orange Juice, whose label, Postcard, was run by one Alan Horne who Stuart would pay tribute to by picturing him on the cover of the *This Is Just a Modern Rock Song* EP and The Pastels,[6] whose 53rd and a 3rd label would introduce the world to the likes of The Jesus and Mary Chain, BMX Bandits, and The Vaselines. His beloved favorites, however, were undoubtedly Felt—whose strict aesthetic guidelines would be a huge influence—and The Smiths, who he first discovered performing "Bigmouth Strikes Again" on legendary British rock show *The Old Grey*

---

6 Underground entrepreneur Stephen Pastel, née McRobbie, encouraged Stuart greatly in his early days, and occasionally let him perform in his now sadly defunct book/record store on Byres Road. Stuart would thank him for his support on the back of *If You're Feeling Sinister*.

Whistle Test—a damascene moment after which he would never be the same. "This is a strand that has happened to me a few times," he says. "Something's come along that's been like a signpost. It could be a person, it could be music, or it could be something to do with religion or faith. A signpost comes along, and at first you treat it with very much curiosity. It's happened with Hal Hartley's films, it happened with religion, specifically Christianity—although I'm still not quite a Christian. You find yourself singing old hymns when you're around the kitchen, cleaning up, and then within six months you've walked into a church out of the blue never to go back. You've walked over the threshold of a church in a momentous decision for you—and that's you. That's a change of the course of your life."

He'd already heard The Smiths, in amongst the Beatles and U2 tapes Michael's dad had brought back from Taiwan, and treated them with smirking—yet privately intrigued—irreverence. But when he finally saw the curious figure of Morrissey in all his flouncing flight, suddenly it all made sense. "In the same way as singing hymns in the kitchen, seeing 'Bigmouth Strikes Again' on *Whistle Test* was the stepping over the threshold of the church, never to return, but you can only see that stuff in retrospect."

And that was it. Murdoch had decided that he "deserved" (his word) a place in the indie firmament; all he had to do was find the people to make his dreams a reality. He had started to teach himself guitar, following the lead of Michael, who was an accomplished classical guitarist, and as he tentatively recovered his strength, he thought more and more—and more determinedly—about forming a band to nurture his increasing arsenal of songs. Somewhat unsure of himself, and still beleaguered by M.E., Murdoch felt that he could communicate more lucidly through his songs. As trite as it sounds, songwriting seemed to supply a kind of therapeutic balm, as he readily admits: "I find it easier now to speak in a more mature way, but certainly in the past communicating through music was a great thing. But there's this otherness, if you have a good song, a good couple of lines of poetry, you can paint a picture that you couldn't explain in pages and pages."

Taking a cue from Morrissey and Felt—along with musical tips he'd learned from the '60s pop he couldn't help but be subliminally influenced by thanks to its prolificacy at the indie discos he would regularly DJ at[7]—Stuart's melodies proved colorful and direct, his lyrics literate and ambiguous, full of poetic irony and unguarded sensitivity. Up until now he'd thought that sport was the only thing he had a natural aptitude for. Turned out he was wrong. Inspired by his long periods of M.E.-induced solitude as well as his innate empathy for the lost and the lonely, he willingly cast himself as bard of the dispossessed, hoping that his songs could touch people in the same way as those of his idols. One such idol, the capricious, enigmatic, and wholly eccentric Lawrence Hayward from Felt, proved particularly fascinating to him, partly because of his utter commitment to a steadfastly defined aesthetic. One day in 1994 Stuart, in a state of increasing desperation, decided to seek out Lawrence and ask him for some words of advice, some pointers, some *anything*. Through a bit of detective work he'd managed to secure the Felt singer's address and promptly took the train down to London, a billion desperate questions buzzing round his head. "I was desperate to meet the right people to make records with," he explains, "and I thought that maybe in the absence of any such progress, that if I met Lawrence he could maybe provide a spark of inspiration; a kind of mentor figure. Give me a pattern as to how I could go about this. Looking back on it now, it was unlikely that this would happen, because you find your own path. If you're going to be anything at all, it's very unexpected, which it was. But at that time I was a soul searching for musical enlightenment. I almost withdrew my hand before I knocked. I could have marched up to his door, but I just got to that point where I thought, 'What am I doing?'"

No, he thought. I have to do this myself. I have to get healthy. Get real. And so he decided, for the first time since The Kintyre Keynotes, that he should bite the bullet and take to the stage. In the absence of an actual band, he made one up, telling anyone who would listen that his band, Le Pastie de la Bourgeoisie (named after some meaningless graffiti

---

7 "I think I've delved much more into the past since the group's got together," he reveals. "It's curious, because when Beans, Isobel, and Stevie would talk about the '60s, I'd shut my ears, I was only interested in what we were doing and didn't want to know about anything else, because to me I had the sound in my head. I remember Beans talking about northern soul right from day one, and just not being interested."

created by John McKeown of local band The Yummy Fur),[8] were about to launch themselves into the Glasgow rock pool. There was no such band, of course: even if he did manage to get through a few rehearsals with some friends, the nascent band were to split up before they'd even played a gig. "I was being too serious," he consents. After so much time spent doing nothing, Stuart was a man possessed. It *had* to happen for him now. Although he was still learning, he knew that the songs he had were at least good enough to unleash. They meant too much to him to keep to himself. And despite the fact that he wasn't a naturally gregarious fellow, he couldn't wait to get up in front of a crowd and play. Wait 'til they hear *this*. "You're driven with your conceit," he laughs. "Conceit against confidence. I didn't know whether the songs were good enough—some of them were pretty terrible—but because you'd put so much store in them you had to do it; it was your reason for living at the time." And as the songs began to gently flow, he began placing adverts in music shops, rehearsal rooms, book shops, his local supermarket, looking for musicians who could bring his vision to life, a routine he would go through time and time again for around three years to no avail. "It got to be a bit of a joke," he says. "I would end up putting up these little cryptic notes, like in *Amelie,* just taking the piss out of myself." And still they wouldn't come.

"Six Months On, the Winter's Gone"

His health had continued to improve, albeit at a pace all too slow for his increasing ambition. In the winter of 1993, he and Michael, housebound and freezing, decided—like Joe Buck and Ratso with their Orange

---

8 "Stuart's like the person I've known longest in Glasgow, since '86 or something," McKeown says in an interview from the Yummy Fur fan site *www.mylegendarygirlfriend.co.uk/yummyfur/.* "He was always like the least likely to succeed, and least likely to do a band. Stuart tried to form a Krautrock band with me and Lawrence [Bradby, also of Yummy Fur and to whom Stuart dedicated *Tigermilk*] once, do this, do that, and it was always, 'Aye, aye Stuart.' Another one of Stuart's mad ideas. In fact they used to be, before they did Belle and Sebastian, they were called Le Pastie de la Bourgeoisie. Me and my sister and Jamie, we lived across from Gregg's [bakery shop], and we spray-painted that. We wanted to do a Jean-Luc Godard meets '68 slogan, but totally empty, really empty, empty statement. But Stuart must've seen it written on the side of Gregg's wall, and took it or whatever, which I thought was quite nice."

County daydreams—to move somewhere with a Mediterranean climate. Perusing an atlas given away with a pack of cereal, the shivering twosome decided upon San Francisco. Their sickness benefits weren't going to take them very far, of course, so Stuart decided to sell off his by now extensive record collection in order to fund their trip. "I had a lot of records from DJing and it was great to get rid of them," he says. "I was glad to see them go, because it was a full stop on all that sort of stuff."

And so a new sentence. Swapping Glasgow gray for California sunshine, Stuart and Michael spent three months in hostels (including a spell in San Diego), their health steadily nurtured by the sympathetic climate. "I'd never really been anywhere before outside Scotland, so this was a big thing for both of us," says Stuart, "coupled with the fact that we were both invalids. It made for an interesting trip."

For both boys, the trip would prove rather fateful. For Michael, it was in San Francisco that he met the girl who would later become his wife. For Stuart, it was where the songwriting promise he'd first shown in Glasgow began to blossom in earnest. "It was good to be in a warm and liberal climate," Stuart explains. "And that was when I'd just started to write songs. In fact that was the first time I'd picked up a guitar. I was teaching myself guitar, basically finding out whatever chords I needed to write whatever song I was working on at the time." Once he'd started, it seems, the songs began pouring out like tears. Songs written then include the as-yet-unreleased "American Schlock," "Soccer in the Free World" ("which didn't have much to do with soccer") and "Quiet Riot," a title which presciently sums up the rebellious sensitivity of his future musical endeavors. For now, however, he continued to dream. "There was a time when I kept notebooks of what I'd written, and when there was nothing going on and no prospect of releasing records, you tended to create your own little mythology, and had ideas for records in your head. So every song was carefully noted. I used to put a little flag beside each song title denoting where it was written," he laughs, blushing slightly. "Because I started writing just before I went to San Francisco, there was a while when I'd written more songs in America than back home."

No sooner had they returned home at the start of '94, Stuart immediately sold some more of his belongings—he can't remember which—and flew straight back out again alone. Basking in the sun for another three months, it was on this trip that he first encountered Monica

Queen, the brilliant Glasgow country belle who happened to be recording an album in San Francisco with her group, Thrum. "Stuart happened to be in San Francisco at the same time, and we just got talking,
we'd bump into one another," she remembers. "And that was my first invitation to the weird world of Stuart Murdoch. Once we'd come back
from San Francisco, we never heard from Stuart, we'd never exchanged
phone numbers—we didn't even know what e-mail was back then. The
next we heard of Stuart was when Belle and Sebastian released
Tigermilk—we got a few tickets in the post—and went down to Ca Va,
and it turns out that it was Stuart and his merry band of bandits."

Suitably bolstered by his trip, Stuart formed another private band
with Michael upon his return to Glasgow in the summer of 1994. Lisa
Helps the Blind were named after a story in the university newspaper
describing the altruistic activities of a beautiful girl who frequented the
Glasgow Art School disco, an essential haunt for every discerning indie
hipster. As Stuart recalls: "Her and her sister—whether they knew it or
not—used to go to the art school and drive the '60s throwback boys into
fervor, just with their beauty. So the fact that she was beautiful and she
helped blind people was perfect."

Lisa Helps the Blind actually evolved into the first of many demo
tapes—starring Stuart on piano/guitar and Michael on guitar—featuring
some of Stuart's best early songs, including "Le Pastie de la Bourgeoisie,"
"String Bean Jean," and "Beautiful," the last of which name-checks Lisa
herself. In fact, Lisa would turn up in a glut of early B&S songs, namely
"Beautiful," "She's Losing It," and "Like Dylan in the Movies." Were
these based on the real Lisa, or a construct of Stuart's fantasy? "Lisa's a
fictional character, just as all the characters are fictional," he says. "They're
composites, but they're all basically fictional." Thus one can presumably
assume that, despite what the song says, Lisa may have been beautiful,
but she probably wasn't slightly mental. Or blind. Or losing it. Or kiss-
ing men. Or anything.

But Lisa Helps the Blind was the name with which Stuart Murdoch
first took to the stages of Glasgow,[9] sometimes with Michael, but more

---

[9] Including spots at the 99p Club run by one Alex Huntley, née Kapranos, who would years
later get his own dream band together with Franz Ferdinand. Huntley/Kapranos also appeared
in an early B&S press shot.

A man about the discos. Photo by Isobel Campbell.

often than not alone, accompanying himself with piano and guitar. Taking advantage of the open mic nights around the city, he became a regular specter on the circuit, sometimes being allowed to play only one song, sometimes able to play three or four of his best. Often, he barely had the energy to leave the house, let alone get up on stage, but he'd be damned if he was going to let this viral bullshit get in the way of his dreams. As over-romantic as it sounds, he knew he'd finally found what he'd been put here for, the reason why what had happened had happened. God decrees everything for a reason after all. As Stuart himself recalls, it was "obviously my time to be reintroduced into the world of work and people." So the days passed in a lethargic blur of inaction and dreams, the nights bringing more and more chances for him to stand in front of strangers and say what he had to say. And people were listening. And people were liking.

And although the curious boy didn't know it yet, his worlds were about to collide in a suitably curious way.

CHAPTER TWO
STUART DAVID

I Dreamt I Had to Go to Mars

The attic was warm and musty, cozy like a tree house, quiet as a church, albeit an extraordinarily cramped church; no room to swing your rosary beads in here, boy. This was where the Space Boy lived, safe and secluded in a world of his own devising, dreaming of the day when his name—not his real name, his made-up pop star name—would adorn the covers of records and books all across the globe.

He brushed the unkempt fringe from his eyes and returned to his notebook. He adored writing, had already written a couple of novels in fact. No one had seen fit to publish them yet, of course, but he wasn't too worried about that. It paid to be patient in space.

He'd lost his place again, thinking now of his new friend, the curious boy from the concrete box who he had begun recording songs with. He was coming round tomorrow to record some more, so he said. They would have to crouch, thought the Space Boy, who, deciding that the words would never come tonight, closed his notebook, picked up his guitar, and sung himself to bed.

"Quiet and Small"

It was a rather special Christmas for Mr. and Mrs. Black of Alexandria. On Boxing Day 1969 they were gifted with a boy child, named Stuart David. And lo, they were a family.

Mother, father, and son were joined three years later by a daughter, Karla, and another boy, Ronnie, who would one day become a Looper just like his brother. The Blacks were forever on the move; even when they moved from Alexandria to Dumbarton when Stuart was just a few years old, they lived in different areas all the time. "I think my mum was on a mission to get to the top of the council house ladder," Stuart David muses. "I think she was seeking the nirvana of council houses. So she stayed on the list notching up the points with each new child, and each new condition each child acquired. And every time they offered her a new house we moved. Each one was a few miles closer to her mum and dad's house too, so it might have been something to do with that." This peripatetic existence meant that the children were forever changing schools, meaning that young Stuart Black wandered through his childhood in a permanently uncertain state. "I wasn't lonely," he maintains. "I was just a bit spooked and bewildered. I was only at my first school for two weeks, and then we moved house and I had to move to a new school. Then when I was getting to know people there another council house came up and I had to go to a different school."

A naturally withdrawn child, he spent these wandering days in a dream, finding his own world easier to deal with than the ever-changing one around him. "I couldn't work out how people knew things that they knew," he says. "Now I realize it was because they had older brothers or sisters. I didn't get bullied or anything," he adds pointedly. "I just say that 'cause it's something people assume about Belle and Sebastian members. I fought quite a lot. I wasn't a great fighter but I wasn't crap. Just in the middle. I threw a few good punches. I didn't back down from anyone, so I took a few good punches too. I felt a lot of the time that I didn't have any outward appearance, and I often wished I looked like certain people in the class. But when I see pictures of myself from then now I looked quite cool."

By the time he was sixteen, Stuart Black had finally found some form of stability, his family having stayed in the same area for a couple of years, meaning that he could at least forge some substantial friendships.

He had become a voracious music fan, immersing himself in the poetic genius of Bob Dylan, Tom Waits, and Leonard Cohen, as well as the more glamorous likes of Duran Duran, David Bowie, and Japan, and the raggle-taggle gypsy blues of The Waterboys. A bed-sit new-romantic, then. Suitably inspired by his idols, he decided, as so many had before him, to become a pop star. For this he would need a suitable sobriquet, having deemed Black too prosaic and unglamorous. And so Stuart David was born. "David is my dad's name, and I was a fan of David Bowie and [Japan singer] David Sylvian at the time—so I thought David sounded like a pop star name. I've always liked the sound of it when people have a first name for a surname too. There was a boy in my class called Mark Craig, and I thought that was cool."

In his final years at school the newly named pop dreamer had gained a particular interest in creative writing, encouraged in his endeavours by an English teacher who he remembers today only as Feargal, on account of his resemblance to Undertones singer Feargal Sharkey. After he left school, when the family moved en masse to Glasgow, he continued to write, eventually completing his as-yet-unreleased first novel, *Francis Point,* when he was just twenty, following that a year later with another called *The Bleach Field,* which has also yet to be published. He'd also been writing songs, which would be necessary if Stuart David were to ever be more than a pop star name in search of a career. "Pop Star and Author" hung quite snugly around his neck, he thought, and so he banished all thoughts of alternative employment to the wastepaper basket into which they belonged. Aside from a year attending an electronic music course at Clydebank College, at which he acquired the kind of basic knowledge he would put to good use with Looper,[1] he signed on for ten years ("I loved signing on"), wrote his songs and stories, and waited quietly for fate to come his way. This he did in the sanctity of his own private world, ensconced in his parents' attic in their "final nirvana of council houses, which they'd decided was such a supreme council dwelling they bought it from the council. I stayed up there for about four years after my college course."

---

1 Looper is the rather wonderful electro-pop group Stuart David would form with Wee Karn and his brother Ronnie Black. Upon first seeing them live Chris was moved to comment: "It's man, wife, and machine in perfect harmony."

"So There Was This Boy and This Girl"

It was during his years in the attic that Stuart David first started to correspond with a girl he would come to know and love as Wee Karn. As detailed precisely in the charming Looper song "Impossible Things #2," the two wrote letters to each other for nearly a year before they actually met. "She shared a house with one of my friends from school when they were both at art college in Dundee," he explains. "He showed her a letter I'd written to him from when I'd been in a 106-mile-per-hour car crash with my friend Steg, and it made her laugh. So she put a letter in with the next one he wrote to me, and we started writing. I was nineteen, I think. We wrote every day for that term, and when she came home to Ayrshire for the summer we met up in Glasgow one day, but we didn't really speak much. We wandered about for seven or eight hours. Then we kept writing after that and met up about once a year and didn't say much."

And they walked out and stood on the edge of the sea there for a while, and when they turned around to walk back to the road the boy said, "Do you want to take my hand?" and the girl said, "Take it where?" And although he afterwards thought he should have said, "Everywhere," he only just mumbled.[2]

Sixteen years on their hands are still entwined.

"You Know This Street Has Lost Its Beat"

In 1994 Stuart David still hadn't made a record, still hadn't published a novel, still hadn't found what he was looking for (Wee Karn notwithstanding). After around seven years of signing on, the benefits office told him, in no uncertain terms, that he had to attend a Training For Work course and get out of their hair for good, or bye-bye benefits. Training For Work was a recently introduced scheme intended to, as its title suggests, train people "unemployed and actively looking for work" in a variety of useful skills so that, by rights, they should have absolutely no trouble getting a job once the course was over, whether they wanted one or not. For a resting musician this proved somewhat troublesome;

---

2 From "Impossible Things #2."

how the hell were you meant to write yourself a lucrative pop future
when you had to go to *work* all week? Fortunately—*very* fortunately—
for Stuart David, one of the courses on the list, nestling enticingly in
amongst the various engineering and catering opportunities, was something called Beatbox, a course designed to offer budding musicians a
chance to become familiar with various aspects of the music business.
What interested Stuart David the most, however, was the opportunity it
offered to record your own songs in the studio. That and the extra ten
pounds a week on his benefit.

So every day (well, almost) he and around fifty other unemployed
musicians from around town would troop dutifully down to a damp,
windowless, wholly uninviting building beneath an underpass, and do
very little in the way of making music. "I liked it," Stuart David says,
"There was one room where you could do sequencing. There was a guy
called Neil who was a tutor and he taught me the Internet, how to build
a Web site, and how to use Cubase and stuff. Then once a month you
could get a shot in the studio to record your songs. And you met a lot of
good people who were on the course."

A blushing boy in a child's jumper being one of them.

Stuart David first encountered Stuart Murdoch at a Beatbox
singing lesson, during which the latter squirmed through a solo performance sporting an excoriating beamer (Scottish slang for blushing)
and a jumper with a teddy bear on it. "I thought he seemed shyer than
me, which is rare," Stuart David remembers. "It turned out he wasn't
really. But he had a jumper on with a teddy bear or something on it,
and I thought I knew where he was coming from 'cause Karn was a
Pastels fan and I thought he seemed to be from that kind of area. I
thought Karn would like him." The two wouldn't really get to know
each other until a while after this first embarrassing encounter, but
something about their shared taste for boldly unfashionable velvet
trousers led them to believe that perhaps they might have something in
common. Stuart David was at this time fronting his own band, a gang
of Dylan/Tom Waits–inspired bohemians called The Ragland Street
Rattle. Remarkable though it may sound, the incredibly softly spoken
Stuart David claims to have been something of a nascent Waits figure
at the time, which must have been something to behold. "I had a very
strange singing voice at that point. Very gravelly and deep," he says. "I

was kind of out of time. I'd been in that little attic for too long, I think."

Fashion means very little to gravelly voiced singers in attics, of course, hence the boy's adopted look of unkempt hair, leather trousers, and waistcoats, which rather conjures up the image of an emaciated Michael Hutchence, or at the very least an out-of-work Portuguese porn star. Stuart M too had clearly decided to go his own sartorial way, with his pudding-bowl haircut, anoraks, and ostentatious trouser-wear (he even had a plastic pair). But just what made these shy blushing laddies wish to draw attention to themselves in such a way? Why would they so blatantly invite ridicule and the disapproving gaze of people who would probably never notice them were it not for their idiosyncratic dress sense? Same reason the similarly introverted Elvis walked the corridors of Hulmes High in mascara and pink, as the crew cuts and pony tails gawked around him. Because he *wanted* to be noticed, he wanted to be different, he wanted to draw a line between himself and the ordinaries around him, even if it meant taking a hiding for it. An introvert with balls, a shy boy in fuck-you trousers. Behind the quietude and manners, the Stuarts were a boiling font of self-assurance. Same as every indie kid, geek, and freak. Same as you, probably. As Jarvis Cocker wrote in "Mis-shapes": *"We'll use the one thing we've got more of/That's our minds."* The geeks shall inherit the Earth. They already have in their minds.

Stuart M had been on the course for around the same length of time as his namesake, and had also begun to find it as intermittently useful, although his early impressions were less than stellar. "I must admit that at first I hated the course and tried to stay away from it as much as possible, and just pick up my money," he remembers. "After going in the first day and seeing someone play a bass solo at me, and going, 'You can do this if you try,' I had a mantra in my head going, 'Don't let them teach you anything.' I was writing songs at that time and I didn't want to know any of that shit. It wasn't until I came back from the States that I thought, 'Well, I've lost here, I have to try something, I've tried to get a band together, it's not going to happen.' I have to go into Beatbox every day and work on my own music, and eventually I got chatting to Stuart because there was a policy that everybody chipped in on other people's demos. There were good musicians down there—I don't think the course realized what they had. I don't think we had that much [musically] in common, and we didn't have that much in common with the scene that was going on around the West End, the '60s scene. Stuart was definitely uncool, and I felt uncool as well, but there was a sensibility in common which was nice. I wanted to sing at the volume I sang at, softly, and I wanted things to be just so, and I think Stuart realized that. He encouraged me because he liked the songs, and he was quite accommodating."

Stuart David prefers to describe this shared sense of "uncoolness" as the "same sense of what was ordinary. At that time, I don't think either of us drank—we didn't have any interest in drugs. We didn't like loud music, or hi-fi music. We thought music sounded best through a Dansette record player 'cause that's how we'd both grown up listening to it. But we'd been listening to different records on them. We both liked songs and music, but none of the bullshit that apparently had to go with it. Most other people you met who were musicians were in it as much for the drugs and alcohol as they were for the songs. But we just liked songs. We had that in common. And we'd both been bowled over by *Catcher in the Rye.*" The peregrinations of Holden Caulfield, with his withering distaste for all things "phoney," his feelings of itchy displacement from his surroundings, would have as profound an effect on Stuarts Murdoch and David as it would/will on generations of disaffected adolescents. Indeed, Stuart David's first published novel, the excellent *Nalda Said,* even reads like a more sociopathic version of Salinger's classic. Both Stuarts clearly owe a debt to Holden Caulfield/Salinger's depiction of the terrifyingly unromantic compromises of adult life, as Stuart D readily admits. "We were probably both just ripping off the same guy in different ways. But the fact that we aspired to rip off the same guy must mean we had something in common."

Whenever the people who ran the course weren't hogging the studio for their own means, the two new friends would go in to record, sometimes alone, but more often than not together. "None of them paid any attention to what me or Stuart were doing," says Stuart D, who had first become aware of Stuart M's talent when he played him "Le Pastie de la Bourgeoisie" at the house of a shared friend called Alistair, who they both made music with. "I think I told him he was lucky because there was already an audience for the kind of stuff he was doing. That probably insulted him," he recalls. The two would also retire to Stuart D's cramped attic, recording Lisa Helps the Blind demos hunched up over the mikes, and would go on to play gigs with Alistair at parties and, on one occasion, at an art gallery with no PA where they were completely ignored. Occasionally they would venture onto the Halt Bar's open stage where they would play only Stuart M originals since Stuart D was still performing with his own band. It was at one of these performances that the latter witnessed the former's exacting perfectionism for the first time. "I remember Stuart stopped one of the first songs of his we did at the Halt Bar halfway through and said he couldn't carry on. I thought that was kind of weird to do that in front of an audience," he says, perplexed by the singer's complete unwillingness to perform his songs if he felt something wasn't quite right. It would be something he would have to get used to.

"He Just Lies in Pieces in the Corner of the Room"

Sometime in 1995 Stuart David left the cozy confines of his attic and moved into a large eight-room house which, in the eighteen months he was eventually there, he would share with a total of seventeen flatmates, one of whom was an amiable ex-professional snooker player and postman from Perth called Richard Colburn.[3] "Richard is hilarious," says Stuart David fondly. "He used to crack me up when I lived with him. And he's a good laugher too, when somebody else is being funny. He certainly likes his drink. Most of the friends I've got who drink, whenever they're drinking I just can't be arsed with them, but Richard doesn't change. He doesn't get more companionable, or more violent, or more open, or more boring, or more energetic, or anything. He just looks a bit more sleepy and he gets a bit funnier. I don't think anyone could not like Richard."

This genial genie had recently given up cue and sack to seek his fortune in Glasgow, harboring vague ambitions to work in the music industry in some capacity. He could play drums a little, but probably not enough to make a career out of it, he thought, so instead he decided to enroll himself in a music management course at Stow College. Like Beatbox, this year-long course is designed to offer students a springboard

---

[3] For reasons best known to himself, Richard Colburn declined to be interviewed for this book.

into the music industry. Every year the kids from Stow (a TV show in the making, surely?) are given the task of running a record label, Electric Honey, with all the marketing/accounting and A&R flapdoodle that entails, resulting in the release of a record by a local act chosen by the students themselves. Initialized in 1992 and overseen to this day by Alan Rankine, ex of '80s art-pop duo The Associates, the course had in 1995 put out an EP by a popular local group called The Moondials featuring one Stevie Jackson on guitar, who also hosted the open-mike nights at the Halt Bar and who would occasionally perform with the two Stuarts. When not playing as Lisa Helps the Blind, the twosome performed as Rhode Island with a Beatbox friend called London (he came from London, y'see) on guitar and Richard on drums, and occasionally with a trumpeter called Mick Cooke who had played on a song called "Dog on Wheels" on one of the Beatbox demos.

In the winter of 1995, the drummer took one of Rhode Island's demos into his course at Stow, hoping that perhaps they might be chosen as that year's project. Alan Rankine had already encountered the Stuarts at Beatbox, with which he was also involved. Like virtually everybody who cared to listen to them, the veteran pop star was immediately enamored. "Everyone on the Beatbox course, no matter what kind of music they were into, were always impressed by Stuart's songs," he says. "I would let people in their forties, fifties, chemistry lecturers, hear the songs and they all appreciated them. He obviously had something very special." Despite his enthusiasm, Stuart remembers Rankine being "quite vague at first. I'd bump into him occasionally at Beatbox and he was trying to sound me out, because I didn't have a group together, so he was probably wondering what the setup was." But this didn't stop Rankine nominating one of Stuart's demos for the students' consideration, unaware that Richard had already done the same. In fact, a total of three Stuart/Stuart David demos were entered that year, the third coming from another kid on the course, a smart and caustic twenty-year-old kid from Banchory, Aberdeenshire by the name of Neil Robertson.

Although he played a bit of bass and had already taken a tentative stab at rock 'n' roll immortality with his obscure and unlamented band, Babycot, Neil had realized that he was born to be a back-room boy, and after answering an advert in the music press from nascent indie label Jeepster Records asking for Scottish A&R scouts, Neil soon found himself with a Converse shoe on the bottom rung of the music biz ladder. Not that he wished to climb up very far, of course. The third or fourth rung would always be high enough; the higher you go the bigger the wanker you become. Must be the altitude. Neil, like most people on the 13th Note/Sleazy's scene, was already aware of Stuart, and had watched him grow from shambling unfocused wannabe to one of the most impressive and individual songwriters in town. He first met him in 1992 through his university classmate Jo, and initially found her boyfriend rather aloof, although this may have been due to some romantic misunderstanding. "There was some guy who was trying to fire into Jo and he thought that was me," recalls the young upstart. "So he thought I was some love rival or something. Also, I kept borrowing lecture notes off Jo and not giving them back. I was seventeen and he was twenty-four; I was very green about the gills." Still, he was astute enough to recognize talent when he saw it, and after getting hold of one of Stuart's '95 demos, quickly sent it down to Jeepster, who immediately flipped over it. "I'd been familiar with the Belle's music before Stow through Peter Easton's *Beat Patrol* program," he says. "I heard 'She's Losing It,' I think, and thought, 'Oh that's really good, I'll try and track it down and give it to Jeepster.' And then it turns out that Richard plays with them, and then it turns out it's Stuart who's known and seen around the place for about four years."

Jeepster had been set up in late '95 by music biz veteran Mark Jones and his friend and investor Stef D'Andrea, their first signing being a band called Orlando, who were then at the forefront of the mercifully brief new-romantic renaissance, which basically amounted to around four or five dandyish London bands intent on reigniting the vacuous spirit of Duran Duran. Thanks to the slavering attention these acts were receiving in the music press—*Melody Maker* were particularly taken with them for some reason—most of the major record labels pounced on them, and Orlando were snapped up by Warner Brothers before they'd even had a chance to record the two singles they'd promised to Jeepster. Jones and D'Andrea took the more powerful label to court, however, and successfully sued them, eventually using the money they received to sign Belle and Sebastian, who they'd set their hearts upon as soon as they heard the demo. "It was just pure songwriting, no gimmicks," says D' Andrea of his immediate impression. "All the tapes we had been listening to were all trying to sound like someone else and concentrating a lot on the musical sound as opposed to real tunes. The thing that jumped out at us was that there were tunes there, real melodies, the fact that these songs were so catchy. It was the best, most original songwriting we'd heard from around five hundred tapes."

Back at Stow, as soon as Rankine played them the Belle and Sebastian (or Rhode Island, or Lisa Helps the Blind) tape, most of them realized that the contest was closed. "I must say, the majority of them went immediately for Belle and Sebastian," Rankine recalls. "And that's the only time that has ever happened. Usually there is quite a bit of debate, but from the moment we put on "The State I Am In," it was almost unanimous that they would be our band. The songs were obviously of such a greater quality than anything else we got that year, or anything else I personally had heard in a long time."

Not long after the group with no real name were placed at the top of the shortlist, Stuart, Stuart David, and Richard (on bongos) trooped into the college to play a short acoustic set in front of the class. "That was the clincher, really," says Rankine. "There was pretty much no contest after that." There were still other possible choices that year, however, including two groups called Motor Life Co and The Ranters, although neither really had much of a chance against Stuart and co. As Rankine says, the voting went almost unanimously in their favor, although no thanks to Neil, who actually voted for Motor Life Co, a decision born from a mix of altruism and self-interest. "I was scouting for Jeepster and I didn't particularly want the Belle's thing to come out on Stow because I thought it would be better if Jeepster got the album," he explains. "I knew they were going to get a record out, but Motor Life Co probably weren't, so that would've been a better tactical thing." Plus, of course, he would receive a not insubstantial commission if B&S signed to Jeepster. The kid was obviously gonna go far.

But despite Neil's efforts, the group chosen for that year's Electric Honey release were . . . well, what were they called? Stuart actually hadn't decided what to call his nascent group. "It was just one of those things that happened, like most auspicious things," says Stuart of the final decision to call the group Belle and Sebastian, a name stolen from the books/cartoon series by French writer Cecile Aubrey.

"I'd been using the name on demos for the previous six months. Radio Scotland had already played a few Belle and Sebastian tracks, they'd played the demo of 'Le Pastie de la Bourgeoisie,' which was a really early demo, and they'd played 'Dog on Wheels' and 'Electronic Renaissance.' This was during 1994 on the *Beat Patrol* program and they'd said that Belle and Sebastian were a boy/girl duo who lived on Sauchiehall Street. At the time, I'd put pictures of Joanne on the cover, so it might as well be me and Joanne. At the time I said we were brother and sister.[4] When we did the Stow thing, one of the kids at Stow said to me that we should just call ourselves Belle and Sebastian. So I thought, 'Why not?' " Who this pivotal gent was has been lost to the mists of time, but if he's reading this, it's probably too late to claim some kind of legal ownership of the name, which, in any case, was already owned by Madame Aubrey, who was less than pleased when she heard about the group. "When I wrote the story, I just thought it would be fun, because it was as far removed from the black-and-white television program as I could imagine," Stuart semi-explains. "That program certainly made an impression on me at a young age." Ever conscientious, Stuart decided to ask for permission to use the name, to little or no interest from the parties concerned. "I wrote to quite a lot of people. I found out that they'd made it into a cartoon and that the cartoon was owned by Viacom, so I wrote to a man there. It's quite annoying, 'cause you try to do all that stuff, and nobody ever wrote back, and Alan and me tried to do it officially, but it wasn't until three years later when *Arab Strap* was released in France that Madame Aubrey bothered, and she wasn't fine with it at all, she didn't want us to use the name, and it was only after we went to Paris to meet her that she grudgingly let us carry on. And it was only because she liked us. Me and Bel and Richard met up with her, and at first she was determined not to let us use it, but she grudgingly let us use it in the end. She was really nice, quite a glamorous older lady, there was something quite Mrs. Robinson about her. The stories had started out as novels, and Sebastian was her son, so in a sense she'd written these books about her son, so we could see why she would be sensitive about it."

---

4 Prescient shades of The White Stripes.

"Sit and Just Be Quiet and Breathe"

"I was happy to play on the record," says Stuart David, whose own band was still technically in existence at this time. "But I didn't expect it to be any kind of ride at that point. Stuart couldn't decide whether to do the record or to go to San Fransisco, 'cause he'd been planning on going there for a few months before the Stow thing came up. I told him he should do it. He thought things would still be waiting when he got back, but I felt more like they might not be, and he should take his chance. So I think me and Richard convinced him of that. I thought we'd just record a single and then he'd go to San Fransisco when we were done and that would be the end of it."

But Stuart Murdoch, tantalized by the opportunity he'd been given, decided to put his California dreamin' to the back of his mind for the moment. He had always wanted a group around him, but now he actually *needed* one, and fast. The sounds in his head could never be achieved by the three stout fellows of Rhode Island alone. So, picturing himself as Steve McQueen in *The Magnificent Seven,* he slipped on his plastic trousers and hit the trail in earnest.

Not for the first time, the Space Boy had surprised himself. This wasn't how he had imagined this chapter to end at all. But imagination and circumstance often led him unexpectedly off course, and he supposed he was happy with the way his story had panned out so far. He even allowed himself a few flickers of excitement when he thought about the music and fun to come. It wasn't the kind of excitement you might feel when told that you'd made number one in Japan or that Tom Waits was in town and wanted to go bowling, but they were undeniable pangs of excitement nonetheless. He'd always wanted to make a record, and here he was about to do just that. Granted, it wasn't his record, but it was at least a step in the right direction, a further step toward the launch pad, closer even still to the thrilling expanse of the space unknown.

The Church up on the Hill Is Looking Lovely

With Christmas on its way, Stuart Murdoch decided, as was his increasing wont, to go to church. In fact, he'd been spending so much time in Hyndland Parish Church of late he virtually lived there, a well-known and surprisingly youthful face amongst the parishioners. The minister, John Christie, had become friendly with Stuart, and one day while chatting in late 1995 he discovered that his young charge was looking for somewhere more permanent to live. He had lived in five different flats in the last year and was desperate to settle down for a while, and so the minister offered him a solution. "The previous church officer was retiring and John the minister rather fatefully asked me if I fancied staying there and doing the job," Stuart recalls. "So I took it. I think they got their money's worth out of me, and for quite a few years during the band I considered my job at the church hall as important and as time-consuming as the band."

And so church officer Murdoch moved rent-free into the flat above the church hall, which lies just over the road from the church itself, paying his way by taking care of hall business. "It was mostly cleaning, clean every morning and late at night, gardening, setting out tables and chairs and stages and platforms for the various organizations, like the Women's Guild, and the bridge club, coffee mornings, lunch club, that sort of thing." Was there any job satisfaction to be had? "From time to time you did actually get a sense of satisfaction, late at night when you were finally tidying up and you realize how well used the place is, and you look around and feel quite good about it."

Richard would later move in with him for a while and would help out with the various duties, although for most of the nine years he spent there he would live alone.[1] The flat was a relatively large affair, with an open-plan living room/kitchen strewn with vinyl, books, guitars, and an upright piano in the corner; anyone stumbling into it would be forgiven for thinking it was the home of a student rather than a venerated

---

1 He would give up his caretaking position in 2001 once Belle and Sebastian started touring in earnest.

indie godfather. The room next to his bedroom would often be used for group rehearsals, as would the church hall itself. "We did a lot down in the hall, and John loved all that stuff right from the off," says Stuart, who continues to sing in the church choir. "He loved that I was involved in music and bringing youngsters around. I mean, it wasn't as if I brought the band into the church, but he would always pop down and things like that. John said he liked the records, but I was always terrified to give them to him because of some of the dodgy lyrics. I've never been so embarrassed as one time when he cornered me and was asking me about some of the words, he said, 'I know you're quite sort of pro-gay rights and things like that.' And I was totally blushing like a bastard," he laughs. "I gave him white label copies of *Tigermilk* and *Sinister* so he didn't see the cover or the lyrics, to save embarrassment, so he's got quite a good stash of collectable stuff."

The subject of Stuart's faith remains something of a thorny issue for some. "God Into Rock Don't Go" is, after all, an equation etched into the ancient tablets of rock themselves. The very idea of someone who plays rock 'n' roll music—with all its ingrained notions of rebellion, indulgence, and excess—also harboring a deep-seated sense of Christian spirituality, seems, on the face of it, all too incongruous to comprehend. After all, as every fool-boy knows, it's the Devil who's got the best tunes. God, according to accepted wisdom, well . . . his tunes are all very nice an' all, but gimme "Highway to Hell" over "How Great Thou Art" any day of the week (even Sunday). The words "Christian Rock" are enough to send a shudder up the spine of any self-respecting rock fan, and this bewildering

"God Into Rock Don't Go." Photo by Mark Trayner.

subgenre—in all its innately reactionary and patronizing glory—is rightly dismissed as a bad joke barely worth repeating. It is, therefore, a bold and foolhardy soul who chooses to embrace guitar and gospel. "I've felt the same thing myself," Stuart admits. "I would still feel slightly awkward talking about it. I would very rarely make an overt statement about it in a public place, but it rarely comes up in conversation, it's something that just arises amongst people of like minds."

Stuart Murdoch is probably the only practicing Christian in indie-pop (or at least, the only one willing to admit it), and while it is to his credit that he's open about his faith in a scene in which God isn't generally granted membership, his beliefs are a source of some contention, especially amongst Belle and Sebastian's detractors. For them, the fact that the group's leader lives in a church, sings in a choir, and reads the Bible is enough to dismiss them out of hand as happy-clappy Christian milksops, but despite the odd lyrical allusion, Stuart has never been one to hammer home his faith in song (with one notable exception, more of which later), being understandably keen to avoid having his band tagged as Christian rockers. And yet his faith is so obviously important to him, and such an integral part of his life as well as a recurring motif in his art, that it's absolutely impossible to disregard.

"I think being aware of my spirituality is a privilege," he declares, although he does add that he isn't "as far up the ladder as people think." And yet Stuart Murdoch's ladder has obviously been an ever-present source of stability throughout his life, and while he continues to skirt the subject with a degree of understandable wariness in interviews, his willingness to even acknowledge his spirituality in a culture where such things are considered so ineffably uncool stands as a prime example of his innate desire to confound expectations, to, in his own quietly rebellious way, upset the status quo (but not the Status Quo, God forbid), and invent his own idiosyncratic concept of what it is to be a gunslinging indie hipster. After all, in the supposedly open-minded awnings of the underground, shouldn't one be allowed to be and do exactly what one wants, even if that involves organizing youth club gatherings and playing Scrabble with septuagenarians?

Amen.

CHAPTER THREE
MICK COOKE

I'll Render Services That You Might Reasonably Require

The boy with the horn looked up from the chart and nodded. It was a simple part, like a melancholy mariachi bolero, but he liked it. And he liked the song it came from. He hadn't really paid that much attention to the words when the curious boy had sung them so sweetly in his flat, something about a dog on wheels, words laced with a slightly unsettling air he couldn't quite place, but he knew that the song—and the few others he'd heard him sing—was, like the boy himself, something out of the ordinary.

He still hadn't quite gotten over the fact that this was the work of that weirdo who used to haunt his music class a couple of years before, the quiet kid in the leather trousers who he later saw performing an almost insultingly shambling set at a hipster bookstore. And he still wasn't quite sure how he'd ended up here in the first place, at some government hangout for doleys, playing trumpet on a song about a dog for a boy he barely knew, when he should really be at practice for his own band, the one with the deal and the future.

But here he was, nodding at the weirdo smiling at him through the studio glass, his even weirder friend (with the same name, weirdly) cross-legged in the shadows, nose stuck in a book. What were any of these people doing here? "Ready to go, Mick?" The curious boy's voice buzzed breezily across the talkback. The boy with the horn flashed a smile; this should all be over in moments. He licked his lips and pursed, set his fingers on the keys and waited for the song about the dog to fill his ears. Rumble, thrum, "Anything goes . . ." Young man, blow your horn.

"My Strength Is in Administration"

Scotland is basically one big raddled blanket of hills, like a vast stretch of Astroturf with varying sizes of mulch hurriedly swept underneath it by a lazy groundskeeper. As such, the mighty Scots have long thought of the peaks as their rightful habitat, treacherous craggy beasties there to be scaled and tamed, often while wearing the kind of clothes more suited to a trip to the supermarket. Which is why Scotland's mountain rescue teams are some of the busiest and most resigned in the world.

Mick Cooke of Dundee was up the hills and down again before he was even out of his pram, such was his father's taste for the outdoor life. A lecturer at Dundee University, Anthony Cooke would boldly drag his flock—wife Judith, sons Alistair and Michael—across the Monros and Cairngorms with the kind of strident alacrity peculiar to a certain kind of Scottish father.

Like most of Belle and Sebastian, Mick comes from a fairly comfortable middle-class background, which you should only hold against them if you're the kind of person who wants to believe that John Lennon really was a working class hero and that Joe Strummer was the bastard offspring of a thousand striking miners. Mick was schooled at Hillside Primary, Dundee, an extremely atypical school in that it had its own symphony orchestra, overseen—in Mick's own words—"by a peripatetic teacher for every symphonic instrument." Given a choice, eight-year-old Mick plumped greedily for the trumpet.

His peers weren't so appreciative of his choice. In fact the kid took a teasing so that we could dig. "Playing music a lot attracted the bullies," he recalls. "I was quite small at school so I got picked on a wee bit, right up until I was about fifteen, when I finally started to grow. But I think I made up for it by telling rude jokes and that kind of thing." Ah, poor wee Mick with his poor wee trumpet. The bullies must've thought him a gift from God. Only jokes about his horn—jokes he probably barely understood—could keep them at bay. Big boys of very little brain like dirty jokes, but are seldom impressed by trumpet scales, however well rendered.

Foreshadowing his later musical itinerancy, Mick would go on to take part in the school orchestra, wind band, choir, swing band, and—Gadzooks!—madrigal band, and his eye didn't come off his trumpet until the age of twelve, when his brother Alistair press-ganged him into learning guitar so that he could play in his band.

His heavy metal band.

But for once he was bullied quite happily, and he set about learning his chops with the same perspicacity with which he'd mastered the trumpet. And so it was that the testicle-shredding allure of the metal bewitched young Mick, just as it had Stuart and countless impressionable adolescents before him. Displaying the same overwhelming lack of clue as so many metal bands, these kids called themselves Terra Firma (Terror Firma would've been better) and churned manfully through the usual 'DC and Purp standards. But Mick, although he'd already written a movement for a string quartet which had been performed at Dundee Music Center, was tired of reading from another man's chart and longed to express his own musical vision. And so he turned songwriter, notably penning (together with Alistair) the trenchant, thought-provoking Titanic tribute, "The Unsinkable," the lyrics for which bear reprinting here:

> *Hence sail the bold Titanic*
> *The princess of the waves*
> *Ploughing through the oceans*
> *Towards its watery grave*
> *Ever onwards to its fate*
> *Never to return*
> *Nearing its destruction*
> *Will we ever learn?*

Oh, the humanity.

Somehow straddling the great divide between orchestra pit and mosh pit, metal Mick found himself more drawn to Terra Firma as the months rolled on, especially as the band were beginning to draw a growing fanbase from Dundee's unavoidably undiscerning metal community. They even got reviewed, in something called *Rhythm* magazine, which described them, a tad harshly, as: "rambling, shambolic, and shamelessly pretentious." They had by this time discovered prog. Lord, one can only imagine the feverish arguments over the relative merits of Roger Dean album sleeves between Mick and Stuart on those long, long tour-bus nights.

For no apparent reason, other than that they probably thought it sounded cooler, Terra Firma changed their name to T.F., and then in 1990 to Tropical Fishes (Totally Fucked presumably being a little too self-critical), when they embraced the emerging tides of baggy. But soon they became simply The Fishes, reverting to Average White Band–style funk, which at least gave Mick a chance to play his trumpet again.

But after a while it was time to put away such childish things, and when Mick left Dundee to study pharmacology at Glasgow University, the Terra Firma saga was finally laid to rest. Not that the Cooke brothers had given up on their rock dreams, of course. No, a new band, Perambulator (their ability to choose utterly shit names hadn't deserted them, clearly), was duly formed and unleashed upon an unsuspecting Glasgow. Influenced by Sonic Youth and The Pixies, the band were regulars at famed Glasgow venues Nice 'n' Sleazy's and the 13th Note, although one journalist did describe them as "antiquated festering wank shit" which made their Terra Firma review look like a five star encomium.

Despite the blindness of the press, they gigged to excess—once fatefully sharing a bill with Babycot, featuring future B&S manager Neil Robertson—Mick toiling in the university labs by day, playing unlistenable songs in 13/8 time by night. Oh, and he'd finally begun to grow, eventually sprouting into a lanky sort with shoulders like a spirit-leveled plank.

Keen to carry on his musical studies, he won a place in first year in the university orchestra and took a class in musical technology.

Then one day fate walked in wearing a pair of rock 'n' roll trousers.

In his third and final attempt at higher education, Stuart Murdoch had decided that, seeing as English hadn't worked out, he might as well try music, as other than sport it was the only other thing which really moved him. Having studied at the university intermittently for five years, he had earned some degree of notoriety, mostly amongst people who didn't really know him very much at all. Which was mostly everyone.

"He was the weird guy in leather trousers that turned up late," says

Mick, recalling his first impressions of this sartorial revolutionary. "I was too scared to speak to him. In fact he didn't really speak to anyone. He turned up late and left early, and as far as I was aware he was just this slightly oddball guy."

Their paths would cross intermittently over the next couple of years, notably when Mick saw the by now budding songwriter perform a shambolic solo set in John Smith's book/record store—run by Stephen Pastel—which hardly altered his opinion of this odd-job. "I thought it was awful, actually, it was absolutely abysmal. It was just pretty shambolic and out of tune—and there wasn't much of a tune. It was just really, really rambling, and I thought the guy had a real cheek to get up and play in front of people."

The next—and in retrospect, more auspicious—meeting came in the Grosvenor Café in late 1995, when Stuart approached Mick and asked him to play trumpet on a tune he planned to record at Beatbox. He'd seen him a year earlier playing as part of a student play at the university, an opus entitled *I Can Smell Liquorice* by one Ronin Breslin, who would also play a part in Mick's future musical endeavors, and which he took part in, again, only at the behest of his brother. Remembering the shambling John Smith's performance, Mick hardly jumped at the offer, but Stuart's contagious enthusiasm managed to win him over. "He said he had this song and that he'd like me to play trumpet on it," he recalls. "So he came out to my flat and played me 'Dog on Wheels,' and he was a hell of a lot better than he was before. He lent me a tape which had 'Dog on Wheels,' 'The State I Am In,' 'Love Has Let Me Down,' 'Hurley's Having Dreams,'[1] that sort of thing. I was very impressed."

Shortly afterwards Mick found himself in the Beatbox studio quickly reeling off Stuart's notated Love/Tindersticks trumpet part. Job done. See you anon. And that, it seemed, was that.

But a couple of months later, in the early stretch of 1996, the oddball came a-calling again, this time to ask whether Mick would be able to play on three songs for an album—an album!—that he was soon to record. This time he didn't need any convincing. Nothing permanent, mind. Just a bit of session work, three hours at Musician Union rates and off back home to his other band, his real band.

---

1 These last two have never been recorded or released by Belle and Sebastian.

"You Said, 'Walk Before You Crawl' "

The abridged history of an abridged band: When Perambulator cease to perambulate, Mick and his brother form a "death metal reggae" band who don't play any reggae and whose only gig is attended by Peter Quinn who, liking the band's musicality rather than their music, asks whether they'd like to back his sister Louise. And so Hardbody are born.

After only a few gigs the band—also featuring Ronin Breslin of *I Can Smell Liquorice* fame—sign to Epic in July 1996, tour with James, record an album in New Orleans which is never finished or released, and finally miss their big chance at Scottish music festival T in the Park when a crew member oversleeps and fails to turn up with their gear. Epic drop them shortly afterwards, almost exactly a year to the day they were signed. Like so many afore and after, Hardbody soared and burned before anyone had the chance to notice. Icarus with a publishing deal, back to terra firma with a crash.

Just as Hardbody were picking up steam, the boy with the horn was understandably wary to get involved with another band, no matter how good. In any case, this curious leather boy was just too, well, curious, to really get anywhere substantial. He liked him now that he'd gotten to know him a little, couldn't deny his charm, and his talent sang for itself. But there was no way he was going to get too involved with this guy. No way this was ever going to become a paying job. No way he'd be bullied into this one.

I'm Coming Over in the Wrong Direction

"We're caught in a trap," sang Reverb in his finest Kingly croon. "Ah can't walk out, because ah love ya too much baby." He built the song to a suitable crescendo—not easy on an acoustic—and for a few rapturous moments the Halt Bar was his Vegas showroom.

"Thangyewverymudge," he slurred, soaking in the applause. For such a shy kid, it was remarkable how at home he felt on stage, how easy he found it to engage with a roomful of strangers when often he couldn't meet a single person's gaze in conversation. Elvis was the same, he thought.

Along with his ex-group, The Moondials, Stevie "Reverb" Jackson had been hosting this open mic hoedown for months, and it had become something of a hit amongst discerning local scenesters. Granted, it probably attracted more hacks and lunatics than it did genuine talent, but even when he spent most of the night trying to hustle overzealous drunks off the stage, Reverb usually had fun, which was all music had become to him of late, since he'd finally come to accept that the toppermost of the poppermost would never be his. He'd been chasing his rock 'n' roll dreams ever since he fell for the Fabs as a kid, immersing himself in the sacred lore and longing to take his rightful place in the pantheon. But at twenty-six, after several valiant attempts, he already felt burned out. With his first group in ruins, his rock family tree seemed to have fallen before it had even had a chance to grow.

Adjusting his glasses he looked to the boy studiously tuning up by the side of the stage. It was one of their regulars, a genuine talent, thought Reverb, whose songs moved and intrigued him more than any he'd heard in a long time. This guy had been trying to get a band together for so long it had become something of a local joke, and if Reverb wasn't so sick of the whole scene, he'd probably be willing to help him out.

But thoughts like that were dangerous; after all, it would probably only lead to more disappointment. "Ladies and Gentlemen," he announced in his finest emcee smarm. "We'd like to carry on now with a very talented act— Lisa Helps the Blind."

And the curious boy stepped up to the mic and sang.

"Spent Summer in the City of My Childhood"

It's all there in the "Wrong Girl" video, the clip made to accompany Stevie Jackson's *Fold Your Hands* solo spot, some thirty-one years after he first blinked into being. Granted, his father isn't Norman Blake out of Teenage Fanclub, nor is his mother Sarah Martin from Belle and Sebastian, and no, he wasn't born fully grown and clad in a duffle coat and glasses, much, no doubt, to his mother's relief. But the early days in Erskine, the lovelorn school-day pining, the playground bullies, the escape to Glasgow, dole-queue bohemia and the dogged search for a scarf and jacket a bit like Bob Dylan's on the cover of *Blonde on Blonde,* that's all true. It's the life of Stevie Jackson in MTV miniature, the story of an introverted, deeply romantic kid forever in doomed pursuit of his dream lover whilst hankering after the distant cool of his idols, a boy to whom reality is merely a bothersome diversion on the endless highway of his imagination. "I can't actually stress enough how accurate that video is," he confirms. "It's kind of indulgent, but I think it's all right. A lot of it is fantasy, but the fantasies are accurate. I was either doing what I was doing in the video, or I wanted to be doing those things."

Those things being, principally, serenading girls with his winsome hepcat rock 'n' roll blues.

"The Strange Affair of the Erskine Cowboy and the Four Lads Who Shook the World"

Stevie popped his Beatles cherry at a very early age, an epiphany which led him onto a lifetime voyage of pop fantasia. The Fabs bewitched him immediately, everything about them was perfect. Their hair, their shoes, that magical aura of Godly glibness, and—most of all—those phenomenal, genius, immaculate tunes. They may have made their music in the decade he was born, but to this '70s child they seemed like a Day-Glo visitation from some unimaginable fantasy land, a place he had to find, and fast. So he asked, and begged, and pleaded for a guitar, and his parents, realizing their son's genuine desire, finally bought him one when he turned eight. While he didn't quite play 'til his fingers bled—this thing wasn't actually worth hurting yourself for, after all—he bent his fingers into as many chord shapes as he could, never really understanding what a chord exactly was, and played and played until he could at least shape something which might almost be considered a song. Or, at best, the sound of someone strumming a guitar in an approximately correct manner, albeit one entirely out of tune. No one had told him about tuning, so everything he played for those first few years was a discordant mess of tuneless clang, albeit a discordant mess of tuneless clang played with an admirable amount of gusto for a ten-year-old.

Once he eventually realized what the knobs at the end of his guitar were for, he found that he could actually play rudimentary versions of his favorite mop-top tunes. In fact, he discovered that a lot of them weren't really that hard to play at all. Even easier were the Elvis songs which had rolled their way around his family home ever since he could remember. Elvis was just about up there with The Beatles for Stevie. The King's hip-sneering charm mixed with his deeply doleful balladeering sensitivity struck him as perhaps the most romantic and attractive attitude a boy could possibly have. And so Stevie began to write some classics of his own, the first being a song called "Get in the Car," an obvious bastardization of The Beatles' "Drive My Car," which when sung to me a cappella years later sounds uncannily similar to Spinal Tap's first effort, "All The Way Home." "That's probably what all first songs sound like," he shrugs.

"It's Not As If I'm Being Sent Off to War"

In his youth Stevie was crippled by a shyness (which is criminally vulgar) which he claims to have gotten over, although in conversation today his body language remains awkward, shoulders hunched and gently squirming, avoiding eye contact like a nun on a first date. He speaks softly, politely, articulately, occasionally breaking into an unconscious Irish brogue, which is rather odd considering the fact that, although he's of Irish descent, he's never actually lived there. And yet still he bristles with the same underlying confidence as Stuart, as Neil, as every damn cat in the B&S court. Make no mistake—although they're far too self-effacing to crow it from the rooftops, Belle and Sebastian clearly know they're something special and remain justifiably proud of their achievements. "I wasn't a tough kid, I was shy," he says, seriously. "I'd stick up for myself verbally, though. But the trouble with winning an argument verbally is they want to punch you anyway. I wasn't habitually bullied, but it did happen." By nature a placid lad, Stevie could still be provoked when pushed, and according to Sarah Martin his temper occasionally flares up to this day. "Stevie's quite measured in most situations, but I think he loses control very suddenly," she claims. "He struggles to control his temper occasionally." It's always the ones with glasses you gotta look out for.

The occasional spat of bullying aside, Stevie's time at Trinity High in Erskine was fairly normal and uneventful, and at the age of thirteen he became friends with another Beatles fan by the name of Ricky McManus, with whom he formed a bedroom band called The Sid Wimpy Experience, which was basically the sound of two teenage boys playing Beatles covers into a tape recorder.

Ricky's elder brother turned the two Beatles fans on to a wider range of music via his extensively hip record collection. Stevie had made the natural progression from Elvis and The Beatles to The Beach Boys, Stones, Who, Kinks, etc., and now added the likes of The Smiths and Orange Juice to his quickly burgeoning trip into the never-ending annals of rock. "There was nowhere else to go in the '80s but the '60s," he says. "I was living in a parallel universe. Even when The Jesus and Mary Chain came out I didn't get it, I just thought, 'That's just The Velvet Underground but not as good.' But in retrospect they were brilliant."

He and Ricky eventually formed a band with Ricky's brother and one of his friends, lending themselves the suitably psychedelic sobriquet The Opal October. Stevie Jackson's first public performance came at the age of fifteen in the hallowed surroundings of Trinity High assembly hall, where he and the rest of the October rattled through a brace of Velvets, Monkees, Stones, and Orange Juice covers, as well as a couple of their own jangling originals. This was it, thought the bespectacled axe God, this is where it all begins. "We thought fame was just around the corner, but things deteriorated after that," he says.

"Destination Here and Now"

After he left school, Stevie enrolled in an HND course at Queen's College in Glasgow for a couple of years, taking the twenty-five-mile commute every day from Erskine. When the course ended he decided it was time to set out into the big bad world, and moved to Glasgow, sleeping on a mate's couch and stacking shelves in a supermarket to make ends meet. And all the while he practiced his guitar and daydreamed about forming a proper group.

By this time The Rolling Stones had become as much of an obsession as The Beatles, and under the former's influence he formed a blues band with Ricky, imaginatively calling themselves The King Bees. Stevie had also fallen in love with Bob Dylan and had begun to teach himself harmonica, playing it in a Dylan-esque holder as he and Ricky mojoed their way through a rootsy selection of classic blues covers. Although the duo managed to blag themselves a support slot with pub-rock legends Dr. Feelgood at Glasgow's infamous Barrowlands ballroom, they were really on a ring-road to nowhere, and at the grand old age of twenty-one Stevie Jackson retired from the business. "I hadn't made it, so I gave up," he says. "Psychologically I shut down and didn't want to be a pop star anymore."

So he returned to the unemployed life ("I was on the dole for years"), sitting on his sofa, strumming his guitar and wondering what the hell he was going to do with the rest of his life. But sometime in 1992 he met a chap by the name of Warren Macintyre who encouraged him to play harp in his country-blues combo, The Moondials. Despite his early retirement, Stevie had secretly continued to hanker after the rock 'n' roll life, and duly joined the band, who over their three-year career became something of a cult on the local scene. "Those were my Hamburg years," says Stevie, never one to pass up a Beatles reference. "It was great fun, we traveled a lot, had a lot of wild times. We'd go to Prague on our giros—we called it giro challenge—our bread and butter was busking, but we'd also try and find a gig, whatever town we were in. We didn't always succeed, but on our steady diet of beer and hashish we always got by."

The Moondials were inveterate buskers, a pastime Stevie occasionally continues with to this day, and it was out on the street, guitar and cap in hand, that Stevie began to develop his tremulous cowboy croon. "With busking I learned to sing better, I learned to project more. And my tastes were developing, I developed a taste for country music, through The Byrds and Mike Nesmith."

The group eventually managed to get enough cash together to record an EP, *Never Knew Love,* which sold respectably locally, and this, along with their burgeoning live reputation, was enough to convince one Alan Rankine and the kids from Stow College to put out another EP as part of their music management course in 1994. But the *Can You See* EP failed to transfer the group's live magic to tape, and by 1995, after being tipped for so long but never really getting anywhere, The Moondials were over. And this time Stevie retired for good. "By that time it was getting beyond a joke, in terms of getting somewhere. I was twenty-six when The Moondials split and I thought, 'That's definitely it, I better get myself a job and a life.' It was all over. But that's when Stuart got in touch."

"How Will I Hide These Feelings Inside?"

In their dying days, The Moondials had started to run open mic events at the Halt Bar, with Stevie becoming the designated emcee at most of the afternoon and evening slots. Although still shy, he had built up enough on-stage confidence to host these events in a relaxed and confident manner, occasionally filling the gaps between acts with the by-now enormous stock-pile of tunes at his disposal. "My job was to keep a handle on the complete nutters who would come in and hassle you," Stevie explains. "Totally drunk guys, guys that were smacked off their fucking heads. They used to call it the nutter shift—the stuff you had to deal with! It was good in a way because to this day nothing ever fazes me on stage, I never get nervous, it seems a natural place to be. It created a confidence thing or something."

"Stevie was the pillar of the Halt Bar as far as I could see," says Stuart, who had become a regular at the weekly Wednesday evening slot. "Stevie seemed to me like a very together guy. Not only was he compering the thing in a graceful fashion, but whenever there was a gap in the lineup he would launch into a country song, an Elvis song, a Beatles song, songs that I hadn't heard. At the time I didn't love what he was singing, the songs weren't my cup of tea—I loved more poppy stuff—but you couldn't help but notice that his voice was really good, and what he was doing with the guitar was terrific. So I'd certainly earmarked Stevie."

In the autumn of 1995, Stuart was beginning to cast out in earnest for the musicians who would join him on his as yet unnamed Stow project. He'd been performing with Stuart David and Richard as Rhode Island, with whom Stevie rehearsed a couple of times. The guitarist had no intention of joining another band, but he had become a fan of Stuart's songs through his regular Halt Bar slots, and agreed to at least come down and play on a few tunes. It was this practice room lineup which Stuart eulogized in "This Is Just a Modern Rock Song," on a verse eventually sung on record by Stevie himself:

Stevie's full of good intentions
Richard's into rock 'n' roll
Stuart's staying in and he thinks it's a sin,
That he has to leave the house at all

Stevie first encountered the two Stuarts performing together—possibly as Lisa Helps the Blind—at the Halt Bar, an abortive performance which illustrated Stuart's diffident nature more than anything else. "I remember it very clearly, because he was working with Stuart David. I remember Stuart David singing something, and I remember Stuart singing 'Le Pastie de la Bourgeoisie,' but after one verse he stopped singing because the sound wasn't right. That was a real sign of things to come," he smiles. "I think at the time I wasn't impressed by that, but over time I grew to appreciate that attitude. About the second or third time I saw him I thought he really had something quite special. It was a

Saturday afternoon and it was still quite quiet and Stuart was singing 'The State I Am In,' and I thought it was amazing. I was just so moved by it and I think I said something kinda corny to him outside the pub that night, 'I think you're going to be a huge star.' He just said, 'Oh, thanks very much.'"

The fact that Stevie liked his songs was enough to convince Stuart that this was the axe-man for him, but rather than ask him in person, he decided to solicit his help by letter. Stevie was flattered by the request, but he still didn't want to get involved with another band, and it took another few letters to convince him that this was something he had to be involved in. "In a sense I wasn't asking him to join another band," says Stuart. "I had quite a nice situation where I had a project, so I asked him to help with that. So I wrote him many letters. I guess very quickly we did become pals, musical pals. I don't know about him, but I really got a great buzz off Stevie, because meeting somebody, a guitarist and a singer to accompany you—to me that was the key element of the group coming together. That's what's going to have to happen, I would have to find a main collaborator, somebody who could listen to your new songs, and add harmonies, and comment on them, and give encouragement, and that's what Stevie was immediately. Stevie's talent was there to see. I guess the rest of us had to prove ourselves a little bit more."

The first time Stevie came round to the church hall, in November of 1995, he and Stuart quickly discovered that they shared a copacetic musical bond. "He was playing his guitar and I had what I still have now, a Fender amp and a Fender guitar with a lot of reverb on it," Stevie recalls. "And I plucked along and sang harmony, and it just felt really good."

Stevie would go on to perform with Stuart on a few occasions, although he remained adamant that he wasn't about to be co-opted into Stuart's nascent group, no matter how impressed he was by his songs. "The first time I appeared live with Stuart it was just the two of us, and we were backing a singer called Helen Reeves in Speaker's Corner," he recalls. "I remember the two of us walked on and he said, 'We're Belle and Sebastian.' And I remember saying, 'No we're not, you're Belle and Sebastian, I'm me.' And he'd play a song, I'd play a song, but his were of infinitely better quality."

But Stuart had a way of wearing people down; his enthusiasm, his assurance, his amazing songs were all too much to resist, and in the winter of 1995, just as Stuart was about to embark on an unexpected and exciting musical project, Stevie Jackson hung up his misapprehensions and tuned up his guitar.

"We're four boys in our corduroys, we're not terrific but we're competent," *crooned Reverb, the afternoon sun casting dusty glass beams through the* *windows above. But the curious boy, strumming his guitar and looking con-* *tentedly around at his bijou band of bandits, knew that they could be more* *than merely competent. With a little more color and shade, some trumpet,* *some piano and strings, they could be* magical. *He could hear it all in his* *head, as clear and fresh and cool as springtime lemonade.*

CHAPTER FIVE
CHRIS GEDDES

He Was Building a Space Rocket

Beans's head lolled back uncertainly, eyes stung and stoned behind his half-steamed glasses, trying to focus on the curious figure circling above him. Music and bodies and banter filled the room, competing to be heard in a swirling funky soup which he found slightly disorientating yet not entirely unpleasant. What was that song they were playing? He'd heard it a million times, a northern soul classic, but still he couldn't place it. Aw, what a joyful sound. . . .

"Beans!" urged the V-Twin, prodding him awake. "Beans, this is Stuart, the guy I told you about." Beans looked blankly at his friend, then, blinking his eyes into shape, turned his gaze to the curious boy, who was holding out a hand. Better shake it, thought Beans. So he did, smiling awkwardly. He wasn't much good in social situations, found it difficult meeting new people, especially when he was this drunk, this stoned, and . . . what is that song?

The curious boy crouched down beside him and said something about a group he was putting together, something about a college course. Was he asking him to sign up for something? "Jason tells me you're a keyboard player," said the curious boy. Beans just shrugged, sliding down the wall a little, and looked bashfully away saying something to the effect of, "Aww . . . no, man . . . nah, not really . . ." He wasn't just being humble. Sure, he knew

55

his majors from his minors, but he was nowhere near as good as he wanted to be. No Quincy, no Stevie, no Ramsey . . . Ramsey Lewis! "Wade in the Water"! That was the tune, a cool soul-jazz piano groove . . . 'cept this was the vocal version, Marlena Shaw, smokin' like a burning casino. He locked into the groove, nodding his heavy head simpatico. Next thing he knew the curious boy was gone, and the V-Twin was up rummaging by the stereo.

So wee Beans closed his eyes and slipped back into his soulboy reverie.

"You Know the World Is Made for Men, Not Us"

It is somehow fitting that the parents of Belle and Sebastian's resident boffin met in a science lab. Over the test tubes their eyes met, baby Christopher Thomas just a blip on their overheating oscillator. Young Tom and Lydia Geddes of Stroud, Gloucestershire saw their experiment come to fruition on October 2, 1975, when their inaugural cherub first set his eyes upon the world. He was followed not long afterwards by a brother, Andy, a child beset by a series of health problems including epilepsy and a bad case of glaucoma that almost cost him his eyesight, something which gave the young Chris an early lesson in the sanctity of good health. "I think that meant from quite a young age I was aware that I was really lucky not to have anything like that happening," he says today. "We weren't perfect brothers or anything, he used to be a really aggressive wee guy and attack me like younger siblings do, but at the same time I knew he was having a much harder time of things than I was."

When he was seven years old, Chris and family moved to Dalry, a town in eastern Ayrshire not far from where Stuart Murdoch grew up. Chris's dad was born in Edinburgh, so the family's Scottish roots grew deep, but still the boy felt like he'd been uprooted to an entirely different climate. "Moving up to Scotland was a big event, because when you start a new school you're kind of an outsider, especially . . ." Especially when you have glasses and an English accent he might be about to say, but he leaves the notion floating. Today he speaks in a fluctuating mix of English and light Scots, punctuating his conversation with a distinctively wheezy giggle of no fixed orientation. Whenever Chris's name is mentioned in conversation, all of the rest of the group attest to his likeability and intelligence, and it's true that in person he radiates a crisp crackle of smarts and ingenuousness, talkative and articulate yet still hampered by an unshakeable awkwardness.[1]

"You Go Disco and I'll Go Funkadelic, Man"

It started with a Casio. A pair of oversized headphones jamming his glasses into his skull, the early-teen Chris, whenever he was allowed the opportunity, would spend his music lessons with his bony fingers wrapping themselves studiously around "House of the Rising Sun" or "Spanish Flea," digging fully the buzz he got from managing a recognizable tune. He loved it, begged his parents to buy him an organ of his own, but still he only managed to get to grade three in class. "It was pitiful," he snickers, humbly admitting that the more practiced Stuart Murdoch can "wipe the floor with me as a piano player in a lot of ways." But in many other ways the kid would find his niche, diligently practicing on his bedroom keys to the finger-funky soul music he began to immerse himself in as his teens rolled on, finding that the more he played the more he could lock into the rolling grooves of Stevie Wonder or Herbie Hancock, Spooner Oldham or Bill Evans. Yup, by the time he was seventeen, he was a soul-boy, a jazz-baby, an insatiable seeker of the funk, stricken with the kind of vinyl-buying habit that has crippled God knows how many less-than-solvent northern soul fans. "It's almost like a mania," smiles confessed funk-hater Sarah Martin. "It's an obsession."

By the time he was eighteen, he'd begun to immerse himself in politics as well as soul, turned vegetarian, and set in stone the ethics which would come to define his adult life, a real gone kid with a conscience so social it had its own club and handshake. "I'm starting to realize that a belief in socialism, or environmentalism, feeling that the world is unjust and the way we in this country live our lives is both unsustainable and contributing directly to the misery of others, only means anything if it becomes an active struggle for change," he posits today, as he expresses his concern over whether Belle and Sebastian do enough to highlight and support worthwhile socio-political causes. "I don't feel I'm sufficiently involved in this struggle, either as an individual or a member of the group. In fact I'm forced to admit that a lot of what we do—flying all

[1] This could virtually be a description of Stevie too.

over the world on tour, producing records that sell in hundreds of thousands, is part of what's going to destroy life on earth if it doesn't stop. We don't very often get asked about these kind of things, so sorry my answer maybe isn't too coherent," he shrugs. "But I'm also not the world's greatest political thinker, just someone who's read a few books and tried to keep my eyes open a bit. Anyone who reads a good newspaper every day could easily be as well or better informed than myself and anyone who lives under western military occupation in the name of democracy, or who lives in an area where climate change or environmental damage is destroying their way of life, or who works in a factory exporting goods they'll never be able to afford to buy probably has a lot more valid points about the way the world is than I do. And I'd rather those people's voices were heard than mine, or Bono's." That said, Belle and Sebastian have performed gratis for the Scottish Socialist Party and for a couple of homeless charity organizations, and Chris hints that they may well be involved in the G8 counter-summit in Gleneagles, Scotland in 2005. "One of the things that first impressed me about Chris when I first met him," says his close friend Stuart David, "was that he was able to be just who he was. If there were things about himself that weren't cool he would just be as open about that part of him as any other. And if he thought something that was a bit weird, he would just say it anyway. He didn't pretend to be anyone else, which seemed to me to be rare when he was so young."

Chris moved to the English town of Colchester (home of Blur) for a year after school before enrolling in Glasgow University where he took a joint honors in physics and philosophy. "I had no idea what I was going to do with my life, really," he says. "I always sailed through maths and physics at school, but as I went on with the course I realized that I was never gonna win a Nobel Prize."

Still, he graduated with honors in 1997, but not before he moved in with the ubiquitous Jason MacPhail,[2] who recruited him into V-Twin in his final year of study. During this time Jason presented a show on the Glasgow student radio station Subcity, which often featured

---

2 MacPhail was responsible for granting Chris his perennial nickname, Beans, a sobriquet based upon the keyboard player's committed allegiance to vegetarian dishes.

zoo-radio-style contributions from the rest of his band. "On the show Jason read bits from books and played old soul records, and a load of us would go around drinking beers while he was doing it," remembers Chris, who first encountered Stuart Murdoch when he was a musical guest on the show one night. "Stuart came along and played a few songs, and I thought they were really good. We had a keyboard in the flat that I was sharing with Simon [Shaw], and the first time he came round and played a couple of songs, I flattered myself to think that I could contribute something to this. They were really different to any songs I'd ever heard anyone just pick up a guitar and play. They just somehow seemed more complete or something."

So it was only natural that when Stuart mentioned to MacPhail that he was looking for a keyboard player to round out the band required for his Stow College project, the V-Twin leader should nominate his young ivory-tickling flatmate. But the next time Stuart encountered him at a party, Chris was apparently too far gone to take in the magnitude of the request. "He was too stoned to register," Stuart exclaims. "Before that I remember trying to pick him up in the Grosvenor Café, but again I think he was too stoned. It wasn't until the third time that I asked him if he was interested in playing keyboards that it struck home." Chris just shrugs uncertainly at these recollections, arguing that he was "probably quite stoned, but probably socially inept as well. I knew I wasn't the world's greatest musician, so if he said, 'What can you do?' I'd have to say, 'Well, I can't really do very much.'" But as far as Stuart was concerned it was "good enough that I'd been introduced to somebody, it was fateful enough. At that time you would take the first person who came along—it was meant to be. It was good enough to me that he knew what a keyboard looked like."

Skinny Beans trickled his fingers nervously across the keys. What was he doing here? The songs were beautiful, but . . . were they for him? The music settled neatly to a close. The curious boy chattered curiously with the other members of the group as Beans twitched in the corner, pretending to concern himself with the unfathomable technical minutiae of his organ. After what seemed like hours he was suddenly aware of a presence at his shoulder. He looked up, startled. The curious boy was smiling yet talking seriously of his song. The way he spoke made Beans think that he was happy with what had been played. The curious boy bustled around the room, gently teasing the responses he required, his quietude never fooling Beans for a second that he didn't know exactly what he was after.

Sometime during the chatter, Reverb whispered over with a shuffling acknowledgment, gangly-armed with a few ideas and questions, respectful, friendly, intrigued.

As he unplugged himself that night, he felt a tingling buzz of excitement zip around his skinny frame. Looked like the wee boy Beans had found another group.

CHAPTER SIX
ISOBEL CAMPBELL

Always Looking for the Sun to Shine

The girl dazzled with romance.

She could be June to his Johnny, Cher to his Sonny, Jane to his Serge. She could be his muse and he hers. They could make beautiful, beautiful music together, hand in glove, bound forever by art and heart. One day someone would eulogize them in film, just like John and Yoko, maybe, in the video she'd almost worn to shreds with endless replay. Imagine.

She snapped cold from her reverie, mockingly chastizing herself aloud for getting so carried away. She didn't even know the boy, they'd only just met. But the way he spoke about music, about books and films—many of which she herself adored—had inspired her, sent her dreaming into wild spirals of romantic supposition. She loved the idea of two star-crossed artists falling eternally in love, it appealed to her beyond all reason. Lord, it was a beautiful notion. She giggled involuntarily, half at her own inner nonsense, half at the notion that this nonsense could be real. "Fertile" even, just as the curious boy had suggested in his curious way.

1996 was going to be a very interesting year, she thought, her forehead crinkling into furrows of bemusement. She slipped the tape into the machine once again. Naw, she almost said out loud, it could be better than that—it could be dazzling.

"For the Presence of the Caterpillar Brings the Butterfly"

The old piano sat enticingly in her grandmother's hall ever since she could remember. Whenever her mum would take her round to visit, the little girl would patiently take tea, nibbling on biscuits and crumbly cake, all the while eyeing the living room door with increasingly obvious impatience. Eventually, after what seemed like an eternity, her grandmother would smile conspiratorially at her daughter, who looked in turn at hers, laughing. "On you go then," she would say, shaking her head and pouring another splash into the china. The little girl scampered off her chair and dashed excitedly into the hall, climbed up uncertainly onto the heavy wooden stool, and plunked away merrily on the old ivory keys until it was time to go home. She was so happy at that piano, so delighted and mesmerized by the simple music they made together. She pleaded with her grandmother to one day let her have it, and her grandmother, sensing the little girl's devotion, promised her that one day she would.

Much to her dismay, Isobel Campbell never did get that piano, denied its pleasures once her aunt and baby moved into the grandparental abode. She'd waited years for it, all for naught. So naturally she whined and stamped her feet, as was her innate right given that she was an eleven-year-old girl.[1] She had to learn piano! Had to play music! Just had to! "I was always like, [whining] 'Mum, I want lessons,' " she recalls. "So she was really supportive in that she got a bank loan to get a piano, and she did the same when I wanted cello lessons, and the same for my brother with his bagpipes. She really encouraged us to try anything that we had a mind to try."

Seemingly deprived of these creative opportunities herself, Mrs. Campbell made sure that her precocious daughter would be allowed to taste whatever whim she fancied. "My mum is a very creative woman," Isobel explained. "But being born in the time she was, in 1953, she probably wasn't exposed to the same opportunities as I have. She always wanted piano lessons, but my aunt did instead, and money was too tight for both of them. So she never had the opportunity."

Once she had become competent on the ivories, Isobel decided that it was time to expand her musical horizons, and so at around the age of

---

1 She was born in Glasgow's Southern General Hospital on April 10, 1976.

fifteen she asked her mother for guitar lessons. Seeing how diligently her daughter had thrown herself into her piano studies, she couldn't help but comply. After being gifted with an old Washburn acoustic, Isobel took some basic lessons from a friend of her uncle, but decided she would need weekly professional tutelage if she was ever to get anywhere on the thing, and so after spotting an advert for guitar lessons in Biggars music store on Sauchiehall Street, mother and daughter trooped trepidatiously into the fray. "My mum took me to this place in quite a rough area," she recalls. "There was quite a dark close, no lightbulbs or anything, and we knocked on the door and it sounded like the guy behind the door was having hallucinations or something." Turning quickly on their heels they raced back home, both deciding that perhaps it might be best if Isobel just taught herself.

"There's Got to Be a Better Song to Sing"

"We'd have these endless summers playing outside all the time," Isobel beams nostalgically, harking back to the innocence she would forever come to crave in her adult life. "We'd play at *Private Benjamin,* all these daft things. We'd have walkie-talkies and things, and I used to dress my [younger] brother up in women's clothes quite a lot, like a pantomime dame, and I used to make him perform. We'd have big sheets strung over a rope and we'd have shows, so I think I always wanted to perform. And I think I was really tough, I was so strict," she laughed. "One time there was a rebellion and all my friends had a concert at their house instead because I was being so bossy." This definite sense of knowing exactly what she wanted would never abate; she would be a team player only if the team played by her rules.

Around the same time Isobel became obsessed with the John Lennon documentary *Imagine,* almost wearing out the tape her parents had recorded off the TV. She adored Lennon's music, his wit, his idealism, and fell in love with the idea of John and Yoko, the brilliant star-crossed couple locked in their eternal cocoon of creativity and romance, soul mates bound by a collective vision. "My dad had a lot of old Beatles records, so I got into them, then The Kinks," she recalls. "I really connected with that period, I loved the style and the whole freedom thing. Then it was Dylan and a big snowball after that." To Isobel, the '60s seemed far more romantic and inspiring a time than the drab, flaccid, cynical times she had been born to, a time of innocence, hope, and really lovely dresses. She began modeling her look on the female icons of the day, her wan beauty suiting perfectly the demure style of a Jean Seberg or Françoise Hardy. She fell hard for the gorgeous gossamer thrills of French '60s pop and movies, immersing herself in the monochrome romance of early Godard and Truffaut; a child entirely out of time, she was nouvelle vogue and loving it.

As her teens progressed she began writing songs on piano and guitar, although she would never be proficient on the latter, as she readily admits. "I'm quite a lazy practitioner. I'm naturally very musical but it's a bit of a shift for me to actually practice, I'm very lazy. I can just about manage some bar chords, enough to write a song. I definitely wrote 'Is It Wicked Not to Care?' on guitar, but I mainly write away from instruments, I can maybe come up with more natural or creative melodies. I'll be in the shower or washing dishes and come up with a tune." Music, it was clear, was in her blood, and although she daydreamed daily of some kind of pop career, never seriously thinking it would ever happen—the music business was too cold and ravenous a beast to nurture a gentle soul such as hers, she thought—she decided that once she left school she would take a more formal musical route at university. She had added the cello to her musical armory and loved the classical music it had introduced her to. Isobel Campbell was going to be a serious musician.

When she was eighteen, Isobel's parents moved to Thailand for work, and their daughter was duly enrolled in George Watson's boarding school for a year, her first experience away from the nurturing bosom of her family and one she found intriguing if not entirely welcome. Divorced from the pack, she described herself as "an observer, observing what goes on in that kind of world," biding her time until she could leave for Langside College in Glasgow where she "relaxed" for a year before embarking on her B.A. in music at Strathclyde University, by which time her parents had returned. "I didn't really love it, to be honest," she says. "I thought it was a bit like the kids from *Fame,* and a lot of acid jazz stuff. If I had a kid and they were musical I wouldn't encourage them to go anywhere, I would just encourage them to do it their own way. I was pretty much a perfect student in the first year, but somewhere during the second year—at New Year's 1996—that's when I met Stuart, and then that's when I started playing with him, then Belle and Sebastian, and pretty much as soon as that happened I wasn't really at uni very much at all."

Tentatively skirting the perimeters of the Glasgow music scene, Isobel longed to make music free from the rigid trappings of her education, and so began to play with V-Twin's Simon Shaw, who after a few weeks of living room jams suggested that she might get on musically with his friend Stuart Murdoch. They seemed to be coming from a similar place, he thought, there was a grace and sensitivity about their songs which he'd rarely heard in person, but Isobel just nodded and smiled, idly putting the name to the back of her mind and beyond.

"Late at Night He Is Wandering for a Poor Misguided Star"

"I'd heard about her a few months previously," said Stuart, who had similarly neglected to pay much heed to Shaw's recommendation. "There was Simon, myself, and Tom who's in The Pastels—we used to get together and play songs, and I think this was Simon's way of saying that they really didn't like my songs that much, because I remember him saying, 'There's this girl called Isobel, she writes her own songs, you should try and meet her sometime.' I just thought, 'Oh well,' and put it to the back of my mind, and then I met her at a party."

Over Christmas 1995, ex–Orange Juicer Edwyn Collins was DJing at Madame Gillespie's, a transvestite club in Glasgow. Not an enormously auspicious happening, you might think, and you'd probably be right, but it was here that Isobel Campbell first clapped eyes on Stuart Murdoch, who was there, no doubt, to play tribute to the former Post-card pinup. "My friend had looked at him [Stuart] and went, 'He's really cute, you should go out with him.' And I thought, 'Hmm, he is quite cute,' but I never really thought any more of it."

Stuart presumably only had eyes for Edwyn that night as he has no recollection of seeing Isobel at all. It wasn't until a few weeks later, at a New Year's party hosted by Jason MacPhail—along with his V-Twin bandmate Simon Shaw—that the two would meet for the first time. The circumstances were suitably romantic, with Stuart approaching a drunken Isobel who was desperately clinging on to a cabinet in the line for the toilets. Remarkably, neither of them realized that they were the people Simon Shaw had told them about. So there were no intentions here beyond a boy chatting to a pretty girl at a party. Albeit a pretty girl in a state of disarray. "I met Isobel on the first of January 1996," says Stuart, quietly relishing the historical magnitude of his announcement. "And to me that's the day when the band came together. I'd met these peripheral people, but something about meeting Bel, meeting a cellist and a singer who wrote her own songs, this to me was the key because I wanted a cellist in the group, and also I was very interested in a girl who writes her own songs, and with who you obviously have something in common, being something of a . . . not a weirdo, but, well, an outcast. It all seemed very pertinent."

Once the awkward and slurred introductions were out of the way, Isobel, as she always did, asked Stuart just to call her Bel. His eyes widened in excited disbelief. Just a few weeks before, he had written a short story about a boy, Sebastian, basically based upon himself, and Belle, a girl, a figment of his imagination but evidently the kind of creative twin he craved.[2] The chronology does prove that Stuart couldn't have based Belle on Isobel, but clearly fate was holding up a sign and waving it drunkenly in his face. "He thought it was quite freaky that people call me Bel and he'd just written this story with Belle," she hazily recalls. "And we just chatted about music, and we arranged to get together to play."

And play they did, a couple of days later, with nary an instrument in site, as they strolled around a closed and frosty Glasgow, drinking too much coffee and getting to know each other a little. "He said we should get together, it might be fertile—and I remember thinking that was a really funny word to use," says Isobel. "I was really intrigued."

There was something charismatic and intriguing about this boy— this *man*—thought Isobel. He was funny, both ha-ha and peculiar, he was imaginative, creative, and very bright, sometimes distant and

---

[2] This story would later appear in the *Tigermilk* inlay and, considering the somewhat autobiographical nature of the tale, most people understandably assumed that Sebastian represented Stuart and that Belle was Bel. "It's not only an easy assumption to make, but again quite a fatalistic assumption," he admits. "It's quite amazing that I was using that name, and then Bel came along. What are the chances of that?"

unreadable, but always interested and interesting. She thought about him a lot. Maybe things could become fertile after all.

The girl stood at the sink and gazed out through the gently frosted window, a snow-sweet melody fluttering around her head. She ba-ba-ba'd quietly to herself, tiny soapsud bubbles tickling her nose. She scrubbed the saucepan idly, merrily distracted by her song. She felt suddenly content as the cold encroached beyond her. "I know where I belong," she thought, smiling in the kitchen heat. And she did. She really, indescribably did.

CHAPTER SEVEN
TIGERMILK

Two Hundred Troubled Teenagers

Almost as soon as the thought flashed through his mind, the curious boy was on his feet and scribbling feverishly on the blackboard. "Five days," he gasped. "In, out, no bother." As he wrote, his thoughts skipping so quickly he could barely catch them up, the '80s pop star sat back with an amused and quizzical look on his face. "The boy has balls," he might've said aloud. "I'll give him that."

Within seconds the curious boy had jotted up a list of songs—his songs—which he gestured to proudly, all the while assuring the '80s pop star that the LP—his LP—could easily be recorded in five days, no problem, piece of piss. It would be the first working week he'd seen in years, and he couldn't wait to get his fingers dirty. He had no real group to speak of yet, of course, at least not the group he would need to sketch his sounds on vinyl, but fate had been dealing him a curiously helpful hand of late, so it probably wouldn't be long 'til he was spreading his full house across the table.

He'd wasted too much time already; not a grain more left to spare.

"We can do this," the boy beamed, as the '80s pop star—whose innocent suggestion that perhaps they had enough material to record an album rather than an EP had sent the curious boy sprinting off into this breathless reverie in the first place—just sat there with his arms folded and his lips pursed.

"Okay," he sighed. "I believe you." And he did, although he wasn't sure why. There was just something about the boy's enthusiasm—his stubbornness and utter conviction that what he was doing was utterly worthwhile—that you just couldn't resist.

And so the curious boy set to work, his magnificent seven twitching in the wings.

Isobel returned to university after the Christmas holidays to discover another letter from Stuart (he'd already sent one to her house after their first "date"). "I thought, 'Hmm, this is interesting,'" she says. "It was kind of romantic. I'm stupidly romantic, like Sonny and Cher, or June Carter and Johnny Cash, it always makes me excited. I think it's because I love music so much and it makes me so excited. If you can have a lover or companion who does the same thing, well it's even better. It's the whole package."

Helplessly intrigued and tentatively smitten, she agreed to meet this boy she hardly knew. "So he came up to the university and we practiced in one of the little rooms. I was really nervous, and I didn't really know him from anyone, he was just this strange person. I remember playing 'Wandering Days' and 'Mary Jo' and maybe 'Expectations.' I was just thinking, 'Bloody hell!' And he gave me the Rhode Island demo and I took it home and thought it was really good. At the time I'd been listening to Buffalo Springfield a lot, and 'The State I Am In' and things aren't in a completely different ballpark, so I was like, 'This is really something'."

Their correspondence continued over the next few weeks; a genuine example of old-fashioned wooing in a world soon to be cut cold by the technological gooseberry of e-mail and text. Until one day he wrote to her about an opportunity he'd been given—without which he'd probably be in San Francisco by now—an opportunity he wished to share with her. "He used to write to me a lot in those days," she remembers wistfully. "With ideas and funny little stories, and one day he mentioned Stow College. There was no thinking about it at all. That's the thing—when I'm not sure about things, I'll umm and err, but when I know something I'll do it."

As per the previous three years, the Electric Honey release was supposed to be an EP, but Rankine was already aware of how much quality material

Stuart had at his disposal and in January 1996 suggested to him that, if they could record it in the allotted five days, the group could make a whole album. "The material was obviously there," he says. "So I gave them the option of doing a whole album at Ca Va studios,[1] which had a recording room big enough to accomodate what they wanted to do, which was to play live together in one room." However, Stuart claims that the idea of recording an album came from him, and that Rankine was initially skeptical. "Alan told me that we could do three or four days in Ca Va, or go into a cheaper studio and spend a bit longer," he says. "There was only a certain amount of cash, but I said, 'I want to go into the big studio, I want to go to Ca Va, and do an album in this time.' And he was, like, 'Weeeeell, I dunno.' But I went to the blackboard, and I was already writing down the track-listing, I was away with it, really excited. And he let us do it." This seems to be a case of selective memory, although both men clearly believe their versions to be the truth. Either way, it was decided that Belle and Sebastian would record their first—maybe only—LP in a single working week, in the spring of 1996. "Stuart definitely has a stubbornness about him, which I don't mind that, you need that," says Rankine. "And he definitely knew exactly what he wanted; he obviously wasn't going to let anyone tell him how to run things."

On the first of January 1996, the day he met Isobel at the Hogmanay party, Stuart picked up his guitar, and flushed with the kind of determined optimism one usually feels on the first day of a new year, wrote a song called "My Wandering Days Are Over," whose brightly skipping melody breezed out of him with ease, his words offering as many personal clues as we care to find.

> *It's got to be fate that's doing it*
> *A spooky witch in a sexy dress has been bugging me*
> *With the story of the way it should be*
> *With the story of Sebastian and Belle the singer. . . .*

---

1 The studio is a converted church in the west end of Glasgow. Everywhere Stuart turned, it seemed, God was footing the bill.

I said my one man band is over
I hit the drum for the final time and I walked away

A chapter had closed, clearly. His quest was over, as he'd finally found the musicians who could make flesh the sounds he heard in his head, and someone willing to record those sounds on wax. It didn't really matter whether or not the group could play that brilliantly—the fact that he had met these people at all was enough to convince him that it was meant to be. On that same New Year's Day he invited Stevie over for dinner and played him another new song, a tender piano ballad containing lines which basically amount to a virtual Belle and Sebastian clarion call.

"Do something pretty while you can," he sang in "We Rule the School," a plea partly inspired by a desire to transcend the everyday drab, but also by a perceived lack of beauty in the prevailing music of the time. *Tigermilk* and *Sinister* were released bang in the thick of Britpop, which although more of a media conceit than an actual musical movement, came to shape the British cultural landscape in a way not seen since punk. But while punk was built upon some root level of political awareness and generational disaffection, Britpop was an apolitical barrage of boisterous celebration of British culture and the self. With a few exceptions it was basically a boy's brigade, one which celebrated the stereotypical male pursuits of beer, birds, and football. The press crowed meaningfully about the whole thing being a refreshing antidote to years of stifling political correctness, but that was only so they could print pictures of oiled tits again, all under some spurious banner of postmodernism. The keynote records at the time were Blur's *Parklife* (although this was admittedly a view of working-class machismo filtered through a patronizing veil of middle-class voyeurism) and the first two Oasis albums, each in their own seemingly oppositional perspective stock-full of galvanizing all-inclusive anthems which appealed enormously to a nation drunk on its own misplaced sense of cultural rejuvenation, a flimsy phenomenon bolstered by the optimism brought about by the generally accepted notion that, come the next election in 1997, Britain's right-wing Tory government would finally be ousted after eighteen years of iron rule, to be replaced by a progressive and energized "New Labour" government headed by the comparatively youthful and clued-in

Tony Blair, the country's first—and they really did bill him as this—"rock 'n' roll prime minister." But Britpop tolled the death knell for "indie" in the traditional sense. As soon as the music industry decided that there was a buck or three to be made out of this guitar-band business, and hitherto marginal acts suddenly became widely accepted, the notion of this music somehow being an alternative to the mainstream became a complete misnomer. Almost overnight, the rebel yell of alternative rock was strangled to a whisper, the whole thing quashed into a glossy paste of blandness.

In amongst all this communal back-slapping and hard-hearted hedonism, there was little room for dissenters, with only Pulp's defiantly awkward Jarvis Cocker managing to inject some much-needed cynicism into the punch, but even he began to find himself co-opted into the carnival, like a class geek being tolerated by the bullies out of amusement.

It was against this brick wall that Stuart Murdoch prayed for prettiness. The crowd heard drums, he heard flutes. *"You might as well do the white line,"* rasped Oasis. *"Reading the gospel to yourself is fine,"* assured the choirboy. Britpop sang for the gang, Stuart sang for the boy and girl alone, and all those people—so many people—to whom Britpop said nothing about their lives greeted Stuart's defiantly sensitive musings with blessed relief, overjoyed that here, finally, was a band they could really believe in. Here was someone who sang for them, who sang of beauty, and ugliness, for the fat girl with the lisp, for the fox in the snow. And in doing so he wilfully cast himself as a kind of conciliatory spokesman for disaffection, a role he took to with gusto. "It's probably partly the reason I started the band in the first place," he admits. "After feeling a certain way at certain times, I had the physical sensation of wanting to guide people away from certain pitfalls—no doubt." The shepherd had chosen his flock.

And while the rest of Belle and Sebastian have often grumbled about being perceived as some kind of torch-bearer for sensitivity—Celtic fanatic Chris was particularly aggrieved by an early review which presumed they didn't like football—it is undeniable that Stuart in particular purposefully cultivated a deliberately literate and unmasculine form of music. He claims, as he always has, that there was nothing preordained about his group, that no plans were ever hatched, and while that may be true to an extent, he clearly had a vision, and there's no disguising the delight he gained in creating a world so profoundly distant to mainstream trends. "What we did came out naturally," he insists. "But I tell you it [mainstream music] didn't deter me any. It made me more determined to make the prettiest sounds, to be as lyrical as possible. It did spur me on, and I loved it. I remember hearing 'Mayfly' in the bath on Radio One and thinking how much it stood out against all the other stuff, and just loving it."

Stevie, for one, was impressed by Stuart's willingness to flaunt his sensitivity. "In my opinion it takes real bravery to sing something like 'Do something pretty while you can.' My initial reaction was, 'You can't sing that, I've just come from a rock 'n' roll band!' But by the time he got to the second chorus, I thought, 'Nah, why not say that? It's brave, it's bold, it's brilliant.' "

The first proper Belle and Sebastian gig, it is generally agreed, was at a party at Stuart and Richard's house on January 13, 1996,[2] for which Mark Jones made the trip from London. It was the first time he'd met the group, and the performance only served to assure him that he had to make Belle and Sebastian the first act on Jeepster Ltd. "When he went up there it was just a case of him trying to sign them any way he could," claims Stef D'Andrea. From the original lineup, Mick and Chris were the only ones not to attend, and even though Isobel had been rehearsing with Stuart, this was the first time she'd actually met Stuart David, Stevie, and Richard. Unfortunately, she couldn't find a taxi willing to transport her cello, and she ended up missing most of the gig, playing on the last song only. "Isobel turned up an hour late, which was a sign of things to come," notes Stevie wryly.

Understandably embarrassed at having missed virtually all of her first performance with the group, Isobel penned Stuart a suitably conciliatory letter the very next day. "The best thing about Stuart's party was Stevie Jackson," she enthused, the guitarist's awkward cool and musical prowess clearly having as much of an effect on her as it did on Stuart. "[He] really was as astounding as you had said. He's also a fan of Nancy and Lee, which makes me extra happy. Stevie spoke about trying out some three-part harmonies, which I've never tried before but it would

---

2 Stuart printed out little flybills for the audience informing them of that night's musical selections.

be good to practice. I reckon you know an ace flirt when you see one," she added, somewhat mysteriously. It's interesting to note that Stevie was already at this point interested in experimenting with three-part harmony, something they would never really develop until Isobel had all but left the group. In conclusion she wrote: "Anyway, I had a good time playing with your band, meeting your dog, and am very sorry if my horrible lateness might have lessened the elegance of your performance. I hope I can hear the 'Stuart and Stevie Baby Songs' very soon." Stuart doesn't know what this last line means either.

Stuart, Stuart David, and Stevie would also play a few songs in front of the Stow College class just prior to the recording of the album, which commenced on March 8, coincidentally the same day as Norma Murdoch's birthday. Despite the time constraints, *Tigermilk*—eventually named after the picture of Jo breast-feeding a stuffed tiger which adorns the cover—was born in a remarkably smooth manner, mainly thanks to Stuart's exact knowledge of what he wanted from the musicians and their ability to realize his instructions. "Stuart knew exactly what he wanted," Alan Rankine agrees. "He's definitely a very creative character. He's different, yes, but that's why his songs are so special."

Of the several songs under consideration, Stuart had eventually whittled the running order down to "The State I Am In," "Expectations," "She's Losing It," "Electronic Renaissance," "You're Just a Baby," "I Could Be Dreaming," "We Rule the School," "My Wandering Days Are Over," "I Don't Love Anyone," and "Mary Jo," a selection which had undergone countless permutations in his mind over the last few months.[3]

Although the group at this point were all virtually strangers, they had found very quickly that they had a copacetic musical relationship, which delighted Stuart in particular. Gently instructing the group in what to play—and what not to play—he marveled as his hitherto private arrangements came tumbling out around him. The music had to be quiet enough

---

3 A tentative early running order ran thus: "Electronic Renaissance," "Dog on Wheels," "The State I Am In," "The Disenchanted Pony," "Sleep the Clock Around," "There's a Place I Want to Be," "Belle and Sebastian," "She's Losing It," "String Bean Jean," "Rhoda." "The Disenchanted Pony" (name-checked in "Wandering Days"), "There's a Place I Want to Be," and "Rhoda" would all remain unreleased, although the latter was performed live on a number of occasions and exists as a bootleg.

for Stuart's fragile yet roundly timbred voice to be heard, and not every song would require the services of the entire group. He didn't want the group to jam and just thrash through the chords as was the usual practice-room norm. Each song had exact requirements, with the various instruments coming in only when required. Sometimes Stuart would take the lead at the piano, leaving Chris to sit aside, thumbing through his keyboard manuals. Often Isobel wouldn't have anything to do at all. But all of them were essential to the cause, essential components of a carefully worked out whole. These songs meant far too much to Stuart to be let down by unsympathetic playing. They were too fragile to be treated without care.

"The music had to be quiet enough for Stuart's fragile yet roundly timbred voice." Photo by Sarah Martin.

So when it was time to record them at Ca Va, the songs were already perfectly formed, meaning that they could nail satisfactory takes in just two or three attempts. "It wasn't fraught, it was pretty straightforward," Stuart recalls, although the very first take of the very first song suggested that the whole enterprise might be doomed. "I remember we recorded 'The State I Am In' first without any singing," Stuart David recalls. "And when it got played back through the speakers it sounded truly awful, and we thought nothing was going to work." These teething troubles were brief, however, and work continued in a surprisingly clear-cut manner, principally thanks to the cool head of their engineer Gregor Reid. "I think because we'd never really done this sort of thing, we let Gregor lead the way," says Stuart. "I wanted someone like Gregor to fall back on, because I didn't really know what I was doing. But Gregor said, 'No, it's all straightforward. We'll record you all at the same time, get a live take.' For example, 'The

State I Am In' is entirely live, with a live vocal—in fact there's only a few tracks where I overdubbed vocals."

Recorded entirely in sequence, the group could barely believe how easy the whole process was. "It was just a big blur of activity," says Stevie. "Then Stuart took a day a couple of weeks later and remixed a couple of things. I enjoyed it very much, it was exciting, it was good fun." Between takes, Chris, Stuart David, and Isobel found themselves strangely drawn to the studio water cooler, which seemed to possess some kind of talismanic charm. "We had a kind of spiritual connection to the drinking-water tank in there," muses Stuart David. "Every time we went back to Ca Va after that we reminisced about how special the *Tigermilk* time had been when we'd felt amazed to be in Ca Va, and somehow it had something to do with the water cooler."

Although Stuart knew exactly what he wanted in the studio, he still wasn't quite confident enough to tell the engineers what to do, as Stuart David reveals. "I remember Stuart had been adamant that he just wanted overhead mikes on the drums, not the whole kit miked up big," he recalls. "But when we got in, the engineer started miking the drums up full, and Stuart was too shy to tell him not to, and I was trying to convince him to tell him—but I was too shy to say anything about it too. So we waited 'til he'd done it all, and then Stuart told him, and he took the mikes off again."

Stuart once again drafted Mick, then busying himself with Hardbody, who reeled off his trumpet parts on "She's Losing It," "Expectations," and "My Wandering Days Are Over" in just four hours. "The kids from Stow were in the control room with some French students who were over on an exchange program," he recalls with a shudder. "So it was absolutely filled with people. It was pretty damn nerve-wracking." Tartly dismissing the exchange students as "a right obnoxious bunch of fuckers," Neil—never one for unnecessary niceties—and a few of the other Stow kids were allowed to "piss about with the desk for an hour or so. I think I got to do a bit of distortion on 'I Don't Love Anyone,' which was probably thrown in the bin once I went."

Aside from flautist Ken Hume[4] and violinist Joe Togher, the only

---

4 As Chris recalls: "When Ken finished recording his flute part for 'Mary Jo,' Stuart said to him, 'Ken, you're a fucking genius.' Ken looked alarmed, and hurried off, never to be seen again."

outside musician to appear on the album is Gerry Campbell, a friend of Stuart's from Beatbox who played keyboards on "The State I Am In," just as he had on the original demo. Chris played keyboard on the rest of the album, however, and on the third and final day of recording, the gawky physics student bustled outside into the cool spring night, hurriedly wiping the tears from behind his glasses. Inside, moments earlier, listening to a playback, he'd become so moved by what he and the group had achieved, he burst into tears. Embarrassed, he ran out into the street only to be joined by a concerned Stuart David who asked him why he was crying. "Because I've never done anything proper before," he said, biting his lip. "But I don't know if that means my life's been really shit up until this point, or if this was just really good." And through the tears and the crisp night air pinching his cheeks, he beamed his wee Beans smile.

"I was already into quite obscure music," he says today. "And I just had this thing that if you make a record and it's really good, whether it's ignored at the time, it's still there for all time. And I felt that we'd done something really, really good."

Even as far back as January, two months before the recording of *Tigermilk*, just as the group were having their first tentative rehearsals, Jeepster had already made Stuart an offer on the strength of the demo Neil had sent them, as the following record from Stuart attests:

> 24 Novar Drive
> Glasgow G12 9PU
> 23rd January 1996

Jeepster
222 Kensal Road
London

Dear Mark,

I was pleased to get your letter the other day. I think it's pretty fair what you're offering. It is in fact close to something that I might feel comfortable with. Right now, however, I can't say much clearer than when I spoke to you in Glasgow. I'm not trying to be coy, simply pragmatic. Maybe it is a fault of the artistic tendency to live in the present, but I usually find that if you deal in the present, the future takes care of itself. Just now I'm absorbed in The Stow College Project, and I'm intrigued and frustrated at the way my ensemble is falling together. I think I would like to record an LP in August, but quite a lot would have to happen in between.

My main criteria is that everything one does has to bear a certain quality, no matter what it is, and I don't think it's too much to ask of the people who are helping you, whether that is musicians or a record company. Nothing gives me more pleasure than when somebody does something which embellishes or complements something I've done. Like Stevie playing "The State I Am In," for instance.

I am against a lot of the practices in pop music today. Not for moral, political, or any other stupid reason. Simply from taste. There are only a couple of people around who come remotely close to the things that I hold dear. I've always liked to get drawn in by something. I would hope that I could draw in my audience, instead of bombasting them. It comes right down to the way you sing, and the problems *that* causes from the start. No regular rock venue is set up to deal with subtlety of singing. Volumes are laughably loud. I have had to put my foot down already, and there have been quite a few musicians unable to deal with it. It's what comes of being passive in an industry which is so obviously aggressive. But in the intimacy of somebody's bedroom, when they've just got the record home, there is no scope for any bullshit. To absolutely absorb somebody as they listen to the LP through on their mono Dansette is what I really want. Who wouldn't?

I think if you have good songs and music, it's a walkover. I really do. Audiences are really attentive. I totally believe that they are crying out for great music. In this decade in particular. It's sad, but it seems that fate was cruel to bands like **Felt.** They produced ten studio LPs in the eighties, eight of which are terrific. The only people who listened to them were bedroom intellects and a couple of doozie bowlie-girls. I feel privileged to follow in their footsteps. It might transpire in ten years' time that I would've preferred their obscure career path, but right now I'm easy. I'll settle for complete adulation! Ha ha!

So you can be assured that nothing *much* will change in the course of the next couple of months. But your suggestions have all been noted, and you may well have planted a seed in my head which will grow as my group makes progress. So cheers for now. I'll keep you informed of my progress, or if I make up my mind about anything. As I say, I like the idea of making an LP in August. . . . depends on Belle & Sebastian I suppose.

Sincerely Yours,
Stuart

It is interesting to note firsthand Stuart's utter assurance of what he did and did not want, in particular his assertions about volume and the necessity for the voice and lyrics to be heard above all else. These are the words of an artist possessed of an absolute conviction in his particular aesthetic, and someone whose jokey assertion that he'd "settle for complete adulation" one suspects isn't made entirely in jest. The message is loud (but not too loud) and clear: The boy wanted to be heard.

After so many years spent in M.E.-induced entropy, and after dreaming of getting a band together for so long, Stuart was finally being given his chance—his due. Understandably, he couldn't have been happier. "At that time I was just high. I was loving it. In a sense, I must've felt a little bit like [British Olympic runner] Paula Radcliffe," he laughs. "You'd been building up to this moment for so long, you could really fuck it up. But I think in a nice way you become more focused rather than freaked out. Basically, it all came together."

Very much Stuart's baby, it was clear at this stage that there would be no room for contributions from other members of the group, which, considering the body of songs that both Stuart David and Isobel had already written, could've resulted in an unseemly battle of egos. And yet both were more than happy to leave the group as a vehicle for Stuart's vision, each realizing that since the world he had created was so utterly distinct, the addition of other voices would merely sully what they were working to achieve. "I was so delighted," Isobel affirms. "I mean, the quality of the first two records—if someone wanted to check out the band, I'd let them hear the first few EPs and the first two records. It was a really romantic time, and I don't really think I understood what Stuart meant when we'd meet up. Occasionally I'd bunk off college and we'd go for drives in the country, and he used to talk about the romance of being in a band. And that's what it really was like. Stuart David is such a character, a one-of-a-kind kind of guy, so funny when he wants to be. And I had a really special affection for Chris as well, and Richard. And Stevie is such a talented guitarist, so it was great meeting these people—it was just really romantic."

You'll note that from this roll call of affection, Stevie is the only one whose musical talent, not personality, is singled out. Although the two had initially got on, the excitable nineteen-year-old had quickly begun to irritate the elder guitarist, something she can only sympathize with in retrospect. "I really respect him musically, but when we were in the group we would upset each other a lot. I remember when we were making *Tigermilk* and he would get the TV remote and turn me off. But I was really young, a bit like a bouncy puppy, so I think he was rubbing my nose in my wee a bit. I think the people who were into being cool were quite put off by me being this bouncy puppy. I was like Aldo, my dog,[5] this golden ball of—love me! But I think Stevie and I kind of buried the hatchet eventually."

The very first moments of the very first Belle and Sebastian record are inescapably arresting. Not arresting in a wham-bam! Look at us! Time to burn your record. Drag your vinyl to the pyre, ye drivelling drones, yea rock 'n' roll as you know it has begun anew! kind of way, but rather in the most cool and understated manner possible, capable of suggesting that what you are about to hear will surprise and enchant you in a way you thought music never could again. Not bad. The voice catches the ear immediately, high and weary, clear and precise, like frosted breath steaming winter windows. *"I was surprised,"* it sings, almost a cappella save for a sparingly strummed acoustic guitar. *"I was happy for a day in 1975/I was troubled by a dream/It stayed with me all day in 1995."* A twenty-year shift in time in the space of a line, from childhood innocence[6] to a troubled adult dream . . . of what?

---

5 As seen in the "Don't Look Down" and "Like Dylan in the Movies" clips on the *Fans Only* DVD, and presumably the dog Stuart claims affection for in "I'm Waking Up to Us." Sadly no longer with us. R.I.P Aldo.

6 Was Stuart alluding to a particular memory of 1975? "For some reason 1975/76 strike me as these sunny mid-70s days," he says. "Supersaturated colors on TV and sunny days. There's a vagueness there. I'll give you my standard answer: All art is abstract."

My brother had confessed that he was gay
It took the heat off me for a while
He stood up with a sailor friend
Made it known upon my sister's wedding day

And in just a few lines, it's all there, the perfect introduction to the world of Stuart Murdoch. Nostalgia, ennui, the inspirational and troubling nature of dreams, the sly nods to ambiguous sexuality; it's easy to see why he chose it as the opening track. He even mentions his brother and sister: Hello everybody, I'm Stuart, meet my family, let me tell you about these funny dreams I keep having. And as his guitar quickens its strum, he's off headlong into the kind of interweaving narrative structure which would become one of his trademarks, wherein a collection of minutely detailed short stories—often mere couplets—dovetail in and out of each other like a child thrumming briskly through a Raymond Carver collection. So, in quick succession, we're introduced to the struggles of the narrator and his unwanted child bride, the "crippled friend" upon whom he callously takes out his frustrations, and the priest in the booth who writes a novel *The State I Am In* based upon the confessions of his unwitting flock. And lo, religion raises its thorny head for the first and certainly not last time, Stuart's ambiguous fascination with Christianity neatly expressed with *"So I gave myself to God/There was a pregnant pause before he said, OK."* Funny, dark, audaciously literate, it's a dazzling lyric. The music, from its hushed beginnings, builds patiently with the kind of spare accompaniment which would come to define "classic" Belle and Sebastian. When the group break Stuart's solo spell after two long verses, they do so graciously, introducing one of the album's signature motifs in Stevie's rippling, reverb-drenched guitar.[7] The verses are just one long repeated thread of melody, but the elegance of the lyric and arrangement mean that it never palls, and when the sweetly aching chorus arrives (announcing the sole introduction of the word "providence" into the pop lexicon), especially on its final extended outing, it is so hypnotically beautiful that the whole song shifts into one of

---

[7] "There isn't anything original about [my sound]," he claims self-effacingly. "There's nothing you won't hear on a Lovin' Spoonful record. I remember Stuart asking me to play in the style of 'Do You Believe in Magic?' for 'She's Losing It.' Can do!"

those inexplicably life-affirming areas into which only the very finest pop songs are allowed. Suffice to say, it's an auspicious introduction.

"Expectations" is a rattling, ragged character study overflowing with detail and parochial references, the kind of colorfully drawn tableau Stuart excels at.[8] The first recorded instance of his empathy—some would say obsession—with beleaguered adolescents, usually girls, "Expectations" takes place, as so many of his songs would, in and around the hormonally confused world of school canteens, playing fields, bus shelters, and classrooms. As has been noted, Stuart was in his late twenties when he wrote the brunt of these songs, some observers finding it curious that he should still be lingering around in the playgrounds of his youth. "I've always thought of him as a sort of Peter Pan figure," muses Mick uncertainly, before admitting that he does find Stuart's recurring lyrical conceits "quite odd." Stevie, although initially skeptical, came to understand these preoccupations, however. "I asked him about it, and he said, 'You write about what you know, and everybody's been to school.' Also, the first couple of albums it's not him that's singing, it's characters. Those songs are all about imaginary people, like Randy Newman or something. 'Family Tree' is written from a female perspective, for example. If you're writing a novel you can put yourself in anybody's shoes or situation. But now his songs seem to be more personal. Why not just make stuff up, like Bowie or Dylan? Dylan was living in a parallel world in his early songs, and I don't think Stuart is any different from that. I think there was only one song where I went, 'No, another song about school kids?' And he said, 'You're either with me or you're not.' And I was with him." Stuart David just accepted the lyrics, neither bothered here nor there. "I didn't find it odd. It was obviously what concerned him. It just didn't concern me."

As for the boy genius himself, he, as you might expect, doesn't think any of this is all that odd. "I don't so much want so much to defend myself than explain things away," he maintains. "But after having M.E. for seven years and living in a vacuum it does amplify things that happened to you before you got sick, and before I got sick was basically school and then a year of university. So at that time I had a lot of time to ponder these things."

---

[8] That's Stuart's zipper you can hear at the beginning of the song. "I was standing on a chair, ready to sing, and I decided I'd be better with my jumper off."

Stuart ponders on with "She's Losing It" one of the group's most irresistibly catchy tunes with a spring-heeled bounce redolent of the *Hatful of Hollow* version of "This Charming Man." It's a saucy little number, full of sly if not exactly subtle gay references (*"where the boys go with boys and the girls with girls"*), a subject matter which would preoccupy him in many of his early songs, even though he describes himself as "straight to the point of boring myself." But in flirting with this kind of gay chic, he could be accused of trying a little too hard, like two sixteen-year-old girls snogging in a pub in an attempt to shock the clientele, who probably couldn't care less, frankly. In treating homosexuality as a kind of bohemian vice in his songs, something titillating and illicit, Stuart threatens to display the kind of unintentional prejudices so common to well-meaning liberals.

The hip pixie specter of Donovan raises its tousled head on "You're Just a Baby," a taut bubblegum punker based around a crisp two-chord riff and an impeccably louche vocal from Stuart. It remains a live favorite to this day, its guitar-heavy energy understandably proving particularly popular with Stevie. "Probably the reason why *Tigermilk* is my favorite record is because it has more guitar on it than any other," he admits with a smile. "I think by the second record Stuart was sticking more to what his actual concept was, the kind of baroque pop folky thing, which is fair enough, but I think the first album is better, because he chose to include songs which were more Velvet Underground-ish. And I think that gives the album more scope, there's hard playing, soft playing, it's more rounded." The comparisons with Donovan and Nick Drake would continue to haunt Stuart although, quite remarkably considering his vocal similarities to both (the former in particular), he claims never to have been particularly familiar with their work until the constant comparisons led him to seek them out. "Our music is nothing like Nick Drake, not even vaguely," states Stevie. "The only thing was the wispy vocal style. But Donovan, 'Jennifer Juniper' in particular, that's just Stuart." It is difficult to accept that he didn't in some way base his vocal style on Donovan and Drake, and as a letter he wrote to Jeepster just prior to the recording of *If You're Feeling Sinister*[9] attests, he was definitely aware and enamored of the latter. Stevie is right, however, in

---

9 See next chapter.

his assertion that their music has very little in common with the pastoral English folk of Drake; only his "Northern Sky" and "Hazy Jane II" could conceivably be seen as an influence, even if in the case of the latter it's mainly as a subliminal inspiration for the title of *Lazy Line Painter Jane*.

One of the standout songs on the album, for its New Ordered musical dressing if nothing else, is "Electronic Renaissance," which Stuart recorded solo using Beatbox computer equipment. " 'Electronic Renaissance' is actually a recording of *Beat Patrol* off the radio, onto a crappy tape recorder," Stuart reveals. "I was listening to the show, dead excited waiting for my song, and I recorded it, as you do, just so you can hear a guy's voice afterwards. But I liked the sound of the tape, because the radio puts your music through a limiter, a big compression unit, and coming off the airwaves like that it's got a nice sound. So I ended up mastering this cassette and put it on the record. I just put it on there because I liked it. There were no rules, no band politics in those days—because there wasn't a band." The song remains an anomaly, not only on *Tigermilk* but in the group's canon as a whole, and yet it somehow doesn't seem out of place here, its plangent melody and waspish lyric bearing an obvious relationship to the more organically arranged songs that surround it.

Cheap synths give way to ringing Who-drenched power chords on "I Could Be Dreaming," a reverberating quiver of power pop which the group would later perform on Scottish Television's *Don't Look Down* program, their first TV appearance.[10] As the title so abundantly suggests, the song was entirely inspired by a dream, the surreal subconscious poetry of which would prove endlessly inspirational. "It was written within twenty minutes of waking up," he explains. "It was one of these rare but happy experiences where, not only do you wake up with the tune, but you have a ready made narrative to pull out. And that's no less valid, because the world of dreams is the world of fiction is the world of fantasy is the world of the abstract, and to me that song stands up, it sort of nailed the dream, and whenever I listen to that I can see the pictures entirely, I can see it like a movie, I can feel it." Stuart's penchant for placing bleak lyrical conceits in incongruously upbeat surroundings

---

10 This lengthy sequence, with each member of the group receiving their own quick spoken-word spot, can be found on the *Fans Only* DVD, although Stevie's segment had to be excised since they couldn't clear the rights to the Nilsson song used on the soundtrack.

reaches a kind of apotheosis here, as he tackles a case—albeit fictional—of domestic abuse with unambiguous ire.

Is he your husband?
Or just your boyfriend?
Is he the moron who's been beating you and keeping you inside?
I've never done this kind of thing
But if I kill him now, who's going to miss him?

It was clearly some kind of anxiety dream, an anxious twitch of paranoia running through lines like *"I'm feeling hunted/I'm feeling haunted/They've got a knife for every time you take the same train into work,"* and the aphoristic *"A family's like a loaded gun/You point it in the wrong direction someone's going to get killed."* The final verse sees Stuart finally trapped by his pursuers outside the butcher's *"with a knife and a bike chain,"* this last detail followed by a carefree *"la la la la"*; a sprinkling of sugar on a pavement cracked with blood. Just as he would in "Like Dylan in the Movies," Stuart implicitly captures, with the merest of suggestion, the creeping fear of impending violence which haunts every geek and weirdo every time they leave the house. Clearly, those geek and weirdo lambs had found a new shepherd.

"One of Stuart's greatest creative spurs is graffiti."
Photo by Sarah Martin.

Aside from dreams, one of Stuart's greatest creative spurs is graffiti, the obscure poetry of which can often be enough to plant a kernel of an idea in his head, as in the case of "Le Pastie de la Bourgeoisie" and "We Rule the School," the song which so impressed Stevie back on New Year's Day. It was while visiting his parents in Ayr that Stuart, sitting on a bus as he so often is, glimpsed "NC Was Here" carved onto a tree. "For some reason that was enough to spark me off," he says. "Graffiti quite often has that effect on me. And the day before on a bus shelter I saw 'We Rule the School.'" Both instances are there, with a little leap of imagination from the author, in this, a quintessential B&S song, with its school play piano and unutterably lovely marriage of flute, string, and xylophone (and, yes, it is a blatant steal from Pachelbel's *Canon in D* and Donovan's "Jennifer Juniper," two composers with more in common than you might think) painting the perfect evocation of Stuart's *"Do something pretty while you can"* tenet. And when he observes sadly, *"You know the world is made for men/Not us,"* Stuart Murdoch, willingly or not, nails his eternal adolescent persona to the mast forever. Although not that it is a exactly a persona, as Mick observes. "He still lives like a student, really," he smiles. "And sometimes he doesn't really seem equipped for life in the real world. Like when rather than get his heating fixed he just kept his oven turned on full with the door open. I've also seen him wear trousers which are just falling apart, like he hasn't noticed. And I don't really think he has." Stevie is no different, Mick goes on, warming to the subject. "I actually heard him say once, in all seriousness, 'I wish I had the wherewithal to load the dishwasher.'" He laughs affectionately, as if genuinely astonished at his bandmates' continuing ability to live their lives in the clouds.

"My Wandering Days Are Over," Stuart's New Year's Day epiphany, introduces the group's winning way with an extended instrumental coda, Stuart repeating the words *"melancholy/Kinda lonely"* as a weary minuet with Mick's Spanish-tinged trumpet; no wonder the Tindersticks were impressed. The neatly solipsistic "I Don't Love Anyone," a loping Roses do the Velvets jangle with lyrics of rather amusingly Scrooge-like misanthropy, is another favorite of Stevie's of course, since it gives him a chance to crank up the reverb and flail. As for the song's desperately cynical sentiments, Stuart explains it as "trying to shrug off sort of relationship detritus, as if to say, 'Look, I just wanna do my thing, leave me alone, I really want out of this.' At the same time, I always thought it wasn't fair that groups like The Beatles, singing about how this girl's messed them up, and I'm thinking, 'Well you're singing from a complete position of strength here.' But [I don't love anyone] isn't a sentiment you want to repeat too much in public." The song also blatantly refers to Felt's "The World Is As Soft As Lace," a typically spectral instrumental featured on their 1984 album *The Splendour of Fear.*

The lilting, wintry "Mary Jo" is the snow on *Tigermilk*'s cap, its fluttering flute redolent of the theme to some quaint '60s children's show, possibly involving puppets. It was inspired "by a blink of an eye," Stuart explains. "I stayed in a bed-sit flat at the end of ninety-five and I was sort of wondering, 'What the hell am I doing in a bed-sit flat, I'm twenty-eight, I don't know anybody, and the guy next door is playing rave music all night. What the fuck?' But it was quite a creative time, you had lots of characters coming and going, and there was a girl who lived across the street and very occasionally I would glimpse her getting in from work, I think she was a nurse, and you know the moment, it sometimes happens in the evening, when somebody turns on the light before they close the curtains? And you catch them, this snapshot of a person, and then the curtains shut. And that was Mary Jo, that was enough to set me off."

Tigermilk is full of such snapshots, full of stolen glimpses and imagination run riot, an utterly distinctive world born fully formed and beautifully drawn in the space of ten short songs and a sleeve bearing no photograph or reliable information about the group—the not-quite autobiographical sleeve notes would become a deliberately unrevealing mainstay. It is the assured summation of years of planning on Stuart's part, as perfectly representative and self-contained a debut album as any in pop, up there with the eponymous efforts from The Smiths, The Velvet Underground and Nico, and The Stone Roses, and is undoubtedly the best album *ever* with a pair of tits and a tiger on the cover.[II]

II The drawings on the back are by Stuart, who dedicated the album to Lawrence Bradby. "Lawrence was a friend who happened to be having a not particularly nice time," he explains. "He was away from Glasgow. It was to remind him we hadn't forgotten about him."

* * *

Stuart could barely believe it, rubbing his thumb over the untouched vinyl grooves with barely conceivable excitement. He had done it. He had made his record. Even in this state, with its white label and white paper sleeve, it still looked beautiful to him. He spun it to Joanne, to his family, to Ciara, to all the ears he could find, and they really did love it, he could tell. As for the band, he knew instantly who he wanted to hear it first. "Stuart brought in a white label and stuck it on," Stevie remembers fondly. "And I turned to him and said, 'We're gonna be rich.' And we're still waiting. It was just a brilliant feeling, it went beyond expectations. There was another couple of songs I would've put on it, maybe for selfish reasons, because they had better guitar parts. The first time me and Stuart were in a room together we did one called 'When the Cynic Stares Back from the Wall,' which is a great song."

The rest of the group were similarly impressed by the album, Mick admitting he was "really quite shocked at how great it sounded. I played it to loads of people, and they were all impressed. It sounded different to anything I'd really heard, it sounded like it hadn't been recorded that year. And I hadn't heard all the songs, which were all great." Neil, not one to shower praise unduly, "thought it was amazing. I knew a good deal of the songs beforehand, and couldn't believe that in a week they could be so well recorded and played."

"When it was finished and I heard it I thought it was great," Stuart D enthuses. "But we went to the Equi Café where we always used to have our meetings, and Stuart wanted to change the first song from 'The State I Am In' to 'I Could Be Dreaming,' and I told him it would be a shit album and talked him out of it. I feel bad about that now." Had the tracks been swapped *Tigermilk* still could never be a "shit album," but "The State I Am In" is the perfect opener, so hats off to the boy David.

Before the album was released, Alan Rankine ferried the group over to France to play for the obnoxious French exchange students. After sailing across the channel with a company called Sally Ferries ("Sounds like a cowboy outfit," grumbled Stevie), the group were forced to sleep two to a bed (Stu on Stu action!) while Rankine took, in Stuart David's words, "a king's bedroom" to himself. They also discovered that they wouldn't be able to get home from London because he'd booked them the wrong tickets. Nevertheless, at the gig they played a slow piano version of Rankine/The Associates' '80s classic "Party Fears Two," which brought tears to his eyes. This, however, was after the band from the French College—the uninvitingly named Loch Ness—played for two hours until everyone had gone home, leaving Belle and Sebastian to perform in front of just three people. This didn't stop Stuart trying to stage-dive from the three-inch stage onto the empty floor, of course. It's an old rock 'n' roll maxim: Whether you're playing in front of three or three hundred people, you've always got to give your all, even if that means making yourself look like an idiot.

Back in Blighty, 1,000 vinyl copies of *Tigermilk* were printed up, many of which were rather badly warped on the second side. The cover, featuring Jo in the bath—no "me and Phil" in sight—breast-feeding a toy tiger, is a perfectly apt image in a way, its curious mix of coy sexuality and innocence neatly encapsulating the music contained within. Although it was basically the job of the students to handle the distribution, Neil remembers most of the group taking bundles of records into shops themselves, Stuart watching forlornly in the coming months as one of his deliveries sat yellowing and unwanted in one particular shop window. This aside, there didn't really seem to be much for the students to do if Neil is to be believed. "I don't really recall us doing very much, to be honest. Me and Richard never finished the course, to devote more time to the band. The only thing I really remember actively doing was posting them out to record labels, which again I did grudgingly because I was on a cut if Jeepster signed them." Rankine remembers sending out at least 150 promotional copies, resulting in an immediate and unprecedented wave of interest. "Everyone wanted to sign them," he says, apparently with little exaggeration. "Sony, BMG, Seymour Stein at Sire, all these people loved the record and were getting in touch immediately, desperate to meet the band and see them live." Fortunately for these drooling hordes, a live launch had been arranged to take place at Ca Va before the album's release on June 6, in the very room in which the album had been recorded. Before this could be taken care of, they played their first low-key paying gigs at the tiny Twa Tam's pub in Perth (Richard treated as a homecoming hero, one hopes), and venue called Stones in Edinburgh, both of which found a scrum of record companies—and Gary Lightbody from Snow Patrol, who would be

Jeepster's next signing (and the next year's Stow project)—in attendance. "They warmed up for half an hour and eventually played four or five songs," remembers Stef D'Andrea, witnessing the group for the first time. "No more than twenty-five minutes, Stuart David sat cross-legged on the floor with his back to the audience." The group had only been playing together for a few months, and despite what they had achieved with *Tigermilk,* the gigs were still awkward, shambling affairs, a problem they would take a long time to iron out.

Their first hometown gig was at the Glasgow Art School in March during which Richard was nearly electrocuted by a live drum stool. The majority of the audience was again made up of hungry record companies, checkbooks at the ready, even if the group's live incarnation fell somewhat short of the relatively pristine nature of their debut album. The group, in Isobel's oft repeated description, were "overwhelmed" by the attention; barely out of the cot, they already found themselves the most feted band in town. "I remember having a pish in the toilet at the art school and this guy turned around to me and put his hand out, going, 'Hi, I'm Zak from Fontana!'" recalls Chris with a laugh, astonished and not a little disturbed by the intrusion.

The launch at Ca Va in June was even more feverish, with even more record companies, including Jeepster, twitching sweatily in the wings. "It was my first experience of London en masse," remembers Neil. "It was a wild, wild night, pretty drunken. There were *Tigermilks* all over the wall and people were scooping them off. There have certainly been times when we all wish we'd done the same. But it was really a done deal with Jeepster by that point. I think we ended up at the art school afterwards, and Beans lived in a flat directly opposite Ca Va, so there was a lot of coming and going from there."

Around three hundred specially invited drunkards crammed themselves into the live room at Ca Va that night, Stuart at the center of it all in his incongruously cool element. "That was a good night," he smiles. "There was no stage as such, a little P.A., but we had a great sound, the blend of the rhythm instruments underneath, and the strings and the piano creating the texture on top—I could tell we were getting to people. Johnny and Monica [Queen] told me much later that they were getting the hairs standing up on the back of the neck. I sound like I'm crowing here, but I would feel the same about another group if it sounded like something new, something good."

"There was a few things that struck me," recalls Queen, who hadn't spoken to Stuart since their San Francisco encounter. "One was complete surprise that someone from Glasgow could create and perform such wonderful, genius-like music, just incredibly beautiful and inspiring. And it really moved me, that particular performance, because I think that anyone who was there at Ca Va was witnessing something that was incredibly powerful, and you just knew that it wasn't going to end at Ca Va, that it was going to go somewhere a bit further. I really enjoyed Stuart's incredibly shy but confident performance. He knew deep down. I think that confidence comes from within, and from knowing that you have actually created something worthwhile."

Alan Rankine had decided to invite the college dean, who was a little bewildered by the unfamiliar rock 'n' roll world he found himself thrust amongst. "I remember introducing the principal to these record company guys and they're all shaking his hand going, 'This is fucking amazing, man.' I think he was quite shocked by it all. I don't think he was expecting any of this. He certainly wasn't expecting to be sworn at," Rankine chuckles.

Isobel has less than rosy memories of the night, however, being already uncomfortable with the amount of attention they were getting. "It was horrible," she shudders. "I remember being overwhelmed—and that's a word I could use to describe a lot of what happened from that night onwards. Before it was quite manageable, it was safe. And these London people cheering got my back up. Those London people are too much for me, always have been and always will be. Where's the fun in that? I know that Stuart and Stevie had probably been waiting for that moment forever, but I felt like I'd been thrown in at the deep end. But that night was a total landmark point because my parents came along, and I remember thinking, rubbing my hands, I can do anything I want now, they think this is good. I can call the tune. But it was just really scary because there were so many people and they were just, like, looking at us. I could tell that Stuart was quite emotional, his voice cracked a couple of times when he was singing. I thought, 'God, he's gonna totally blub! Oh no!' But it was scary because it was like being on the brink of something, and before that I wasn't really sure how involved I wanted to be. From that point on, within the band people stopped taking care of each other slightly."

And this at the launch of their first album. Just five months into their career, Isobel claims she could already see the cracks which would simmer beneath the group like equatorial fissures for the next six years. Not that anyone else seemed particularly aware of this, with Stuart being particularly content to bask in the sudden and overwhelming acceptance of his vision. "To be quite honest, a lot of the early gigs were emotional for me," he admits. "Just the whole experience of actually succeeding in what I'd been trying to do for so long. Singing your songs to so many people, as you can imagine, was quite an experience."

As the room emptied that night, drunken kids and music bizzers tumbling merrily into the street, a dazed and delighted Belle and Sebastian in tow, the significance of what had just occurred wasn't so immediately apparent for anyone to treat the group or their album with any great reverence. "At the end of the night people were frisbeeing their *Tigermilks* down the street," remembers Chris. It wouldn't be long until copies of the record were going for as much as £400, many no doubt chipped and scratched from their aerial flights through the Glasgow night.

On June 4, two days before the album was released to a not entirely rapacious public, Stuart David spotted a copy lying a record shop, later writing in his *Ink Polaroids*:[12]

> We had a sweepstake to try and guess who in the band had sold their own personal copy, and favorite was Chris—because he needed to buy a new powercard to have some electricity in his house. Second favorite was Richard—who would no doubt have spent the money on chicken soup and pasta. And in third place was Isobelle [*sic*]—just because she probably wouldn't have much listened to it anyway.

---

12 The limited edition fans-only pocket book he released in 1998 along with *Little Ink Movies of Belle and Sebastian in New York,* which was written in screenplay form and told of the group's trip to visit U.S. record label The Enclave in late 1996.

Chris still has his copy under his bed ("Obviously there have been times when I wish I had a box of them under my bed"). Richard was unavailable for comment. Isobel probably doesn't even know where her copy is, even if she still does have one.

Now that Stuart had joined the pantheon, it was time to alert his peers, and so he sent a pair of *Tigermilks* to Lawrence and Morrissey.[13] Lawrence was taken enough to get in touch and come to their first London gig later that year. Morrissey has presumably been busy. As of writing, the following is the only piece of correspondence, written or otherwise, to have taken place by Stuart Lee Murdoch and Steven Patrick Morrissey. It is reproduced entirely as written.

The Church Hall
Hyndland
Glasgow G12 9PU
16th July 1996

Dear Morrissey,

In the spring, my friends and I toiled to produce the record that you will find enclosed. There was only a thousand records produced for a college label. It happened so quickly. The group had only been together since January. During this time, the previously supposed *sense of importance* of making our first album was dismissed as sentimental. We never stopped to think what we were doing. I think things went as well as I could have imagined, though the finished record is flawed in my opinion. What could I do? Maybe one day I will come to love the record, as a *record* of the bands first months together.

You loved your first record as everything you hoped it would be and more. I know this because I read an interview with you, on the train on the way to London. I had also read in the past about the way you and Johnny felt when you went to London

---

13 Separate copies of course. They don't live together, although one does like to imagine them squabbling over the marigolds, locked into an endless cycle of bickering yet affectionate domesticity.

with the tapes of *This Charming Man.* On the way to cut Tiger-milk, I wanted to feel the same way . . . as if you had something new and perfect, something you loved and were sure of. I didn't though. My friend asked me intermittently if I felt like The Smiths yet. No, I replied.

I'm sure of certain things though. I'm sure of the band. There are seven of us. They are the best *band* in the world. Each of them came to me from the stork. I'm soon going to record some more, but for the moment I'm in the kind of lull that always separates the good bits for miles and miles. There might be exciting times ahead, but they might as well be on the moon as far as this morning is concerned. I haven't had any romance for a long time, and it struck me just now that *that* is maybe what happens to people to intoxicate them out of the notion that everything is bland and worthless. Is there anything else? Bungi jumping? Green bowling perhaps? I dunno. The only thing that I really like is playing with the band. They are very good, when they've all bothered to turn up. I just start to enjoy them, but then I think that one of them is bound to leave or die or turn into a junkie. So I start brooding over them like little chicklets.

I think there is a special kind of PMT that comes to you just when you are about to record an lp. I think that's what I've got. Do you get like that? It's rubbish. You promise yourself that you'll have fun after it comes out. But that's when tiresome people want to rip you to shreds if you're good, or stamp on you if you're bad. Oh well.

So anyway, you've got the record, probably along with ninety-five others today alone. If I was you, I probably couldn't be arsed listening to them at all. You are probably fed up with music completely. I know what though. I think we are making a twenty minute film to accompany five songs from Tigermilk. Maybe you would like to be in it? I suppose you'd have to pretty bored, but you're welcome to if you like.

I'm in the student library even though I'm not a student. There are people opposite talking about birds they've shagged, so I can't concentrate. I can't be bothered asking them to shut up though. I'm going to go to the swimming baths to relive the tension.

Cheerio for now,
Stuart

Of the other copies of *Tigermilk* sent out to the Great British media, two of the most significant were those which ended up in the hands of Radio One DJs John Peel and Mark Radcliffe.[14] Peel was/is a broadcasting legend, a tireless champion of the outer fringes of rock without whom the likes of The Sex Pistols, Buzzcocks, The Smiths, Joy Division, Pulp,

John Peel launched the careers of bands like The Sex Pistols, The Smiths, Joy Division, Belle and Sebastian, and countless other rockers on the outer fringes. RIP. Photo by Mark Trayner.

and countless other underground luminaries would probably never have made it. If this sounds like an exaggeration, bear in mind that there are still no national alternative radio stations in the UK, meaning that the holy approbation of Peel was the only hope most marginal acts had of widespread attention. Peel supported Belle and Sebastian from the off, and would have them in for three of his fabled Peel sessions over the years until his death from a heart attack in 2004.[15] Mark Radcliffe is another dry and irreverent northerner whose excellent late night show in the mid '90s—replete with surreal comedy skits, cult film/book reviews, and poetry readings—was, along with the Peel show, a comparative beacon of esoterica throughout the Britpop years, and as soon as he heard "The State I Am In," he was immediately smitten.

---

14 Stevie claims that Richard and Stuart—briefly flatmates at the church hall—drove down to Manchester to deliver *Tigermilk* to Radcliffe in person, although the DJ remembers receiving it through the post. The former account is rather more charming, of course, although the latter is probably the more prosaic truth.

15 Stuart attended the funeral, alongside the similarly grateful and respectful likes of Jarvis Cocker and The White Stripes.

bands that sounded kind of sub-Nirvana at that time," he laments. "And we were always looking for stuff that broadened the musical spectrum, bands who looked further than the last Nirvana album for their influences. But Belle and Sebastian were braver to paint from a broader pallette. They weren't afraid to appear as sensitive balladeers, trying quite ambitious arrangements, which didn't always come off, certainly live, but I think that's still one of the charming things about them. They've got very pretty songs and arrangements, but sometimes they fuck 'em up a bit by putting a few wrong notes in there. But the easiest thing in the world once you've established a certain standard is to hire competent musicians, but that kind of spirit which is engendered by keeping the same bunch of mates is a much more precious commodity." Radcliffe spun tracks from *Tigermilk* regularly throughout the summer of 1996, and booked them in for a pair of live sessions later that year, during which the public first got a flavor of the group's slightly diffident and circumspect nature. They could often come across as rather prickly and suspicious, an attitude which, although undoubtedly justified when dealing with the music biz and certain representatives from the press, was hardly necessary when dealing with sympathetic souls such as Radcliffe, although Stevie does admit to the debt they owe him. "We got famous through the radio, thanks to Mark Radcliffe and John Peel—we bypassed the press completely."

The initial release of *Tigermilk* went almost entirely unheralded in the press, with only the Scottish arts magazine *The List* deigning it worthy of a review (they were probably one of the few who actually listened to it, to be honest), who mentioned Nick Drake, Love, and Tindersticks, concluding with the hope that "Belle and Sebastian reach the size of audience they have the potential to seduce." And that was it. As far as the press were concerned—and they weren't, clearly—this was just another cheapo record from another lo-fi Glasgow band; probably wouldn't even fetch that much at the record exchange, in fact. So what really was its point?

The curious boy was so wrapped up in his own expanding bubble, he barely had time to think about the papers or the wireless or the record company suits with their dubious promises and intrusive over-friendliness. All he could think about were the stories in his head and the songs he had to write around them. And write he did, voraciously, excitedly, nurtured by the knowledge that he now had a group, his very own group, to wrap his troubles in kind.

"Sebastian wrote all of his best songs in 1995," he wrote of his alter ego in the sleevenotes for his first LP. But he wrote too soon: The songs he wrote in 1996 would knock the curious boy, and more besides, for six.

Photo by Stuart Murdoch.

CHAPTER EIGHT
SARAH MARTIN

Waiting for the Moon to Rise

Wee Sadie listened to the voice drifting softly from the tape, and let the goose bumps ripple. Shock and awe, it was.

The curious boy's girlfriend, the one she knew from class, the one who had almost bared all on the cover of her boyfriend's record earlier that year, had told her how good he was, but that's what girlfriends of budding singer-poets are meant to say, isn't it?

But then she listened and found he really was that good. Odd, perhaps, but good.

Taking her violin from the case she began to play along. She could do this fine.

"The Days Are Long Where I Come From"

There she is, up a tree again. A little blond girl, nestled amongst the heavy thick branches of an ancient oak, singing softly to herself and tripping merrily through the dales of her imagination. She was happy and contented, alone but not lonely, safe in her natural habitat. The ground was just too flat and dull for Sarah Martin; treetops were freedom, just like the ocean, where she could spend hours merrily splashing around, finally wading back to shore at her mother's insistence, pruned and beaming.

She was born in Blackburn in the north of England, before the Martin family upped sticks to Liverpool when she was four, the year she began learning the recorder. By the time she turned eight, the family were back in Blackburn, leaving Sarah's early school friends behind. "When we moved back to Blackburn there were no other kids of my age anywhere near," she recalls. "There were a lot of boys my brother's age, two years younger, so I entertained myself a lot."

By this time she had given up on the recorder, an instrument she picked up only when her music teacher told her that she was too young to master the flute, an instrument she adored. "I was obsessed with the flute from when I was tiny," she says. "My mum used to take me to the ballet in Liverpool. I was completely, single-mindedly obsessed with playing the flute, but I was much too little. So they told me I should start playing the recorder, but I jacked that in when I was eight. I hated performing for people." And she's still never really managed to look truly comfortable on stage, frankly. When the equally ill-at-ease Isobel was in the group, the two of them would barely move during gigs, sitting shyly in their corner staring at their shoes. When Isobel left, Sarah was left out there alone, looking more exposed than ever. The rest seem at ease up there, especially in recent years, but Sarah still looks like she'd rather be up a tree, and when she shuffles up to the mike to sing, your heart almost breaks for her, as the eyes of the audience divert en masse in her direction, and when she sang the Brazilian pop standard "Baby" in South America in front of thousands in 2002, the crowd singing lustily along with her nerve-cracked, slightly off-key vocal, it's a moment both touching and awkward; the poor girl must've been terrified, but still she can't disguise her pleasure as the sun-soaked throng cheer her to succeed. Charming is the word.

"I Thought About a New Destination"

Towards the end of her primary education, she began learning violin, the instrument which would eventually win her a place in Belle and Sebastian. And although she writes her songs on guitar, she claims to know only a smattering of chords.

Once school was over, she moved to Glasgow to study at the university, initially to take courses in politics and philosophy, but eventually she ended up studying linguistics and astronomy. "Probably not worth the paper they're written on," Stuart wryly noted of her degrees in the liner notes to *If You're Feeling Sinister,* the first record she would play on with the group.

While at university, she shared a flat with Jason MacPhail, the cap'n of the band V-Twin, who unwittingly brought Chris and Isobel into Stuart's orbit. Before V-Twin formed, Jason was just as keen to form a band as Stuart. In fact, Stuart had asked him to form one with him. "Jason was like, 'Oh that guy's crazy,'" says Sarah, who occasionally would be dragged by Jason down to a practice room on a Sunday morning, where, along with various cohorts, they would drone their way through chords in search of a song. This would be Sarah's first and only taste of band life—such as it was—before she met Stuart, whose girlfriend, Joanne, she knew from an Old Icelandic class she took at the University. Jason had already suggested to Stuart that he recruit Sarah on violin, but when he eventually asked her, she wasn't particularly excited by the invitation: "Until I heard some of the songs, which were totally amazing: 'Expectations,' 'The State I Am In,' 'Put the Book Back on the Shelf,' really great songs."

As Stuart explains, "The fiddler on *Tigermilk* was moving to Ireland, so there was no prospect of him being involved on a daily basis, so I took a copy of *Tigermilk* round to Sarah's house. And she was very keen. And again, it wasn't as if anybody got auditioned or anything, it was more like a feeling, and I'm glad that it went more by feelings than anything else, because there's a sensibility when the group together, us being, in a sense, the musical dregs. Not being particularly interested in musicianship, but interested in capturing a feeling."

Like most folks, Sarah thought Stuart "quite odd, but pretty interesting," certainly odd and interesting enough to agree to play violin on the record he and his barely year-old band were about to make.

And Wee Sadie found that when she played with the boys and girl in the band, it was like dreaming up a tree, like bobbing in the surf, like love and freedom combined.

CHAPTER NINE

IF YOU'RE FEELING SINISTER

Make a New Cult Every Day

The group settled into a clean and robust thrum, huddled in a vague circle in the recording room which, in days gone by, would've thronged with the clatter of church collections and the hearty blare of Christian hymns. It was a very different kind of service they were conducting today, however, the only prayers being made were those of the rock 'n' roll kind: please, Lord, no bum notes, I hope I can remember my part, let's nail this take in one, that sort of thing.

Three months previously they had convened in this very same room to record their first LP, a task they had undertaken with minimal fuss and maximum result. Now they were recording another, with songs about girls and God, dreams of horses and stars of track and field. And just as before, their task would be over in a week. No point beating around the burning bush when the iron is hot.

Reverb picked at his Fender, serious as cancer; Beans frowned at his keyboard dressed in a yellow cape which looked suspiciously like a bedsheet; Bel giggled behind her cello at a joke only she could hear; Wee Sadie sat cross-legged, head nestled sleepily on her violin; Richard affected that curiously constipated look he wore whenever he sat on a drum-stool; Mick stood head-bowed, holding his trumpet like a golf club, waiting for his cue; Stuart David hid himself behind an amp, playing his bass almost as an after-

thought as he tried to turn the pages of his book with his feet; and the curious boy listened carefully to the sound they made and knew that it was good. Catch him in a particularly tender moment and he'd tell you it was the best he'd ever heard.

It was all going disconcertingly well. Those scattered copies of *Tigermilk* were slowly beginning to disappear from whatever racks had them stocked, as word got around about this mysterious gang from Glasgow who some were already whispering in the same breath as The Smiths. This was enough to pique the flagging interests of those who prayed nightly for a new band to come along and nurture their sensitive, introspective ways. Thanks to the airplay from Radcliffe and Peel, as well as Radio One's early evening indie show the Evening Session, which had also started championing the group, their cult was growing by the hour. But since copies of *Tigermilk* were so hard to come by, their nascent apostles had no choice but to contact the group directly—not in itself an easy task, necessitating some judicious detective work—and ask for more information. Duly flattered by the attention, Stuart would endeavor to answer every letter personally, evidently recognizing something of himself in their desire to make meaningful contact with favored musicians. The following letter, for example, enthusiastically answered the kind of query typically found in most early fan correspondence.

> Dear Rhys,
>
> Thank you for showing interest in Belle and Sebastian. I'll tell you what's happening with the record. Initially we put them around Glasgow and Edinburgh.
>
> When Mark Radcliffe started playing the record we did mail order from Stow, then we got a distribution deal for the UK. Because there's not many of the records pressed, you are best to send a cheque for £8 (that's all inclusive) to Stow, payable to Electric Honey Records, *quite* soon. We may reissue *Tigermilk* (ten songs, either way) on CD if things go to plan, but that may be in years rather than months, because we are already concentrating on other projects . . . see below.
>
> We got together at the turn of the year to do the Stow College

project, which turned into *Tigermilk*. It occurs to me now that I should have just called the record *Belle and Sebastian*, but what the heck. We are all slaves to impulse! Perhaps the third LP ought to be eponymous, like the Velvet Underground.

All the songs were written last year, apart from "My Wandering Days," which was written on the first of January this year. I've written the second LP, which we are recording at the start of August for Jeepster Records of London. I'd like to call the record *Falling Sentry Blades,* but it depends on the picture I put on the front.

(*Tigermilk* was called *Tigermilk* because the wee tiger was getting his milk on the cover.) The record will be ten songs long, which is as long as my mind can accomodate. It will be available on all formats, though I recommend the vinyl, as that is how the project has been conceived. It will be available everywhere! The songs were written between January and June.

I think we'll leave off playing live till October, and then, depending on the demand, we'll try and play a few nice halls the length of Great Britain. At some point, I'd like to do an LP titled *Lazy Line Painter Jane: a Sympathetic Rendering of Old Favourites!* For this, we might rework some older songs, and put a couple of lengthy new ones in, to make a six-track LP reminiscent of Felt.

That's about all there is to say. I hope that you enjoy the record if you decide to buy one.

Sincerely,
Stuart

Falling Sentry Blades would never make it as a title, of course, at least not yet, nor have they released an eponymous album, although *Lazy Line Painter Jane*—sans the above suffix—would eventually be the name given to the EP collection released in 2000. As for that *Tigermilk* reissue, it would turn up sooner than Stuart seems to have assumed: A remastered CD version became widely available in 1999.

In January of 1996, three months before the recording of *Tigermilk,* Mark Jones met the group in The Grosvenor Café, that fateful vortex at the center or thereabouts of the Belle and Sebastian universe, and more or less begged them to sign with Jeepster, keen to secure their signature before anyone else had the chance. "He was so London it was unbelievable," laughs Stuart. "He came up in a big silver puffa jacket, sitting in the Grosvenor Café going [in motormouth cockney brogue], 'What it is, man, what it is . . . ' He stood out like a sore thumb, hanging himself by his own rope."

Jones frothed about how unique he thought they were, and how important and successful they deserved to be. This was all very flattering, especially for Stuart, but being innately obstreperous, the group had no intention of showing Jones that his overtures meant anything to them. Call this indie-cool, if you like, but it should be remembered that the Scots are by nature a circumspect race, suspicious and paranoid, with a self-deprecating irreverence which may well suggest an easygoing acceptance of some perceived inferiority, but actually masks a knowing sense of superiority over, well, pretty much everyone who isn't them. Plus they have a keen nose for bullshit, especially when it emanates from London. So to the London-based music biz and press, Belle and Sebastian always seemed infuriatingly obstinate and precious, whereas up in Scotland, they were generally hailed as canny cats getting one over on the Man. "All that media-London thing is just nonsense," scoffs Stuart David. "And we knew it was nonsense, so we approached it with a sense of humor. But media-London don't really understand a Scottish sense of humor."

So the Scots let the man from London sweat. "We gave him a hard time, we really put him through the wringer," admits Stuart. "We didn't tell him that we were gonna sign to him, but he was terrified that a scrum of people were hot on his heels, and he didn't have any money to offer us up front. The thing was we knew we wanted a fifty/fifty indie deal, rather than take the money now. We wanted to own half our records, and that's what Mark gave us. Mark was hungry, and so was I." In a fit of unnecessary desperation, pen twitching in his pocket, Jones offered the group anything—anything—they wanted in return for their signature. Chris asked for a pair of forty-inch flares, Celtic to win the league cup, and a date with Kate Moss. He's still waiting.

Island Records also met with the band around this time, but Stuart had already decided that Jeepster were the label for them. He had trusted fate to lead the way so far, and had yet to be disappointed, so the fact that he'd been led to Jeepster via a guy he'd met on the Stow course which he'd been led to via the flatmate of the boy he met on Beatbox, was enough to convince him that it was meant to be. But although they agreed to become the first signing to the label—Jeepster wouldn't actually come into official being until June—the group refused to sign until August, when it was decided that they would record their second LP. Stuart wrote a letter fully demonstrating the determination of his intentions.

24 Novar Drive
Glasgow
G12 9PU
15th May 1996

Dear Mark,

I have been thinking about our meeting last Friday, and I have been trying to consolidate what our best way forward is. I think we should stick to what we know, and what we are good at. To sway from these things would be daft. I'll explain.

I've been trying to turn my thoughts to recording at the beginning of August, rather than at the end. This will give you more time to manouver. A sleek operation like Jeepster should be able to move pretty fast anyway, and I'll help with the knowledge I've gained from *Tigermilk*. I'll do the artwork, and lay it out with Andrew Symington in Glasgow, for instance.

The main thing is that we get the record recorded in August. The project will change if that doesn't happen, and perhaps some things will be lost. I see it as being the band's work, something that just has to be done to establish our relationship with you. It was a complete idea as soon as I thought that we were going to work with Jeepster. As Stuart [David] said yesterday, we'll probably have more fun recording subsequent singles, but that is a luxury we will enjoy once we've recorded a cracking album.

What you do with the album should depend on the circumstances at the end of August. How much work did we do with *Tigermilk*? If you will have to break us from zero, then perhaps we could take a single from the record. This is something I really want to avoid though. If you spend prudently, I think we can afford to put the LP out on its own. We won't need that much dough to record.

I think we will have time to put the record out in the autumn. I will be sad if that doesn't happen. I want to make the MM and NME end of year charts, twice! I don't go with all that was being said about scheduling. If that was true, then everything would be released in one week in October, or one week in January, every year. We can afford to be less shackled I think. A wee bit anyway. It's all relative. If you start selling bags, you could make a point of releasing your album on Christmas Day every year for a decade!

I think you should start making plans for recording. We won't need three weeks. I'd like to ask for eight days, scheduled as follows.

Day1 Day2 Day3 Day off Day4 Day5 Day off Day6 Day7

The last day would only be an option to take, maybe three days after we had finished, in case we had to remix anything. We'd like to use Ca Va, Studio 1, with Gregor Reid as the engineer. What about a producer? I'm going to send forty copies of *Tigermilk,* if Alan allows. You will probably hand some of them on to producers you might think suitable. See who takes the bait.

We will have all the parts arranged before we go in, but I think care has to be taken with the live feel that we get when we record the backing tracks. Also, the singing has to be given special attention. I'd like some of the songs to have a Northern Soul feel, coming close to the Blue Cat and Red Bird recordings in the sixties, and some to be closer to the sound of *Tapestry* by Carole King. By chance, I tuned to the end of Radcliffe's show two nights ago. There was what I assumed to be a Nick Drake song playing. I'd never heard it before, but the sound of it was flawless. It seemed to be up to date, and classic at the same time. I know that his singing and playing was exceptional, but if it was Joe Boyd that produced the record, he must come in for some praise too. Is he still alive though? Did anyone think of that? Poor Nick Drake. His songs were tragic from start to finish, but he had such a beautiful voice.

I think I've gone on enough. The main thing in the long run is that we should have fun. Although I don't think of it as work, I think I will feel a bit worn out by the time the LP's finished. But that's OK. I will feel a lot better when people are buying and listening to the songs.

The LP might be called *Cock Fun*. Ha ha ha! It depends on how my photography goes! I'll probably change it about six times more. Here is a possible running order. I can't give you a tape yet. Sorry.

"Like Dylan in the Movies"
"If You're Feeling Sinister"
"Me and the Major"
"The Fox in the Snow"
"The Sunday Gang"
"Seeing Other People"

"Get Me Away from Here, I'm Dying"
"The Stars of Track and Field"
"Mayfly"
"The Boy Done Wrong Again"

Best Wishes,
Stuart

With "Judy and the Dream of Horses" taking the place of the mysterious "The Sunday Gang," a song inspired by the Sunday school kids Stuart had got to know at the church hall—"It came along like a friendly Labrador and could not be ignored," he claims—these would be the songs which made up *If You're Feeling Sinister* (and not *Cock Fun*, sadly; "Isobel did *not* like the idea," Stuart unsurprisingly declares), which was eventually recorded almost exactly as Stuart had dictated. It's both interesting and perplexing to note that, despite Stuart's claim that he had no interest in Northern Soul at this time ("I didn't care, I didn't want to know about that stuff"), he should reference two cult Northern Soul labels as example of the kind of sound he was after, a sound notably missing from the finished record and one, which, in any case, hardly seems suitable for this material. It wouldn't be until "Dirty Dream Number Two" on *The Boy with the Arab Strap* and, more obviously, "Woman's Realm" and "There's Too Much Love" on *Fold Your Hands Child, You Walk Like a Peasant* that the appropriate Northern Soul influence would be achieved. And although he wasn't as familiar with his music as many initially assumed, it was clear that Stuart had fallen under the spell of Nick Drake (aided by the ever influential Mark Radcliffe, it seems), and his desire to work with

Drake's famed producer and mentor Joe Boyd—who was and is very much alive—was certainly a tantalizing one, although with hindsight such a collaboration would doubtlessly bring about the kind of comparisons Stuart would be understandably keen to avoid.

As the band's only songwriter, Stuart was the only member of the group to receive a publishing deal once they did—much to Jones's relief—eventually sign with Jeepster, although once the band became a growing concern and it looked like it might be something which the rest could

The band eventually signed to Jeepster. Photo by Stuart Murdoch.

give up their day jobs for, he eventually split the publishing between them. Stuart David, however, in a tellingly prescient move, had his own separate contract from the start. As Stevie says, "Stuart David was in it for himself, but at least he was honest about it." The boy David had never made a secret of the fact that the group wasn't the be-all and end-all for him ("nothing is the be-all and end-all for me"), and that really the most important things to him were his writing, his own music, and the right to live his life, which wouldn't be dictated by group activities. "I'd been working on being free and not having a job for ten years by then," he explains. "And I'd been working on my own songs and my own bands, and the contract implied that both of those things could conceivably be curtailed if I signed it how it was. I was quite happy not to sign at all, and just play with the band as normal, and not take any of the money. But they all decided we all had to sign or no one would, so I got a contract that would still let me do my own music, and not be someone else's property." A man wanting to do things on his own terms in a band wanting to do things on their own terms—it was never going to last.

"I was just high, I was loving it," exclaimed Stuart of the excitement of 1996. His creative juices spiked by *Tigermilk*'s small yet telling success, the songs continued to flow, and between January and summer he had enough songs ready for another LP. And they were good. Better than that, they were the best he'd written yet. One of them, "Get Me Away from Here I'm Dying," was even a self-deprecating yet affectionate testament to the group themselves.

> *Think of it this way*
> *You could either be successful or be us*
> *With our winning smiles, and us*
> *With our catchy tunes, and us*
> *Now we're photogenic*
> *You know, we don't stand a chance*

Don't stand a chance? They were hardly freaks. Indeed, if they had been so inclined, they could've easily sold handsome Stu and lovely Bel as indie pinups du jour, with maybe rugged Rich as the housewives' favorite. "At the same time I knew we weren't going to play any industry games," counters Stuart, by way of vague agreement. "It was so obvious we didn't fit any industry mold, and in an industry sense we didn't stand a chance. The thing is, we still don't stand a chance. We've done it the hard way, we haven't had a leg up from fashion promoters or anything."

But it wasn't all aw-shucks-ma-we-suck. *"Nobody writes them like they used to so it may as well be me,"* he declares, almost unwillingly, as if so disillusioned with the dearth of decent new music around him and the lack of anyone willing to do anything about it, he has no choice but to step up to the plate. This could easily sound like hubris were it not for the fact that, quite obviously to anyone with a heart and ears that worked, this kid was the best songwriter to breeze out of the gates since . . . well, take your pick. "I'm not saying, 'Hey, I'm much better than these dudes,'" he protests. But self-aggrandizement doesn't come naturally to him in conversation, and one is never in doubt of the confidence and creative self-esteem simmering under that self-effacing surface. He did admit, however, that the song was inspired by his annoyance at the arid state of most popular music at the time, sending him off on a determined mission to write something more substantial. "'Get Me Away from Here' was more like, get me out of this place because I can't stand the music. Getting out of a club—bang!—into the street. Let me have the music in my head rather than the music in here, because it's driving me nuts." The title could also be taken as the anguished cry of a housebound M.E. sufferer, but Stuart claimed that "by the time we recorded *Tigermilk* I was pretty much functioning like a normal person," and although he would occasionally have off days—without the group's knowledge: "I'd hide away from them and lean against a wall for a bit"—he had come a long way from the invalidity of the early '90s. The trips to San Francisco, the final realization of his pop 'n' roll dreams and the ensuing adrenaline rush of creativity must have done his mental and physical health a world of good, and so he had been reborn as a restless spirit desperate to make up for lost time by cramming in as much activity as he could into every waking moment.

With eleven fine new songs in place,[1] the group—including newest recruit Sarah Martin—reconvened at Ca Va studios, this time working with in-house engineer Tony Doogan, since Gregor Reid was unavailable. Reid had done a remarkable job with *Tigermilk* and the group was sorry to lose him, but Doogan was a safe pair of hands, a copacetic collaborator who would go on to record nearly all of their subsequent records.

The album opened with one of the group's signature tunes, "The

---

[1] "This Is Just a Modern Rock Song," recorded at the time, was eventually dropped from the track-listing at Jeepster's suggestion.

Stars of Track and Field," an alternative radio hit on both sides of the Atlantic and for many their first introduction to the perfumed gardens of Belle and Sebastian. As would be the case on the opening tracks on all of their first four LPs, the song begins with Stuart alone, as if welcoming the listener personally into his private, personal church, the group joining him in gradual rising steps. A tale of playing-fields jealousy, Stuart pitches himself into an athletic landscape he knows and loves all too well, carefully noting the *"blue velour and silk"* and *"terry underwear"* of the athlete's uniform as if they were garments of the most splendid quality.

If You're Feeling Sinister could almost be thought of as Belle and Sebastian's sex album, hardly something to bother Prince's twitching jockstrap, perhaps, but a record preoccupied with the—often frustrated—pleasures of the flesh nonetheless. The subject raises its sweaty little head for the first time here, with this gym-slip femme fatale, this *"honey with a following of innocent boys"* giving herself up willingly to the stars of track and field. The most joyous moment comes when our jealous voyeur shifts up an octave into *"And when she's on her back, she has the knowledge to get her into college."* Rarely has a voice so pure sung words so soiled. Great pop is made up of little special moments, and Stuart Murdoch lilting into *"on her back"* is one of them.

Stuart described "Seeing Other People" at the time as "one of the most personal songs I've ever written," something he still maintains to this day. "That *is* autobiographical," he maintains. "I like that song, it still feels quite fresh to sing it because I picture a time and a place, caught up in a little scenario. I have fond memories of the cast of that particular song." One can only assume, judging from the lyrics, that he and Jo were in some state of confusion at the time, as well as suffering some sort of awkward sexual stalemate (he did say it was autobiographical, so let us force conjecture). *"Seeing other people at least that's what we say we are doing."* Who knew what was going on? Isobel, a peripheral but significantly observant player on this scene, claims to have witnessed a few curious goings on. "I saw him lead her on a merry dance quite a lot, cat and mouse kind of stuff. So I thought, I've got your number, mate," said Isobel. But in this song the narrator seems neither cat nor mouse; a fur ball, maybe.

"Me and the Major" is a catty and vilified put-down of the generation gap from the perspective of a nice young boy irritated by the knee-jerk prejudices of the older set. *"Me and the Major could become close friends"* sighs the church-going cherub, if only it weren't for the old man's narrow-minded, tabloid-fed beliefs, the right-wing major being determinedly unaware that the unkempt youngster before him is in fact a God-loving soul with a passion for poetry and prose.[2] These frustrations were originally sparked off by Stuart's encounter with an actual real life Major, a regular at Hyndland church, who actually turned out not to be as blinkered as he originally thought. "The Major is a chap that comes to our church," he explains. "He's a great guy, but when you meet somebody for the first time you can let your imagination run away with you. I remember going into the church and the minister said something about, 'If you want to volunteer for Christian Aid collections, leave your name at the back.' And I thought the Major was one of the elders so after the service I asked him if he knew where I could sign for Christian Aid. He said [affects disapproving colonial brogue], 'Hmm, Christian Aid, that's a left-wing organization, I think.' As if that was a really bad thing!"

And so to "The Fox in the Snow," Stevie Jackson's favorite Belle and Sebastian song, and perhaps the perfect example of their ability to wrench impossible sadness from the simplest of conceits, is ostensibly the wonderings of Stuart Murdoch witnessing a family of foxes *"illuminated so clearly on a snowy night on the waste ground behind the hall,"* but the song drifts off into lanes of such indescribable beauty it transcends specific meaning to become something quite impossible to define. Quite simply, it's a ridiculously beautiful song rendered in such a way—piano, cello, and heartbeat Velvets toms—that its meaning becomes irrelevant, and all that ultimately matters is the aching winter magic of the whole. Stevie, probably Stuart's staunchest and most loyal fan, can only quote in awe. " *'Second to being born, second to dying too,'* it's as good as Dylan, as good as anything I've heard," he says, shrugging in subservience. It is a song which, in all its aching grace, creaking and glinting like frosted railings, perhaps sums up more than any other why this is a group which can make the hardiest hard-nut weep.

---

2 Any nice young boy or girl who's ever held a door open for an oldster, only to be greeted with impolite indifference, will grit their teeth in recognition here.

Since their records had been designed for vinyl—a determinedly traditionalist conceit which their critics would dismiss as a kind of stunted luddism—the group would place an approximately ten-second gap on the CD between the end and beginning of each "side," where one could mime the flipping over of an LP if one were particularly desperate. This obsession with the smallest aesthetic detail was actually one of the group's most charming and commendable facets; the fact that they care about these things makes them worth caring about. So side two opens with "Get Me Away from Here I'm Dying," Stuart's autobiographical tribute to the group and a willful disassociation from the frigid airs of contemporary pop, a song as spry and contagious as a contaminated monkey, and a particular favorite of Stuart David. "I still can't quite work out how Stuart did that," he enthuses. "The triplet rhythm of the vocal melody and the structure of the vocal melody—it's very special."

This bumptiousness in turn fades into an inexplicably touching ambient recording of children at play, which when overlaid onto the gently thrumming intro of the title track creates a tender mood of happy/sad nostalgia with Chris's piano glissando skimming like a hopscotch stone. This sense of playground ennui actually has very little to do with the actual song itself, but is a beautifully judged opening nonetheless, drawing us into another of Stuart's overlapping character traits, starting with Anthony, who is dropped after the first verse in favor of Hilary, a confused girl into *"S&M and Bible studies"* desperately seeking some form of religious salvation at the crux of the song. "This was me writing about characters that I saw around me," Stuart explains. "People that were hanging out in the clubs, kids that were into music. As far as I can see, this was a little story about what one of these people might think about religion. It was interesting to me, because I was starting to go to church every week, I was really getting into this. I knew what I felt, but I wanted to paint a picture of what some kids might've felt, maybe if they were a bit younger, a bit more disillusioned and out there."

Following the gleefully upbeat "Mayfly" and the somber "The Boy Done Wrong Again" (the only song in the B&S canon that actually does sound like Nick Drake), the album closes with "Judy and the Dream of Horses," a celebratory bauble of pop and one of the group's most irresistible songs. Based around one of Stuart's favorite narrative conceits—a smart girl gone bad and loving it, with the quivering narrator alternately lamenting and celebrating her newfound licentiousness. "I always thought 'Judy' was a bit about me, but not all of it," posits Isobel, a notion Stuart refutes with stunned disbelief. "Isobel? No, it's not about Isobel." This will become a common reaction every time it is suggested that Isobel might have inspired a particular song. "If she thinks that, then fine. Maybe I'm wrong. Maybe a line might have been suggested by something she told me. In a writer's conceit these things can be forgotten. But that song I was really pleased with, it came during a long walk to Cambuslang along the Clyde, the whole song was there. But it's definitely a fiction."

Even more so than *Tigermilk, If You're Feeling Sinister* was a fairly staggering showcase for Stuart Murdoch's not inconsiderable songwriting skills. It is a near-perfect collection, the whole thing utterly of a piece yet with each song strong enough to stand on its own: the mark of a truly great pop record. Generally regarded amongst fans to be the group's finest hour, oddly it has never been popular with the group themselves, who remain disappointed with the production and performance. "I think we thought we could just play better," Stevie bemoans. "And with *Tigermilk* there had been someone cracking the whip, but on this one people had their own ideas of how things should be done, and maybe this wasn't the time to see it through in that kind of exploratory manner. It was probably the first freely creative thing the band had done, and it was with a different engineer, who was a bit of an unknown quantity at this stage. I think Stuart really wanted to do that album with Gregor, but he was working with The Pastels, and so initially there was a little nervousness about working with somebody different."

Chris expressed similar reservations in regards to the album: "I was still thinking that the songs were amazing, but we could have maybe opened out a bit more and made the music stronger. But I didn't have a strong enough personality to grab a song off Stuart and say, 'Your strummy acoustic guitar way is not the best way of doing it.' And I had neither the confidence nor the ability to come up with a better way of doing it." Even the man responsible for the superior contents of the record felt that it could have been stronger. "The first one was quite clinically worked out in terms of parts," he says. "Everything went to plan. And also you've got the energy of this new bunch playing together, the enthusiasm and naïveté which you can hear on the LP—it's got a lot of energy. But at the same time they were following my set ideas. By the time we sat down with the second LP, we were getting to know each other, we were beginning to acknowledge that we had a bit of a band going on here, and instead of me working out the parts for everybody, they were quite capable of working out the parts themselves. Obviously this is going to pay dividends in the long run, but at the time, trying to record a second album and make it better, we ended up coming up short. It's not a bad thing. We were trying to make *Tapestry,* trying to make *Court and Spark,* a great second record. I knew I had a great bunch of songs, which I'd written so quickly, and I felt they were my best songs at this point. I think now when we play those songs live we have a better feel for them. It's just a simple case of production—we produced it ourselves in essence; it's a tall order."

Granted, it's a much sparser record than its more stylistically varied predecessor, but the one thing the group do all agree on is that the songs on *Sinister* are uniformly stronger, each one a beautifully sculptured tumble of melody and prose. *If You're Feeling Sinister* cemented Stuart Murdoch's vision and aesthetic to such a degree that, eight years on, it's still considered today to be the essence of Belle and Sebastian, and until *Tigermilk* was released on CD in 1999, it was the record upon which the group's reputation rested and the one which introduced them to a far wider set of eyes and ears than their limited-edition debut.

On the day they finished recording the album, Mark and Vanessa from Jeepster brought them presents to celebrate, and in Sarah's flat they sat happily amongst a scattered pile of wrapping paper, spark guns, chattering teeth, and fake cigarettes, each nursing a bottle of champagne and a specially made B&S T-shirt, which they all take to Oxfam the very next day. The T-shirts, that is, not the champagne. Some things are too good for charity.

During the mastering stage for *Sinister,* Stuart and Bel ended their tentative ambiguous courtship and began an equally ambiguous relationship. Although not officially. It would never be official. And it would never be easy. "We never really officially went out, but we were involved with each other, which was really upsetting for me and the source of a lot of grief," sighed Bel. "We were involved on and off for five years, but by the last year it was petering off. I was so exhausted, I remember just waking up, being twenty-five, and just being exhausted with it all. I thought, 'This is just going to finish me off.'" Although there had always been some kind of mutual attraction between them, Isobel had never been entirely sure of Stuart's feelings towards her until she started seeing "this wee guy who shared a flat with Stuart David, and I remember Stuart M's reaction, like he was jealous or something, and I thought, 'Oh.'"

Stevie seemed vaguely aware of his intentions—"After *Tigermilk* I didn't see him for months, he was chasing Bel," he says with a hint of resentment—but didn't actually realize there was anything going on between the two for the first year until Sarah had to spell it out. "I'm naïve and stupid," he shrugs, perhaps wishing he'd stayed that way.

Recalling the early days of their relationship, Isobel grins: "I had a few irons in the fire at that time. Y'know, when you're nineteen and you're just a bit of a case. I thought he was really intriguing but I kind of had his number as well. God, I wish I'd stuck to that. . . ." And his number was? "I think some artists are complete malcontents, there's always something *better*. Artistic people can be very seductive, and even though they can be very bad, there can be these amazing highs and intense lows. He would say, 'I love you, but I can't be with you.' And I would be, like, 'What am I supposed to do with that? Are you gay? What are you?' And we'd maybe not see each other for a while, and say someone would ask me out, I'd go and meet them and my heart wouldn't be in it—but Stuart would turn up on the day! What do you do?"

Romantic entanglements within bands are often problematic affairs, and the tryst betwixt Isobel and Stuart was no different, causing no end of resentment and divisions within the Belle and Sebastian ranks. "Their whole relationship was ambiguous at best, with regards to how it affected the group, and it was one never-ending problem," Stevie complained. "It veered from awkwardness to complete nightmarishness. I mean, really, really terrible. Essentially it didn't work. It worked in the sense that we made good records, but I think pretty early on the records started going downhill. Their relationship got in the way of business all the time. Initially when I first met Isobel I thought we were going to be good friends, I liked her and felt quite close to her, but when the Stuart and Isobel thing started it created a complete division. It became Stuart and Isobel and the rest of us. It caused complete resentment, not just by me but from everyone."

Stuart was obviously a good deal older than Bel, and while it would be remiss to blame him for all their problems, one has to wonder whether he took some advantage of this girl who, by her own admission, was clearly starstruck by this enigmatic elder poet. Stevie, for one, is in two fleeting minds. "I blame both of them," he complains, before turning on a dime. "In fact, I mostly blame Stuart to be honest, because he should know better. My one regret is that I was always complaining to him about everything, and I wish I had complained to Isobel a bit more, but by that point we didn't connect at all. Maybe it's the inverse of that old adage, when you look back you only remember the good things, but when I look back I only remember it being completely horrible."

Stuart, by his own admission, became a doormat upon which Isobel could stamp her every whim, which more often than not went against the group's best interests. Arguments between them would regularly flare up backstage at gigs and in the studio, creating the kind of tense atmosphere which was hardly conducive to group harmony, and days in the studio could often be wasted as a result of their personal preoccupations. "As far as I was concerned that mainly caused problems in the studio, rather than musically," claims Neil, before adding with a rueful smile, "I must have rose-tinted glasses. I don't think [their relationship] hugely shaped things other than Stuart looking out for Bel in a way he might not look out for other people. She wouldn't put her hand up to say no about something for fear of being seen as the one putting the spanner in the works. I can totally understand why she didn't want to be seen publicly as the one putting a stop to things like touring. She possibly should've had more courage and faith in the rest of the band to know that they wouldn't all think she was a bitch for sliding their ideas. But when she didn't, Stuart would step in for her. And I think that was a positive side of the relationship. When Stevie's sitting there going, 'Let's do six months on the road,' she didn't want to be the one going, 'Well, you can't have your dreams, Stevie.'"

And yet Isobel still felt unfairly vilified, exacerbating her already burgeoning desire to flee the coop and spread her own songbird wings.

* * *

Prior to the release of the album the group played a gig at Café Soma in Glasgow, an occasion Stevie recognizes as a turning point in their fortunes. "I lived at the end of the street at the time," he recalls fondly. "And I remember walking down the street straight into Café Soma and finding the place just packed out. There was such an atmosphere that night, it was really exciting, it really felt like this was turning into something. It was a beautiful night." Suitably bolstered by their rapidly growing fanbase, they played their biggest gig yet in the suitably bookish climes of the Mitchell Library in Glasgow's Moir Hall on October 18, exactly a month to the day before the album was released. The library wasn't used to accommodating rock 'n' roll bands, of course, so the group had to set up their own stage; in fact they set up two, one for the main body of the group and another at the opposite end of the room for Stuart David and Chris. Why? Because they could, frankly. Unfortunately, the sound delay between the stages meant that the two factions were rarely in synch, resulting in the kind of technically inept performance which the group were becoming frustratedly used to. "I think me and Stuart came up with that," recalls Stuart David hazily. "Whenever I went into a place we were playing I always looked for a way to use the space. It sounded fine to me, because I could hear the band the way I could hear them, and my bass amp was right next to me, so I played in time with what I could hear, and everything was just right. But that probably wasn't the case if you were in the middle of the room. It was still great though because Stuart had to do a keyboard part in one song and he had to run through the hall to our stage. Then I think there was a fight on our stage between Stuart and Chris or something. That was always more what interested me. Just the event of the thing. Other people in the band got fed up with that stuff because they were musicians, but I can't really play anyway. I just like the event." As did the majority of their audiences, it would seem. Indeed, despite the critical brickbats which rained upon most of their early performances, the fans would never really have a problem with the technical glitches and longueurs, all of which were worth it for those magical moments when the group got it together—which in truth was more often than legend would have you believe.

As if celebrating the refined, distinctly un–rock 'n' roll nature of the library, Stuart printed up concert programs welcoming the faithful to their leather-bound hootenanny:

Ladies and Gentlemen,

Welcome to our little evening's entertainment in the plush munici-pal surrounds of the Mitchell Library. I'm certain Mr. Mitchell would turn in his book-lined grave if he knew what we were doing here tonight. We are privileged to have Falkirk's Arab Strap playing with us tonight. They will open with a short set of acoustic obser-vations. They are good, but quite rude, so it is suggested that you position your hands over the ears of small children in readiness. Next come Belle and Sebastian. Recording on the Jeepster label, this group (all active members of the T.A.) will play songs from the record *If You're Feeling Sinister.* In fact, they will play the whole record in sequence. This is the sort of indulgence that gives rock a bad name. To give you something to do while you listen to ten songs which you probably don't know, we have provided a handy checklist opposite. The band have stuck the encore onto the end of the set, so you can be assured that there will be no ugly surprises to come between you and your Saturday gins.

True to their printed word, Belle and Sebastian proceeded to play their new album in sequence with an encore lost to memory, wrapped up in books and out-of-synch. "We were really D.I.Y., which is proba-bly why the first gigs were so bad," muses Neil. "We had a crew of three, including me." As far as Stuart was concerned, this no-frills setup was presumably a way of—if you'll allow the expression—keeping it real. "Keeping it shit," retorts Neil, who ever since the group had begun had been an ever-present conspirator, taking a more and more prominent or-ganizational role with every passing day. He would never really "offi-cially" become their manager—he still refers to Stuart as "the gaffer"—but he quickly fell into the role in all but name, displaying an amazing amount of aptitude and confidence for one so young. As stub-born and ambitious as Stuart himself, he became an ideal ally and facil-itator, a man who knew what he wanted and didn't mind telling anyone to fuck right off if he didn't get it. All in the most charming manner possible, of course. "Neil became our manager in the same way as Mark became our label—by attrition, by being around," Stuart explains. "We didn't call Neil our manager for ages, he was our helper. And we were managing ourselves, but later on I was quite happy to hand the reins to Neil. Obviously, he'd proved himself and continues to prove himself. He was just a kid—much younger than me—managing this group of adults and kids, an unwieldy bunch. Rough Trade claim he's the best manager they've ever dealt with."

A few days after the gig, on October 26 to be exact, Mark Jones and the group—sans Stevie who by this time was working as an occupational therapist in Erskine and couldn't get off work—flew to New York to visit The Enclave, a Virgin/EMI subsidiary interested in releasing their records in the States.

Stuart David's faux screenplay *Little Ink Movies of B&S in New York* adroitly captures the—in this case, literal—innocents abroad nature of Belle and Sebastian at this time, with the group depicted very much as wide-eyed if irreverent strangers in a strange and not entirely welcome land.

Affectionately known as "the Kids" amongst the group's elder members, Chris and Isobel, although both twenty years old, still slept with cuddly toys, a stuffed owl and rabbit respectively. Stuart David quite rightfully found this somewhat disturbing, dryly chastizing them for their cutesy immaturity, as recalled in this New York taxi exchange:

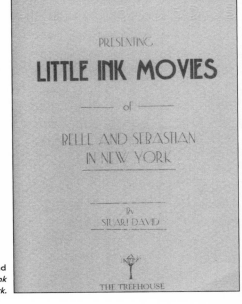

PRESENTING

LITTLE INK MOVIES

—— of ——

BELLE AND SEBASTIAN
IN NEW YORK

By
STUART DAVID

THE TREEHOUSE

Stuart David's screenplay of Belle and Sebastian's first New York trip *Little Ink Movies of B&S in New York.*

Chris
What you've got to remember is, myself and Isobel haven't long turned twenty and are still entitled to behave like children the majority of the time.

Isobel
Yeaaaah!
She falls silent.

Isobel
I didn't even hear what you said then, Chris. I just cheered.

Chris
See what I mean? I rest my case.

Between meetings with The Enclave the group amused themselves, like The Beatles in *A Hard Day's Night,* by running a quiet riot through

Ink Polaroids
of Belle & Sebastian

by
Stuart David

...it used to be I had a camera called a Zenit—but now I just take photographs with a cheap old pen...

here are some I took of
Belle & Sebastian

Belle and Sebastian on their excursion to New York. Photo by Stuart David.

the city, messing around in charity shops—where Chris bought the ankle-length ladies' fur coat later so admired by Seymour Stein—and dancing in Central Park, an incident filmed by Stuart David on Wee Karn's Super 8 camera and later used as backup footage at his Looper gigs. The aerophobic Richard, strongly against his better judgement, spent a terrifying journey in a helicopter with Mark Jones (and a qualified pilot, of course) during which they swooped between the twin towers, while down below, Stuart, a huge fan of revered U.S. independent filmmaker Hal Hartley, dropped a demo tape off at his office in the hope that he would use the group in one of his films. He never heard back. Meanwhile, Mark Jones somehow managed to arrange a lunch for them with legendary ex-pat gay icon Quentin Crisp, a rite of passage seemingly required of all visiting British bands. Not that B&S seemed particularly excited by the prospect: "Who's the old woman?" asked Stuart David as they entered. It was all downhill from there. Crisp talked to his friends, B&S listened. B&S talked amongst themselves, Crisp listened. Neither party took anything from the table apart from the bill.

When they did meet The Enclave, they let Jones and Stuart do the talking, while Chris did handstands against a wall and Isobel looked at plants. Everyone else looked bored. One of the few things which seemed to genuinely excite them about the trip was the prospect of seeing Woody Allen perform live at the Le Parker Meridien hotel, but their excitement eventually turned to disappointment when they trooped into the ballroom only to discover that Allen had left after his first set.

Stuart David summed up the trip thusly:

> The gap between this and our real lives has been just too wide; the main meeting in The Enclave's conference room—which I chose not to film—just too . . .
>
> The conversation which cannot be heard is specific. Before long Sarah falls asleep on her bed, sucking her thumb, but everyone else remains animated; fidgeting, swapping places . . . Chris cries twice. Stuart curls up a little, I chew my way through a clear plastic drinks stirrer. Isobel often looks confused.
>
> The scene fades on everyone who is still awake looking intensely tired.

"It was never quite the same again after that," he says today, with a twinge of sadness. "So I was glad I'd captured that happening."

Once safely home, Jeepster continued to field foreign licensing offers from the likes of Virgin Europe and Seymour Stein's Sire label in the U.S. A genuine music biz potentate, Stein was the man responsible for signing Madonna, The Ramones, and The Smiths in the States, so the fact that he was interested in signing this lot was both slightly incongruous and entirely apt. The guy had pretty good taste after all, and like pretty much everyone else who'd heard it, *Tigermilk* had obviously worked its magic on his learned ears. So he flew in from Frisco in the late summer of '96, booking himself into a five-star hotel just around the corner from the church hall. He'd asked Jeepster if he could sit in on a rehearsal, but as the band hadn't planned to rehearse that day, they told him he could go see a show like anyone else. In the end a compromise was reached, and Stein was treated to a couple of songs at Stuart's house. This "big loveable cliché," as Neil calls him, only had to walk a few hundred yards from his hotel to the church hall, but for a man whose feet probably hadn't touched concrete since disco, he nearly didn't make it. "I was waiting for him at the church, and I remember seeing this bright red guy coming round the corner," says Neil. "We thought he was going to die. We used to make all the record companies walk." Stein managed to puff and splutter his way up the stairs where the group took a begrudging jaunt through "Judy and the Dream of Horses." Irritated by the imposition, Stuart later vowed never to grant anyone such special treatment again. "I didn't really know who he was, he was just a guy who came over," said Stuart who, unlike Stevie, cared little for rock history. "Once you met somebody you would treat them with the politeness that you would treat anybody, and we did, I think. But I didn't enjoy playing a little set for him. Once I did that I thought, never again, I'll never bend over and do something extra special for someone like that. It just felt like we were trying to sell ourselves."

Later that night, Stein took the group and—whether he liked it or not—around fifteen of their friends to the Crème de la Crème curry house, mainly with a view to convincing Stuart of his intentions. But there were so many people there, they ended up sitting at opposite ends of the table, as the hungry dole-kids greedily devoured their meals, and since Stein ordered the entire menu, they ended up going home with doggy bags full of food, enough to keep them full for a week. The difference between this cigar-chomping mogul and these stuffed urchins couldn't have been more vast, as Neil laughingly recalls: "We were out with him and Elton John comes on and he goes, 'Elton actually wrote this song in my house, on my piano, which my ex-wife's got now. It should be in the Rock and Roll Hall of Fame, but that bitch got it in the settlement!' " When the After Eight mints arrived Neil and Stuart David stuffed as many as they could into their pockets, hoping he wouldn't notice.

The incident was later immortalized in Stevie's first song for the group, "Seymour Stein," which alluded to his admiration for Chris's jacket, that ankle-length Brooklyn fur which apparently reminded him of something Johnny Marr might wear. Not that Stevie was there to witness any of this; he was over the road in Ad Lib, unable to get out of his dishwashing shift. Still, Neil, Stuart, and Stuart David did pop over with a couple of doggy bags for him, so it wasn't all bad. Being the group's resident rock historian, Stevie was perhaps the only one who genuinely wanted to hang with Stein—if only for the kudos by proxy if nothing else—so when he crooned, "Sorry I missed you," he isn't being ironic, as some have assumed. Thanks to a lifetime of reading rock books, Stevie is a man who understands the significance of things.

Despite the dinner and the chocolates, the group would eventually be signed to The Enclave in the U.S. Seymour Stein's thoughts about his days in Glasgow and the song written in his honor are sadly unknown.

To mark the release of the album, Jeepster had organized three London dates between the 7th and 11th of November, including two dates at the ICA as support to Tindersticks, whose elegant string-laden bed-sittery marked them out as one of the few contemporary bands with whom Belle and Sebastian shared compatible DNA,[3] followed by a headline show at the Borderline a few days later. Just as they had at Moir Hall, the group invited mordant post-folk duo Aidan Moffat and Malcolm Middleton, aka the boys with the Arab Strap, the booze-sodden Falkirk duo who had become something of an underground cause celebre that year with their terminally dissolute Chemikal Underground album *The Weekend Never Starts Round Here* and its classic attendant single "The First Big Weekend." This inaugural trip to the nation's show-biz capital would inspire Stuart to write "The Boy with the Arab Strap," an abstract snapshot of the trip during which the group shared a rented house with the Strap.[4] "I remember having a really good laugh with Arab Strap, who came down," said Chris, who remembers the group treating their first trip into the beating heart of the music media with their usual degree of unconcerned irreverence. "We had quite an insular attitude at that time. We were in a bit of a bubble." Stuart viewed the fact that the group lived miles from London a key factor—probably the key factor—in their ability to do things exactly on their own terms, which is undoubtedly very true, although it's certainly not true that all London bands are doomed from birth to remain shackled to the unforgiving strictures of the Man. Any band who wants to can do their own thing their own way if they put their mind to it, surely? So why don't

---

[3] Stuart had marvelled at their majestic 1993 single "City Sickness," praising it as one of the few contemporary records aiming for the kind of organic grandeur which he so desperately wished to achieve in his own music.

[4] Stuart wasn't feeling particularly well, however, and stayed instead with Stef D'Andrea from Jeepster. A flat with the Arab Strap is no place for an ailing boy, obviously.

more bands try? By way of his own explanation, Stuart waxes analogous. "You're watching a football match, professional footballers, and somebody does something spectacular, scores a great goal, and you think, why can't they do that more often?" he ponders, working up a metaphorical steam. "The thing is it's *hard* to even make it that far. It's really hard to train and work to get where we are. And sometimes you get the one with just a little bit more talent, who can score a great goal, rather than being grafters, grafters, grafters." He stops and frowns; evidently his analogy has escaped him. "Actually, I've put that badly because it makes it sound as if we're the extra-special players." He pauses briefly before opting for a more straightforward tack. "I think it's hard to be in a group. You're up against record companies, an established system, and to get away from that you've really got to step right outside it, and it's easier to do that in Glasgow 'cause you're right outside it anyway. But if you're in London, *forget it.* If we played the game we could've been up and running within a year and been playing big shows and festivals, but it took us four, five years of fighting the record company—and this was a record company who was on our side! We fought to get our way, paranoia all the time. Everything from production to record sleeves to press pictures. Doing it our way was not a small thing, but it was the basis on which the band was built. But it's not an isolated thing at all. You quite often find with filmmakers, bands, writers, there's always a story there. Pick a great filmmaker, someone you have respect for, say Truffaut—did he just come through the studio system, and just make films? No, he was a soldier and he dropped out and then he was a filmmaker who thought he could do better, and he did. Originals I really have respect for—they've got to do it the hard way." Even if that means sound-checking for up to eight hours at a stretch, and having just three people, the singer included, to take care of the gear and sound.

The night after their Tindersticks support, the group commandeered the venue in their own right, and after deciding that the sound was just so (although the ever exacting Stuart could be heard asking the soundman to make his vocals "brighter" during the gig) they ambled on before a packed London crowd including various journalists, scenesters, and pop stars, including Jarvis Cocker's and—be still his fluttering heart!—Stuart's hero Lawrence Hayward. "Somebody told me before I went on that Lawrence was there, and I was high," he gasps, reeling at the memory. "The whole gig was for him." Fortunately, he didn't disgrace himself, and the gig went pretty well, cover of The Beatles' "A Day in the Life" and all, with *Melody Maker*'s David Hemmingway giving them their first major national review, rapturously declaring that "hearing Belle and Sebastian is a pleasure, a joy. A new band to exalt!" Lawrence's thoughts are unknown, but judging by the amiable chat he and a starstruck Stuart shared after the gig, one assumes he was happy with what his genes had begat.

The next day, lost on their way to the Borderline, Stuart, Isobel, and Chris wandered into a record store to ask for directions. The Australian girl behind the counter who helped them on their way happened to be a big B&S fan, and had virtually elected *Sinister* as the shop's in-house soundtrack ever since it came in. "We'd be sitting wondering what to put on," Katrina House explains. "But nothing else seemed as good as *If You're Feeling Sinister*. I hadn't felt that way about a record in a long time." After realizing that these wayward travelers were in fact the group she had been falling in love with these last few weeks, Katrina sent them on their way, unaware that this was the first encounter on a voyage which would eventually take her from behind the counter and out into the wonderful world of Belle and Sebastian for good.

The gig that night was another success, a buoyant Stuart dancing ecstatically during the closing song, hammering Chris's keys with his feet and nearly crushing the keyboardist's nail-varnished fingers in the process. The next day they traipsed back to Glasgow, the dreaded London lying conquered in their wake.

After witnessing the show that night, and the number of devoted fans who had crawled unexpectedly from the shadows, Katrina, the girl from the record shop, decided, along with her boyfriend David Kitchen, that these people needed a clubhouse to accommodate them. And so the first Belle and Sebastian fan club was born, which became a much-needed meeting place for the myriad fans all around the country, some of whom had no idea that anyone else out there shared their precious and private infatuation. Eventually, Katrina would move on and work with Jeepster and, after moving to Glasgow in 1999, worked hand-in-hand with Neil, initially as merchandise coordinator, before going on to take care of general office admin and accounts, press, stamps, envelopes, tea, and taking out the trash, eventually becoming a kind of surrogate manager and all-round indispensable cog in the B&S machine.

The group's first widespread release, *If You're Feeling Sinister* was released to, in classic rock biz parlance, a fanfare of glowing reviews. *Melody Maker* urged its readers to "buy, play, read along, swoon," and *Entertainment Weekly* praised its songs "so potent they could make Morrissey cry." It was also featured in *Q* magazine's "50 Best Albums of the Year" and eventually *Rolling Stone's* "50 Best Albums of the '90s." For Belle and Sebastian, the season had arrived.

It was a very good year. For Stuart Murdoch in particular, a quite remarkable one. On January 1 he had sat in his flat, entertaining the guitarist in his new group with tea and song, telling him excitedly of the pretty cellist he had met the night before, the one who could very well be the final piece in his jigsaw. Three months later the group had recorded their first record in less time than it takes most bands to set up the drums; five months after that they were recording their second album with similar briskness, this time for a bona fide record company. People, lots of them, were falling in love with his music, justifying the fluctuating faith he had had in himself for years, telling him with every letter and article they wrote, every record and ticket they bought, that all of it had been worthwhile, that all of it *meant something.* It was beautiful, just as he had hoped.

The group couldn't wait to unwrap Christmas and drink down Hogmanay, couldn't wait to play together again. They had come a long way in a short time, floating in a bubble of their own devise, bouncing high and loving it and praying it would never burst.

CHAPTER TEN
EXTENDED PLAY, 1997

Playing Songs for Children

Despite the praise heaped upon *Sinister,* the press still didn't mean squat to Camp Sebastian, for two principal reasons. Firstly, Stuart felt he had been misquoted and misrepresented in two small articles in the U.K.'s two influential music weeklies, *Melody Maker* and *NME,* and henceforth refused to blot his carefully created world with the messy pens of unsympathetic journalists. And also, the group had been so spoiled so quickly, with record companies drooling at their feet before they'd even received a review, and with the likes of Mark Radcliffe and John Peel waxing their praises on national radio and *Sinister* becoming the most requested album on college radio in the U.S., they didn't really think that they needed any favors from the press. And they were probably right. Granted, this made them act in an at-times misguidedly difficult and self-righteous manner towards press-folks, but they were understandably full of themselves. They'd managed to create a buzz without leaping through the usual media hoops, with their dignity and integrity intact, and all in a matter of months. All they'd had to do was make a coupla great, great records, all without any press campaign whatsoever—indeed, with something the press viewed as an anti-press campaign—and still the business came groveling like some forelock-tugging serf around their grounds. "We were just amazed at what was happening," says Stuart David. "We were all either long-time dole merchants, or very young people straight out of university. So none of us felt that it should be happening to us, all the attention. It just seemed bizarre. Particularly since we'd only been together for about ten minutes. We hadn't even decided if we were a band yet, so it was just, 'What the fuck are you all talking about, get a grip!'"

After reading those first two features,[1] Stuart decided to shut himself off entirely from the press; he'd been dreaming of this for so long, and it all meant so damn much to him, he wasn't prepared to let anyone stamp their cynical fucking London boots all over his creation. So he went ostrich: If you don't read it, you don't know it's there, and the dream can flow unfettered. "If you felt you were creating something particular on record, then why talk about it?" he shrugs. "I didn't talk to the press or deal with the press, so it was all above my head. It just felt like it wasn't necessary and wasn't worth it, because you would get into all sort of strops when what you had said hadn't been represented in the piece. Papers like *NME* and *Melody Maker* were interested in having their own angle, they weren't interested in reporting what you said or what you were about. But to their credit they were the first papers to take an interest, but I had a bad experience with the early interviews."

To Jeepster this refusal to play the game was a mixed blessing. On the one hand they were excited to be working with such a principled and rebellious act, but still they couldn't understand why Stuart seemed to be willfully depriving the group of its potential. "Both Mark and I as very young teenagers had been punk fans," says Stef D'Andrea. "We totally liked the idea of a band that you couldn't see play, that refused to have their photographs taken, all these anti-establishment things we thought were kinda cool, we loved it. But there's only so many times you can say no to everything. All of the standard things that you need to do to get a career off the ground, Stuart refused to do," he sighs wearily. But didn't Jeepster in some way respect the way their wayward charge stuck so doggedly to his guns? "I respect it inasmuch as he understood

---

1 To be fair to the journalists concerned, the articles were both pretty small, rendering it necessary for them to somehow capture the essence of the band in a few sound bites. Predictably, this meant concentrating on Stuart's religious leanings and government-funded background, which he presumably found somewhat misrepresentative.

how good his songs were, and he understood that it was important to keep control of the situation," D'Andrea concedes. "But I think he went too far in protecting that situation, I think it lost them a lot of chances in the early days, things which it has taken them many years to be happy to do. With them I always think it's a big trade-off between what they could've done and what they were really able to do personality-wise. They always thought they weren't ready in the sense of having a career. It was kid-gloves stuff, we were coaxing them into the idea that this could be a career for them, something that he could enjoy doing, but in the beginning they wanted to believe that they had nothing to do with the music business whatsoever."

"I'm glad that we didn't play the game initially, because we didn't have the strength of character to do it then," ventures Chris, who rightly views the group's unwillingness to follow music biz etiquette as a manifestation of their innate punk spirit. "Our tour manager Stevie Dreads said to me once, 'Belle and Sebastian have got the least punk rock sound, but the most punk rock attitude of any band I've ever worked with.' Him being a lifelong Ramones fan, I took that as a huge compliment. But I think it's true. We do have a rebellious attitude, and when any kind of authority comes into contact with us, it does bring out that side of us where we want to stick two fingers up." Stuart David puts it more succinctly: "I think we were the only punk band in a long time, and there haven't been any successful ones since," he says proudly. Isobel's feistiness perhaps best sums up this attitude. "I think it's just part of my spirit, like a kid, don't tell me what to do, *I'll* decide what I want to do," she attests, displaying the stubborn nature which would also cause her to butt heads with the group as well as the business.

Asked whether the whole thing was basically a protracted attempt to piss people off, Neil is in no doubt. "Fuck yeah," he grins mischievously. "I wasn't in it for the music . . . only joking. Sometimes it was out of sheer belligerence. I don't know if I can speak for everybody, Stuart always gives different reasons, but personally you'd do things only if the conditions were so ridiculous. You go in with such a position of power, not caring about things, and there's no stronger position than not giving a fuck, so you say I want this, this, and this, and sometimes you got it. And that's great fun." So it was all just a deliberate shit-stirring game? "Oh yeah. I certainly got a buzz off it. Although

I don't think that was Stuart's motivation. But that was a happy aside for me."

And it wasn't Stuart's motivation, so he claims, although his innate anti-authoritarian streak must've been piqued in some way. He was, after all, the brains behind the operation, and being a bona fide artist, with all the ego and integrity that entails, well, he must have taken some satisfaction from the fact that all he had to do was paint his picture, keep his mouth shut, and watch the thing explode. But Stuart, he was so wrapped up in his own blossoming world, he really did seem to have no interest in outside interference. No time to lose, gotta keep moving, keep the magic flowing, don't let the real world peek in for a second. No energy to waste. No energy to waste. "We never tried to wind anybody up," he insists. "We just had a notion of what we wanted to do, where we wanted to play. To us, if it was a choice between playing King Tut's or hiring out a function suite in the Mitchell Library, there was no choice. We just wanted to do everything different. We had this great chance, this great band, this great music we wanted to play, so it was natural. We weren't daft, we had all these ideas. The press might not have got it, but I didn't give a fuck. The kids who came to see us, they got it. We didn't have to play any of these small gigs, we just played a couple of gigs in Glasgow, and because we had this record out, we sold about four hundred tickets for the Moir Hall gig. This is within six months of getting together. You show me what other groups have done that."

And in all his confidence and naïveté, in all his excitement at this buzzing hive of newborn opportunity, how could he be bothered with the accepted norms of music biz etiquette? Interviews? Why be interviewed when nothing he could say couldn't be better expressed in song? And pictures? Pictures to flash the mundane reality of their given flesh across the press, like every other spotty band of nobodies you couldn't care to mention? *"Now we're photogenic, you know we don't stand a chance,"* he would self-effacingly sing on the title track of his latest LP, but there was more than mere humility behind his reasons for refusing conventional band photos. He'd created a world in his songs, so why not illustrate that in pictures? A keen photographer—he followed up Beatbox with a stint on a photography course—he saw press shots as just another way of expressing his very particular vision.

So there would be no moody monochrome shots of the group being all deep and existential against a brick wall. Fuck that shit. There would be pictures of two or one of them or less, like Isobel in a surgeon's mask, or Beans doing the ironing, or Stuart David crouching over a dead nun. And sometimes the pictures wouldn't feature any of them at all. The music, the artwork, the press—it was all part of the same precious package. "There was nothing conceived," he claims. "Maybe it's my extreme naïveté, but I didn't know about press pictures, press angles, about what you were meant to say. It just occurred to me that if they needed an image to accompany the record that was out, it might as well be another image of someone who was maybe on the record, something vaguely artistic that would say a little bit more about the record, the band. It was just something I wanted to do. It's fun. I like taking pictures."

Rather than risk having his words twisted in print, Stuart sent out a "handy" Q&A, the ostensible purpose of which was to helpfully answer the questions he assumed most writers would want to ask, although you don't have to read too closely between the lines to recognize the satirical intent.

Belle and Sebastian Interview Technique

How did the band get together? Stuart M: They were the first five people me and Stuart met after we were asked to make a record. Stuart and I met on a government training scheme. We made the first record for Stow College, for their music business course.

How did the name Belle and Sebastian arise? Stuart M: Belle and Sebastian are two wee guys, aged seventeen and twenty-three. I wrote a short story about them. I nicked the names from an old French program about an orphan and his dog. That's where the similarity ends. I think about them a lot, so I don't mind telling you a bit about them. Sebastian is a bit of a misfit. When he met Belle, his schedule was pretty empty. He was getting into all sorts of trouble, just letting himself drift along. Belle, on the other hand, still had her life regimented by school and family. It is this as much as anything else which attracted Sebastian to Belle. He is as envious of her as he is fond of her. There is a side of Belle which wants to be like Sebastian, but she would never think about that. She is quite happy to learn off him. To Sebastian, Belle represents grace and privilege, and the allure that goes with it. Belle could do anything, he thinks.[2] It's not as simple as that, though. Each Belle and Sebastian song is written by either Belle or Sebastian. Have fun trying to guess who wrote which.

What are your influences? If you were to ask us this, we would move uncomfortably in our seats and shirk the question.

Why? Because you're not going to like the answer. What are our influences? Our mums, our dads, the boy in school who told us about sex. . . . You'd like us to give you a big list of music that we like. You can bet that that is the last thing we are thinking about when we are playing. Does Eric Cantona think about George Best when he is sticking one away against Liverpool? I don't think so.

"Maybe we were a bit up our own arses, but it didn't seem like that way at the time," says Stevie, who quickly realized that, since the press were only really interested in speaking to the man behind the songs, and since he wasn't willing to talk, there wasn't really much point in any of the rest of them doing interviews. And so the myth began to grow. The press, denied an angle, created one out of the fact that the group wouldn't speak to them. A group who didn't want to see their faces splashed over the front cover of the *NME,* who didn't want to see their faces splashed anywhere? How desperately odd, they thought. And the more mysterious they seemed, the more people wanted to know, and the more successful they became. This may not have been Stuart's actual intention, but he must have been secretly delighted. In just a year he'd achieved his goal completely, and all entirely on his own terms. And it had been the easiest thing in the world. "I still maintain it was an accident," says Stevie. "We never ever once sat in a room and said, if we don't talk to the press, it'll make us more mysterious. There was no contrivance like that. But it just seemed to get out of control."

---

2 It's tempting to wonder whether Stuart was at this point feeding his own feelings towards Isobel into her fictional namesake.

Sometimes it was hardly surprising they shunned the press, especially when the journalist in question would so fundamentally, sometimes almost willfully, fail to understand what the group were about, they'd end up forcing their own warped agenda upon them. When interviewed by a French rock mag, for example, the quite patently disturbed hack sent to interview them ended up vomiting his Gallic neuroses all over Isobel's polka dot pinafore, resulting in a piece which should probably have resulted in some serious psychiatric intervention. Granted, he was unfortunate enough to find himself interviewing the group en masse—the only time anyone has ever been brave or foolish enough to do this—and, perhaps overwhelmed by the novelty, they could offer nothing more insightful than, at best, aimless, uncertain answers, and at worst, utter silence. Thus denied the frisky badinage he'd probably hoped for, Pepe Le Punk instead decided to vent his sexual spleen upon the prettiest member of the group. "The interviewer wrote in the piece that he'd stopped listening and started to fantasize about lots of sexual ways of killing Isobel," reports Neil, shuddering with disbelief. "If Bel's dad and brother had read it they would've kicked his ass—they're not the kind of guys you want to mess with. There's also the review of *Arab Strap* [from the *NME*] which has a drawing which appears to be Stuart wanking over Isobel. . . ." All of which says more about the sordid sexual peccadilloes of yer average music journalist than most of us probably care to know.

The fact that the group hardly played live also added to the allure,[3] although again the reasons for this had nothing to do with some deliberate myth-making plot. It was because the group, thrown together so suddenly, hadn't really worked out how to adequately perform in front of an audience. They hadn't rehearsed enough, for one, so gigs were often a shambles. And—lo—another angle for the press: Belle and Sebastian, the shy, shambling live band who spend more time tuning up than actually playing, which was reported as either charming or insulting, depending on the writer.

It was also around this time that they became saddled with a description which has dogged them ever since. Yes, brave reader, we have staved off this evil Jabberwocky for as long as we can, but now we must tackle

---

[3] Eight gigs in 1996, twelve in 1997.

and dispatch it as soon as we can so as to carry on with our journey un-fettered. Let's catch butterflies.

Twee—affectedly dainty or refined
Synonyms: dainty, mincing, niminy-piminy, prim

—From WordNet.com

Frankly, they should count themselves lucky they're never described as niminy-piminy. With its emetic connotations of gurgling girls in Hello Kitty hair-slides sucking lollipops and arrested boy-children writing flaccid poetry in purple Biro, the word "twee" has been batted like a recalcitrant fly around the heads of Belle and Sebastian ever since they crawled from the womb, and while it is not entirely unwar-ranted regarding certain aspects of their phenomenon, it is ultimately a tiresomely inaccurate generalization. Basically, "twee" is a British colloquialism, a kind of baby-talk corruption of "wee," which, in mu-sical terms, first came to describe the fey, jangling sounds of the bands compiled on the *NME*'s legendary *C-86* tape, including Glasgow's Primal Scream and The Pastels, which then gave birth to an entire genre, epitomized by the almost translucently brittle pop of Sarah Records in the U.K., and K Records in the U.S. Belle and Sebastian are seen as the natural successors to these bands, and yet stylistically they have very little in common bar a shared desire to "do something pretty." The vast majority of '80s twee-pop bands were irritatingly flimsy things, both musically and lyrically, peddling pat, wispy love songs with all the substance of dandelion spores. If we must talk lineage, then Belle and Sebastian share more genes with the likes of The Velvet Underground, Felt, and The Smiths, bands with a dark, humorous, subversive bent far removed from the la-la blah of twee-pop. "Twee" is a generally disparaging adjective, and not something any serious group would ever wish to ally themselves with, despite the presence of fan sites such as twee.net, which, in lumping B&S to-gether with the aforementioned acts, really aren't helping matters. But then, as Stevie notes, several of the clichéd assumptions surrounding the group have more to do with the fans than the group themselves who—and some of their more sensitive fans may want to reach for the smelling salts here—actually LIKE FOOTBALL! AND DRINKING! AND SOME OTHER NAUGHTY THINGS, INCLUDING RUTTING LIKE STAG-BEETLES WITH MEMBERS OF THE OPPOSITE GENDER! JUST LIKE REAL FUCKING ADULTS, EVEN! A shocking revelation, perhaps, but one which needs be told.

"I honestly don't get the twee thing," Stevie says with a shake of the head. "The only reason I can gather is because of the music. People assume that a band that says something like, 'Do something pretty while you can,' has got to be twee. Maybe the songs attracted a certain kind of person who could be described as twee and gentle. Which is fine, but none of us were ever really like that. I think maybe the stereotype was more about what the press perceived our fans to be like. But as far as I can see, our fans are a mixed bag. A lot of them are quite cool and good-looking, and some of them are quite shy, the people who are perceived as twee."[4]

Members of B&S would never do something like play FOOTBALL!!! Photo by Sarah Martin.

---

4 A lot of the antipathy people feel towards B&S is undoubtedly aimed less at the group themselves and more at the self-regarding, smugly exclusive nature of much of their fanbase, many of whom will no doubt be reading this book. It's all your fault, you dolts.

Granted, the twee tag could occasionally be justified. "Mayfly" is, ostensibly, a song about befriending an insect (whereas "Dog on Wheels" is actually a neurotic little song about lost innocence, rather than the titular stuffed mutt) and a couple of Stuart's early recorded vocals perhaps err a little too close to child-man territory for comfort, while the video for Isobel's "Is It Wicked Not to Care?," with the group lolling around in the long summer grass, Isobel with stuffed lion and hair-slides reading *The Lion, the Witch, and the Wardrobe,* is virtually a twee-pop fashion reel, and in fact Isobel wouldn't have been particularly out of place fronting any number of girly-gosh Sarah bands ("Critics used to always talk about Hello Kitty hair-slides and that dreadful, redundant 'twee' word," she grimaces. "But I used to really like it when girls would turn up to gigs and my friends would say that they dressed a bit like me, I'd think it was really funny."), but these are fairly isolated examples from a rich and varied eight-year career. Belle and Sebastian are just too fucked up to be considered twee, frankly. "Some of the music's really dark," argues Stevie. "Some of the lyrics are hilariously funny. This idea that it's twee and sensitive, well, people obviously haven't got it. As a songwriter he's certainly sensitive and very poetic, but he's no fucking wallflower. There's real bravery in some of the writing, real hilarity, and there's always been a bit of dirt in there, the odd sexual innuendo. So I don't really understand the twee thing, but ultimately I don't really care."

Neil, who is about as twee as shite in a pint glass, is also unsurprisingly aggrieved at the notion. "They're not twee in any way," he grumps. "When we all get together we're a right bunch of bastards. It might all seem very cliquey and in-jokey to an outsider, but it's the same with any group of friends."

Stevie: "I wouldn't be in this band if it was twee. I remember hearing *C-86* and thinking it was garbage, [sings listlessly] 'La la la la.' Fucking hell! In the early days the press interviewed people we were so-called influenced by, and one of them was the guy from Sarah Records, and I said to Stuart, 'Oh, this is your department.' And he said, 'No, I don't like any of that stuff.' Stuart is meant to be taking the baton on from this guy! It's just assumptions the whole way. We're into soul music, all kinds of stuff, which you can hear on the records, and yet we get this *thing.*"

* * *

But as for the "shambling" tag, well that couldn't really be denied, as they themselves admit. "The gigs *were* a total shambles," allows Mick. "We never rehearsed, we didn't have a crew, if the cello broke down it would take seven minutes to fix between songs." The crew at that time basically consisted of Neil, Stuart, and whoever they could get to help at the time. Stuart used to roadie at the Queen Margaret Union, so he knew a thing or two about humping amps and mixing desks, and being the dyed-in-the-wool old-school indie dude that he is, he thought it only right that the "artist" should get his hands dirty. But he was taking too much on, and after a long day's load-in and sound-check—and Belle and Sebastian's day-long sound-checks have gone down in legend— he was often too tired to deliver a decent performance. Plus his very definite ideas of how he wanted the group to sound actually worked to their detriment, as Stevie explains: "Stuart always sang quite far back from the microphone, with the effect that the gigs were always painfully quiet. That worked beautifully in a room full of a hundred people. Part of Stuart's original ethos was that we had to draw the audience in, and the early shows were amazing because he'd be singing gently and the audience would all be really quiet. But the difficulty of having more people come to see you is that it didn't work, it was too quiet."

A case in point were their three gigs at the Manchester Town Hall over the 27th and 28th of December, 1997. Such was the demand for tickets, the group had decided to play a matinee show before their evening performance on the second day, and like Moir Hall the year before—and at a gig at the Oxford Zodiac in August 1997,[5] where a hapless Chris found himself adrift in the middle of the crowd on his own Hammond island—thought it might be fun to play with the stage layout despite the fact that the earlier gigs had been technical disasters. So with the group assembled on the main C-shaped stage, Chris and Stuart David once again found themselves across the room on their own small stage, in an almost bloody-minded refusal to learn from their mistakes. Just as before, the distance between the musicians meant that they were hopelessly out of synch, which predictably

---

5 At the same gig, Richard, taking a pre-show dump, knocked a syringe out of the toilet-roll holder. Hey—Belle and Sebastian fans can be skag-heads too.

Belle and Sebastian performances were tagged as "shambling." Photo by Mark Trayner.

ended up infuriating the by now at the end of his tether keyboardist, who smashed his equipment to smithereens at the end of the gig— generally regarded by the group as the worst they've ever played—much to the astonishment of the crowd. "[The keyboard] was a piece of crap," he shrugs. "I knew I was going to have to get something better so you might as well go out with a bang, you know? I did also once throw a volume pedal out of the window at a practice, but it had already packed up, so at worst I'm guilty of dropping litter in that instance." He was in even worse tune at the next day's matinee performance when, after getting blind drunk following the previous night's show, he spent the entire show vomiting into a bucket hidden in amongst his keyboard enclave. On the other stage things weren't much better. Stuart, in his tireless if impractical quest for the perfect sound, had decided to position the group in amongst the amps so that they could hear what the audience were hearing, hoping that this would result in a copacetic aural oneness for all concerned. "And that was not helpful," argues Neil. "Because it's no good hearing what the crowd is hearing if what the crowd is hearing is shit." In future, the group agreed that it would perhaps be best if they were at least within spitting distance of each other on stage.

Stevie, for one, although he respected Stuart's desire to create a special mood at each gig, was becoming increasingly unhappy with the singer's increasingly insular onstage demeanor. "Initially when I met Stuart I had done the Halt Bar and I wasn't frightened of an audience, I talked to them," he says. "But he was the best I'd ever seen, he was so funny and really sharp. But when we started to become successful—and I think his relationship with Isobel had something to do with this—he totally clammed up on stage." Thus it was left to Stevie to plug the often embarrassingly lengthy longueurs between songs, cracking jokes and chatting to the crowd as Isobel restringed her cello, Stuart methodically tuned his guitar, or Chris picked a fight with his keyboard.

Why Stuart's relationship with Isobel should affect his live performance is not clear—arguments before the show, perhaps?—but Stuart has his own explanation, arguing that he was concentrating so much on what the group were playing and how it sounded, he ended up all but ignoring the audience; wholly ironic considering that the group's relationship with the audience was so important to him. "I think it must be reiterated," he reiterates, "that the reason for our group being a shambles—apart from our ambition—is that we grew up in public, we were playing quite large gigs within six months of forming. And we were non-musicians apart from Stevie and Mick. I would challenge anyone to do that. Even The Smiths had time to tighten up their sound before they were thrust into the public eye."

Chris agrees, also blaming a basic lack of rehearsal for most of their problems. "We'd worked really hard on rehearsing for *Tigermilk,* but we hadn't really learned how to put a performance together. We hadn't connected with each other and couldn't really engage with an audience. Most bands build up an audience first before they release a record, but we did it the other way around, and when we did play live we weren't very good, which probably put us off doing it more."

Not that the gigs were all a complete disaster, of course—the atmosphere could often be pin-drop electric, something far transcending your usual gig experience[6]—but it quickly became a problem when the group's lack of professionalism became something which threatened to define them. "To some people that was some of the charm—not me personally," argues Neil. "Some people got off on the sheer amateurishness of it all. I didn't think it was brilliant when they fucked up, any more than they did. Some funny moments came of it, and they could get good repartee with the audience, but being known for that isn't as good as being known for songs."

"Most of the gigs were pretty disastrous," Stevie concedes. "Those gigs probably added to our reputation for being difficult, for being shy and precious. And for a band capable of making great-sounding pop records like 'You're Just a Baby, Baby Girl' [sic], and especially 'I Could Be Dreaming,' I knew how we could sound on stage, but we never showed that part of our ability."

And yet Stuart's desire to create a particular atmosphere at gigs, as flawed as it was, should be applauded inasmuch as it mirrored the care and attention with which he approached every aspect of the B&S mosaic. From arrangements to production to record design and live performance, the pursuit of perfection was all, and while it often didn't work—particularly live—their failure was always well-intentioned. As for Stuart David, however, he always thought, with a good deal of justification, that the group's supposedly shambling nature was a huge part of the appeal, lending their music a tangibly human quality which was lost amongst more practiced musicians. "It was very freeing, and it gave the songs some air and a delicate quality," he posits. "It made them quite alive. I remember one song where Isobel played the bass, and she played it quite tentatively and quite often made some mistakes, and Neil said one of the sound guys was always saying, 'I don't understand why they don't let Stuart David play the bass on this. He's tight.' And Neil said about the sound guy, 'He really doesn't get it.' And he

---

6 My first B&S gig was at the Assembly Rooms in Edinburgh in March 1997. Apart from feeling profoundly irritated towards the overly solemn kids sitting cross-legged on the floor, it was an extremely enjoyable, moving experience. Apart from Stuart stopping "Dylan" a few bars in—he felt it was too fast—there was nothing particularly ramshackle about the performance. The gaps between songs weren't too lengthy, and seemed reasonable at the time. The music was all that mattered.

didn't. There was a lot of courage involved at that point, to be that vulnerable, and I think as it went on and some people in the band started to feel we should be more professional because we were getting a certain amount of success, some of the life went out of it. That was where a lot of the life came from."

Disappointed with the sound of *Sinister,* the group decided to shun Ca Va and set up amps in the church hall. They'd always rehearsed in a room in Stuart's flat above, but after a few tryouts in the hall itself, they soon fell in love with its acoustics. A large rectangular room with high walls and windows, it possessed a natural echo which, when properly recorded, blessed their music with the kind of tangible body and depth they felt *Sinister* had been denied. As Stuart explains, "When we recorded in the church hall we had a stereo pairing of ambient mikes on these two channels on the left of the desk, and all you had to do was turn up the bottom on these mikes and then you suddenly got this Spector-esque quality coming in, and this wasn't displeasing. We felt—and it's an unfortunate word—but there was an organic sound to *Sinister.* We're being hard on yourself, because if you look back, it takes people many years of playing together before you can come up with an LP like *Court and Spark* or *Tapestry,* which are maybe the benchmarks of what *Sinister* could've been. And we thought the best way to get the sound we were after was to be able to hear each other and look at each other and feel each other, so the idea was that we'd get together in a room which had interesting acoustics."

And so in early 1997 Belle and Sebastian decamped to Hyndland Church hall and set to work recording a batch of songs, not for an album, but for a planned trio of EPs to be released throughout the year. The first, however, would not consist of new recordings, indeed would not consist of anything actually recorded by Belle and Sebastian. Instead, the *Dog on Wheels* EP would feature the songs Stuart and Stuart David (and on the title track, Mick) recorded at Beatbox in 1995—with help from Michael, Gerry and David Campbell, Mark McWhirter, Brian Nugent, and Steve MacKenzie—including the original version of *Tigermilk*'s opening track, and the song of the story which gave the group its name.

Very few listeners at the time probably realized that these were basically Stuart Murdoch solo recordings; such was the completeness of Stuart's vision, his demos already sounded almost exactly like the group he had yet to form. "The State I Am In" does lack the liquid lightness of the *Tigermilk* version, and Stevie's trademark reverb is missed (plus Stuart sounds a little hoarse in spots), but the lyrical grace of the song is undiminished.

"Dog on Wheels" would become one of the group's most popular songs, a charcoal-brown lament which more than any other song brought them the not unwelcome Love comparisons which were made in almost every early review. There's something slightly insidious about the song, something vaguely unsettling and not quite right. The protagonist is damaged, depressed, possibly suicidal, curling up on the pavement in an exhausted attempt to ignore the harsh reality around him, longing to reclaim the dog on wheels which kept him happy and contented as a child. *"See my dog on wheels, he seems a mile away,"* he laments, before intoning with an air of mysterious portent, as the bare backing rumbles like a Spanish dust storm beneath him, that *"anything goes,"* suggesting untold avenues of dark intention. Sarah Dempster in the *NME* thought this character a "pathetic child-man whose only confidante is the toy of the title," a not entirely unwarranted if somewhat harsh judgement; certainly, the grumbling clouds in which the tune is immersed conjure up something far more sinister than mere immature whimsy; a nimbocumulus namby-pamby, maybe. In any case, Mick's tequila sunset trumpet break is sublime.

"String Bean Jean," a tender twang of Morricone drama, is one of Stuart's most autobiographical early songs, an abstract diary entry alluding to his time at Beatbox *("Got my fingers dirty at the school of rock")*, and the flat he shared with Joanne *("Jo")* above Nice'n'Sleazy's in 1995 *("I left the keys down in the caf ")*. And yes, she really did wear trousers that small. Part of Stuart's peculiar genius is being able to bestow a shroud of inexplicable poignancy upon the most prosaic phrase or observation. *"Well she asked me, 'Do I need to lose a little weight?' "* he sings. *"Well I said, 'Now don't be stupid 'cos you're looking great'/And we call her String Bean Jean because the label on her jeans says,/Seven to Eight Years Old—well that's pretty small."* This last line he repeats three times into the chorus, as if it were the most profoundly heartwarming thought he's ever had. "These songs were a pleasure to write," he says, alluding to the autobiographical nature of the lyrics. "Because you're leaning on events. They're always fun to write and sing because you can go back and imagine the real life characters. If Joanne's ever around I always sing that song. I don't think she even cares," he laughs.

The song "Belle and Sebastian" takes the struggling songbird lovers of the Tigermilk inlay, adding a hint of gaudy rock star demise—Sebastian crashing his car in the rain: shades of Bolan—and professional jealousy. This is another carefully arranged glimpse into the sound Stuart would patent with Belle and Sebastian a few months later, the piano trills and flute again showing that the boy knew exactly how he wanted his records to sound. It's not quite there, however; the drums are a little busier than Stuart would ever allow Richard to play on the first couple of records, but the melody is typically wonderful, replete with a distinct chorus, whereas many of his songs are instead made up of repeated melodies and refrains—the kind of effortlessly free-flowing tune Stuart could probably write in his sleep, and often does. Although the song, as ever, subscribes to Stuart's "all art is abstract" dictum, there's an unavoidable impulse to find autobiography in the lines *"Oh Sebastian wrote his diary that/He would never be young again/But you will/Fellow you are ill."* He goes embarrassingly flat in the first chorus, of course, but when he sings/soothes *"But you will . . ."* no amount of bum notes could steady the flutter in your heart.

Released on April 28, with a cover starring Jo and her real-life dog on wheels Patch,[7] "Dog on Wheels" trundled into the grateful hearts and minds of a voracious army of believers hungry for more, including James Oldham at the *NME* who judged it thus: "This might only be their third release, but already they're starting to sound timeless." Oldham would be less impressed, however, when he would take the trip to Glasgow later that year for an ill-fated feature in which the group (sans Stuart, who was still in the midst of his press embargo), with perhaps some justification, came across as precious, pointlessly contrary snobs. After this, Belle and

---

[7] Patch is now owned by B&S fan Lisa Carr, who also bid successfully for Stuart's car Max, which he auctioned for charity in 2002. Max made a farewell appearance on the artwork for the "I'm Waking Up to Us" single, and earns tribute on the self-explanatory "I Love My Car."

An outtake from *Dog on Wheels* cover. Photo by Stuart Murdoch.

Sebastian would never again be revered in quite the same way in the pages of the *NME*. Hell hath no fury like the feeding hand scorned.

One spring Saturday morn, a hungover Monica Queen received a call from a typically enthused Stuart Murdoch garbling something about a great song they'd just recorded which was in need of her urgent vocal attention. "I kind of recall him saying that he couldn't quite get it to work, and he instantly thought of myself," La Queen recalls hazily. "Having seen Thrum and having heard the records, he sort of knew what I was capable of. He just felt that this was what 'Lazy Line Painter Jane' needed."

The song itself was powerful enough, a booming Spector-esque wall of teetering city soul, undoubtedly the most epic and expansive thing the group had yet recorded, but Stuart's pastel-pallored vocals seemed swamped amid the blare. "It had quite a big sound, and my voice didn't come up to the standard," he confesses.

Still groggy from the night before, Monica nevertheless rose magnificently to the challenge, belting out an excoriating country-soul vocal of shiver-inducing power, her presence booting the song into shires of previously unimaginable majesty. "I love singing with Stuart," she enthuses. "We've sang on other occasions with other kinds of song.[8] I feel that we do sing extremely well together—not to say something as vain as saying we're in the same vein as Gram Parsons and Emmylou Harris—but I think when you're looking for boy/girl singing, you have to find some sort of connection, and compatibility, and offering something different. And I think when Stuart and I sing together we do provide that black and white." Hungover or not, Monica Queen didn't need much convincing to tumble down to Ca Va that spring morn. "If someone like Lou Reed, Nick Drake, or David Bowie had said, 'Do you want to come and sing on a song with me?' of course I would say yes, and I hold Stuart in the same regard," she says. "I mean, obviously it wasn't completely apparent back then, but the respect was always there, and having witnessed beautiful, wonderful moments within Stuart's live performances and records, I can identify that being asked to sing with Stuart is a wonderful thing."

After listening to the song a couple of times, Stuart simply encouraged the country chanteuse to do her own special thing. "I just did the recording, went for something to eat afterwards, never spoke about the track in detail," she shrugs, her job done in just a couple of takes. "I just got word a few months afterwards that the record company had loved the track—and the band had loved the track, how it had turned out—and felt confident enough to release it."

The second of that year's EPs (or the first, if you count "Dog on Wheels" as a solo release), *Lazy Line Painter Jane* surprised fans and critics alike. Those who had passed the group off as peddlers of twee whimsy scratched their preconceptions in disbelief at this throbbing

---

8 "We've sung more in a Sunday morning at church way," she explains. "Which takes you out of that whole pop sensibility. And between myself and Stuart we're eternally looking for maybe something spiritual, and we feel very happy within that environment. I think we both grew up with that background. I feel extremely relaxed and at one with it, it's something that we both enjoy doing. There's some beautiful tunes within that church set, and I'm a big lover of gospel music."

blast of white punk soul. Those already on the group's side were similarly stunned. Where were the acoustic guitars, the cello, the violins? Where the hell was the Stylophone? But it was still Belle and Sebastian, only bigger, bolder, and with a big-voiced woman on top. Aside from "You're Just a Baby" and "I Could Be Dreaming," the title track was the first B&S song you could properly dance to, and as such remains a big club and live favorite. Quite simply, it's one of the greatest songs in the Belle and Sebastian canon, a magisterial convoy of blue-black Spectoresque cool which, just in case anyone hadn't realized it yet, announced these people as a genuine force to be reckoned with. It remains an anomaly in that it's the only song they've recorded to feature a guest vocalist (bootleg recordings of fan-assisted covers don't count), and it's as much Monica Queen's record as theirs—when she bleats *And you hope that they will see*" it's pleading divinity incarnate—but it stood at the time as further proof of their ambition and remains a shining example of their ability to transcend their influences to create something magical all of their own. As Stuart and Monica unite on the final chorus call, the song building and building in an interlocked two-chord groove the equal of The Velvets at their droning syncopated best, the swirling boom of the church hall virtually becoming an instrument in itself, it reaches a point of such vast life-affirming joyfulness that when the "River Deep" riff which signals the song's closing moments starts bringing it all back home, it's almost an affront, a rude reminder that this manna can't groove on forever. And when it does end, in a clanging bucket of spent echo, you're left exhausted, exhilarated, just like Painter Jane on her back doing it for the joy of giving.

After that "You Made Me Forget My Dreams" is the perfect postcoital comedown. Featuring one of Stuart's most angelic vocals, it's an impeccably touching performance, weighted with a sadness as heavy as the weather. Again it's swaddled in the church hall's municipal echo, with Stuart, creaking chair and all, catching more of his dreams alone at the piano, joined later by the briefest hint of guitar and tom, and a quite ridiculously lovely swathe of heavy synth strings, ending in a jarringly unexpected snatch of cheap techno; the space rocket blasting through sleep and bringing us back to Earth. The cameo appearance in the second verse from *The boy who plays bass guitar/With the boy who's wearing flares,"* explicitly references a dream Stuart had about inveterate gigglers Stuart David and Chris. "I was having a dream about Chris and he was building a rocket, Stuart was there as well. They were just having a good laugh to themselves; those two when they got together, Chris would just be giggling like a madman."

"Photo Jenny"—which was briefly touted as the lead track—dates back to 1995 (quote from *Tigermilk* inlay) and is, in its own breathlessly rollicking way, an archetypal B&S pop tune. It's named after a girl, who the lovelorn protagonist—who doesn't take drugs—wants to photograph (photographing pretty girls being one of Stuart's greatest pleasures in life), and it contains an unlikely reference to a British '70s pop culture totem (*"What's on the box?* Man About the House *with Paula Wilcox"*).[9] It's also one of the most ragged things they've ever recorded, especially in the deeply untogether vocal harmonies, but this merely adds to its knockabout charm, with a touch of Bill Forsyth[10] about it, especially in the gormless "I dunno!" overdub towards the end.

The EP ends with Stuart David's first foray to the mike, with his shaggy dog story "A Century of Elvis," a spoken-word piece concerning a mystery dog and its regular visits to the house of Mr. David and his by-now fiancée Wee Karn.[11] Set against the backing of the at-the-time unreleased "A Century of Fakers," it almost works, but not quite. For one, Stuart D is mixed too far back in the mix, which renders part of his monologue almost inaudible, and since the tune wasn't actually devised for this oratorical purpose, it doesn't really offer the story any support. It's all rather arbitrary; just a bloke talking over an unused backing track. But as the first evidence of Stuart David's lightly surreal, whimsical writings, and as a clear precursor to the style he would hone so well with Looper, it obviously has some historical significance. "It was Stuart's idea," Stuart David concedes. "I think he'd heard Arab

---

9 An unremittingly saucy '70s British shit-com.

10 The Scottish director responsible for *Gregory's Girl,* one of Stuart's favorite films. Quite unsurprising considering it's virtually a celluloid evocation of his prevalent lyrical ethos.

11 They would be wed later that year in the Winter Gardens on Glasgow Green. The rest of the group were all in attendance, with Chris as best man—dressed in his New York fur coat—and Isobel playing cello for Karn as she walked down the aisle.

Strap's 'The First Big Weekend' and become quite taken with it." A typically blunt and candid evocation of a booze 'n' drug fueled weekend, that song, with its mordant, conversational Moffat vocal, obviously seemed to Stuart like a style which would suit his bass-playing chum's literary leanings. "So I went into the studio myself one morning to do that, but I forgot to take the story I'd written," Stuart D reveals. "I didn't want to admit that to the engineer, 'cause the studio was sixty pounds an hour. It would have cost me about a hundred pounds to go home and get my story. So I just got the engineer to record, and I talked 'til I lost my place, then I got him to stop and start again from there 'til it was finished. It just took about ten minutes. I thought it was shit, but some people liked it. So I thought maybe I thought it was shit just the same way you think a photograph of yourself is shit. And I thought maybe it was quite a natural thing to do. So I did some more. I'm still not entirely convinced by the format though. It might just be shit."

Although this oratorical style has continued to sustain him throughout his solo career, he still seems genuinely unconvinced of its worth. "I feel as uncomfortable with it as when anyone sees themselves on a video tape or something. You just think, what a fanny. But I have an idea for one now and again and I just do it. Like if someone has curly hair, and they hate that and they always straighten it. But whenever you see them with curly hair you think it looks great and they should just leave it like that. I do the spoken-word stuff on that basis. I'm taking other people's word that it's all right, and they might just be taking the piss to laugh at me looking like a curly haired wanker," he smiles.

Lazy Line hit the streets on July 28, 1997, with a cover starring one Thea Martin,[12] stalling at number 41 in the charts, much to the amusement of Chris, who had bet Mark Jones it wouldn't reach the top forty. One hopes he used his winnings to buy the enormous flares Jones still owed him.

---

12 Thea also appeared in one of the group's early press shots, holding a "Stop Children" sign, as well as on 2000's *LLPJ* EP compilation. When playing a gig in Australia in 2004 Stuart was unaware 'til afterwards that the girl chosen from the crowd to sing Monica's part on *LLPJ* was actually the EP's cover star, who he hadn't seen in years.

* * *

Having spent so much time in the eyes of the Lord over the last few months, you would be forgiven for imagining that the non-gospel-reading members of the group (that'd be the other six) would be keen to ply their wares somewhere a little less cloistered, but three days after the release of their latest non-hit platter they found themselves amongst the pews of the Union Chapel, playing before an audience agog with almost religious devotion. Excuse the prolonged metaphor, but by this time the reception B&S were receiving upon their rare public appearances had become truly devotional, obsessive even, a phenomenon most of the reviews concentrated on. As had become the rather tiresomely predictable norm, the sound was bad and the group were under-rehearsed, tuning up endlessly between songs, leaving Stevie desperately thinking of something to say as the crowd gazed silently at them through the murk. During a particularly awkward gap towards the end of the set, between forthcoming single "Century of Fakers" and "Seeing Other People," the guitarist launched into a solo rendition of "Like a Rolling Stone," before Stuart abruptly cut him short to begin the next song. The usually reliable Chris Roberts in *Melody Maker* witheringly cited this as the highlight of the gig, going on to lambaste what he saw as the smug, willfully amateurish disrespect with which the group treated their wildly partisan audience. What Roberts misses is the fact that the audience really didn't care how long it took the group to tune up; they were there for the pleasure of seeing their beloved Belles perform their beloved songs in private. True, they often didn't perform them particularly well—opener "Wandering Days" was botched from the off—but that's not because they didn't care, it's simply because they couldn't. Yet. There was a communal respect between group and audience here, a very particular relationship, which, to an outsider, might have seemed ridiculously one-sided, but to those involved, made more sense than anything in life.

With the *3 . . . 6 . . . 9 . . . Seconds of Light* EP—its title another allusion to Stuart's passion for photography, and with a cover featuring a young Stuart (the first time a member of the group had graced a cover) and his then-girlfriend Victoria Morton ("We set the timer and put the camera on a rock. We were at a little beach near Ayr"), the U.K.'s weekly music press (i.e. *Melody Maker* and *NME*) finally realized that something very special was going on under their noses—and beyond their prying eyes—each naming it as their Single of the Week upon its release on October 13. Tania Brannigan, writing in *MM,* saw beyond the usual clichés, saying "It's not fey, it's not twee: just simple, straightforwardly beautiful," before chucking any trace of objectivity into the pond and pronouncing it "So heart-piercingly perfect, I can only prostrate myself in awe." Upstairs at *NME,* Tommy Udo wisely chose not to curse them by branding them the best new band in Britain, but could hardly contain his shower of praise, reserving special mention for "Beautiful": "'Beautiful' could so easily have been some smarty waspish sneer, like Morrissey at his worst, but Stuart Murdoch's mellow Donovanish voice carries such emotional depth and sincerity it saves all their songs from this." It was also their biggest hit to date, reaching the hallowed heights of number 31.

Track one, "A Century of Fakers," is actually one of the group's weakest early efforts, and one of their most poorly recorded. The shuffling backing track had already been heard on the last EP, but Stuart's vocals don't add very much, being buried far too low in the mix. The lyrics—a witheringly caustic tirade against an apathetic, irony-obsessed generation—hit the mark, but the melody isn't one of Stuart's most memorable, and the whole thing has a slightly knocked-off air about it, as if the group had already become so used to their standard sound, they could churn this stuff out in their sleep. "Le Pastie de la Bourgeoisie" is one of Stuart's earliest songs, of course, dating back to Lisa Helps the Blind, and rocks like a French '60s garage band choking on their Salinger. Plus the lyrics are virtually a Murdoch master-class, containing reference to a mousy girl with buck teeth and split ends, *Catcher in the Rye,* Judy Blume, Kerouac, and, of course, those twin Murdochian pillars, school and church. No sex, though.

Lisa appears to be in need of her own assistance in "Beautiful," which is the highlight here, a prime tragicomic Murdoch mini-drama with Lisa not merely losing it but now slightly mental, who tries (nudge-nudge-wink-wink) photography before going blind, possibly as a result of excessive masturbation. The delicate arrangement is silver and brass perfection, Stuart's voice at its wearily empathetic best. What's more, the reference to *"two hundred troubled teenagers"* would give its name to one of the first major B&S fan gatherings in London the following year. After this, "Put the Book Back on the Shelf" seems like another rake over old ground, a feeling encouraged by the return of Sebastian, who has now written a book *(The State I Am In?)* which nobody wants to read, and who sees God in the crumpled face of this week's '70s pop culture icon, Sid James.[13] Remarkably, after just one year together it almost seemed as if the group were in danger of settling into a creative rut, a fact evidently not lost on their ever-contradictory leader.

---

13 Cackling star of the legendary *Carry On* series. See also: Morrissey, S.

CHAPTER ELEVEN

THE BOY WITH THE ARAB STRAP
Color My Life with the Chaos of Trouble

By summer 1997, as Belle and Sebastian were about to begin recording their third album, Stuart Murdoch had decided that his group had grown to such a point that, for them to fully prosper, the established order had to change. Worried that their standard working practice—singer brings in songs, group rehearses them—was becoming stale, he began encouraging other members of the group to come up with material. "To be quite honest, the group were kinda bored with me just coming out with song after song," he claims. "It doesn't matter how good the song is, they were bored with it—we'd recorded a hell of a lot."

Having already stockpiled a delicate arsenal of tunes, Isobel was relatively happy to contribute, although she'd always known that Belle and Sebastian would principally remain a vehicle for Stuart's songs, and had begun setting her sights instead on the freedom of a solo career, while Stuart David, who had made it clear from the start that his main concern would always be his own music, still decided that there would probably be no harm in giving away another of his story-songs to the group. Stevie, on the other hand, was horrified, fearing that the carefully orchestrated identity they had built up so far would be compromised by the intrusion of other voices. "I just fought other people contributing songs all the way, I thought it was a terrible idea," he says, although he has always been somewhat unjustly critical of his own efforts.

The guitarist bowed to democracy in the end, however, and dutifully set about trying to come up with something to match his master's voice, but before work on the new LP could begin in earnest, the group took their first working visit to the States for two CMJ shows with The Pastels at the Angel Orensanz Center in New York. On the day they arrived, Stevie—who had missed out on the trip to see The Enclave—was accosted by a girl proffering him a bundle of fanzines, which she later managed to interview him for. The publication in question was called *Chickfactor,* so at least he now had an idea for a song, albeit one he would never be happy with.

Jeepster had booked the group into the relatively fancy Paramount Hotel, whose staff were apparently incensed by their inappropriately casual posture. "We got in and sat down in the foyer and immediately got in trouble for not sitting properly on these Phillipe Stark seats," Neil recalls disdainfully. "We used to piss the doormen off by asking them to open the door and then we'd give some money to the beggars outside and go back in. They soon stopped acknowledging us."

At the first show, the ever-unfortunate Chris narrowly missed injury from a large chunk of ceiling which crashed down past his ears as he played. Insert your own "bringing the house down" gag here. Even before the show, things seemed typically uncertain, as Stuart David went AWOL on a sight-seeing trip, forcing Neil to fill in on bass during the soundcheck. "He'd been up the Empire State Building and lost track of time," Neil recalls with a mix of affection and irritation. Sight-seeing was obviously far more important to Stuart David than playing some bothersome sound-check. "He's not a dreadfully unpunctual guy, just a kind of weird guy," laughs Neil. "He would rather have been somewhere else." Which would appear to pretty much sum up that air of detached disinterest which Stuart David seemingly carried throughout his tenure with the group. "I don't know if I had that air, but it wasn't how I felt . . . except for the time I was in bed with Stuart," he smiles. "I enjoyed all the times we played, and a lot of the trips, some of the recording and some of the rehearsing. No matter what I was doing when I was younger though, now and again I'd get seized with this claustrophobic feeling, and panic that I wasn't somewhere else, doing something else. It wasn't particular to

Belle and Sebastian, or any more prevalent when I was with them."

Always a shadowy presence on stage—he always looked like he was trying to hide himself behind the amps, en route to the bus home—and in videos—he's basically asleep in both *I Could Be Dreaming* and *Lazy Line Painter Jane*—whether he wanted to or not he always gave the impression of a man for whom this was all just too much effort, a tiresome inconvenience standing in the way of what he really wanted to do, which was scribbling down his daydreams or polishing off a novel or making his own music or staying in at home with his beloved Wee Karn. And yet . . . Stuart David really did enjoy his time with Belle and Sebastian, and while he would never pretend that it could ever be more important than his own private creativity, he was, in the early days at least, probably more committed to the group than the likes of Isobel and Chris. "The only thing I didn't enjoy was when I felt I was squandering time, sitting about or traveling, or waiting at sound-checks, or waiting at recording sessions. I kept feeling I didn't have the luxury of squandering that time and I should be at home writing."

The gigs at the Angel Orensanz were the first chance for Belle and Sebastian's intimate New York fanbase to witness their Caledonian idols in the flesh, and it was clear that they expected to be in the presence of a troupe of translucent prophets rather than the irreverent bunch that they really were, such was the audience's slightly awkward reverence throughout the shows. "You're so very quiet," announced Stuart towards the end of their first show, slightly disconcerted at the over-polite reception. When the crowd cheered, presumably in an attempt to show that they were still breathing, Stuart silenced them with a swiftly raised hand. "No," he hushed. "We like that."

Following the gigs, the group somehow managed to find themselves invited to that year's MTV Music Awards after-show party, an event they invaded in typically understated and naïve style. "There was a huge red carpet, the first one we'd ever been at," remembers Neil, sniggering at the incongruity of the group rubbing canopes with the likes of The Smashing Pumpkins, Marilyn Manson, and Janet Jackson, whose bouncers jostled them in a quite unnecessary manner. "Everyone pulled up in limos and we arrived in a yellow cab. I was wearing a white jacket which I'd been wearing at [Scottish music festival] T in the Park the week before, and it had grass stains all over it. When the bouncers stamped our hands, it was with infrared stamps, so Stevie's going to them, 'Oh, this hasn't worked, this hasn't worked.' They just looked at him like he was an idiot. We couldn't believe it. Infrared! No way!"

Neil feels they perhaps played up this "innocents abroad" image from time to time, but after all, if you cast yourself as the underdog, it makes it all the sweeter when you get the girl. They were actually far from innocent, of course. Cynical buggers to a man, whenever they would find themselves at occasions such as this, they would sit in the corner in their own bubble of mirth, laughing at the ridiculousness of the people and behavior around them. "I always remember Stuart at that party in New York," recalls Stuart David fondly. "And he was walking about with his anorak and his bag on, saying to me, 'What's all this about then? What are we doing here?' He has no pretense. Chris's sense of humor comes from that, and that's the kind of humor I like. When it's just about how ridiculous everything around you is. And in the early days Stevie had a huge irreverence. He was always saying to me, 'What are we doing here?' when we were in some millionaire's house or something. But I think Stevie likes to do things the orthodox way, follow in the footsteps of people he admires. I don't like to do that."

The next day, a bleary-eyed Belle and Sebastian stumbled into a TV studio situated at West Fifty-fourth Street for a planned session which would eventually remain unbroadcast on account of the group's apparently unprofessional conduct. "It wasn't a shocking show, it was very indicative of the Belles at the time," Neil protests. "Well, [apart from] Stuart forgetting his lyrics, which he still does today. Some kids had brought an album sleeve to be signed, so he was singing off that. It was deemed an unsatisfactory performance. They wrote us a really pompous letter. But it was us at the time, someone just hadn't researched us to find out that we were like that. It could've been their best performance ever and it still would've sounded substandard to them. Also, half of them were hungover." Indeed, Richard only made it with moments to spare, his MTV hangover still buffeting rudely around his head.

"There's No More 'Wait and See'"

With Hardbody gone to the great rehearsal room in the sky, Mick Cooke had decided, after years of hard-rockin' struggle, that perhaps it was time to look for more gainful, permanent employment. He there-fore decided to return to college and settle down for a future in the safe haven of information technology. He had, however, agreed to play on Belle and Sebastian's third album, which he was more than happy to do. It was extra money after all (although Musicians Union rates were hardly the stuff dreams were made of) and it was fun. No, he could never give up the rock 'n' roll life entirely, of course, but he'd begun to realize that it was far too transient a thing to base one's future upon. He'd also agreed to tour Germany with a local group called The Kare-lia, which featured Stuart's old friend Alex Huntley, and who would be joined on this trip by the ever amenable Richard Colburn. Before he set off, however, he called up Neil and asked him whether he would be al-lowed some royalties from the next B&S album. "On that topic," Neil replied breezily. "Come along to the next band meeting."

And so, intrigued, he did. When he got there he quickly found out that the group were very keen to have him join as a full member. It was an exciting offer, one he couldn't possibly turn down. He thought for a moment. "Err, no thanks," he said, to a collective sigh of disbelief, espe-cially from Stuart David, who had been particularly vocal in his desire to bring Mick on full-time. "I brought it up at a meeting and convinced everyone else that it wasn't fair he wasn't a member," he says. "Mainly 'cause he'd been making me laugh on a New York trip. So the next time we saw him we asked him to join and he said he didn't want to be a member. It had taken me ages to convince the rest of the band, and I was thinking, Cooke, you fucker! But then a few days later he came back and said he'd changed his mind. He did want to join."

And then there were eight. For Mick Cooke, the suit and tie would have to wait.

"My One Man Band Is Over"

As the group very quickly became a growing concern, and as the various members gradually got to know each other and make their voices heard, Stuart decided that, not only did he want the group to solicit material, he also no longer wanted to be the one leading the way, and therefore began to encourage some form of nominal democracy amongst this seven-headed creature he'd created. So sometime in 1997, B&S matters ceased being the sole collusion of Stuart and Neil, as the floor was opened to the band as a whole, hopefully resulting in decisions which the majority could be happy with. Or at least that was the plan.

Seven people attempting to agree on one common goal—attempting to agree on anything—proved immensely problematic, and today the group still talk about the meetings between 1997 and 2000 with a mix of horror and disbelief. There was clearly a severe lack of communication going on between them, and the idea of some kind of democracy being in play was soon dismissed as a sham by certain members of the group, who felt that no matter what was said at meetings, the ultimate decision would be taken by Stuart and Isobel anyway, which meant that the group existed unsteadily on a constantly shifting plain of uncertainty, confusion, and resentment.

Stevie, Chris, and Stuart David in Hyndland Church hall, 1997. Photo by Stuart Murdoch.

"I just recall pain. Anguish. Torture," winces Stuart, who according to Stuart David genuinely did encourage group democracy although he wished that he had a group of more like-minded people to work with, perhaps thinking that he actually did have such a group. "If it was me in charge, like it was at the start with a clear vision of everything from songs to sleeves then there's no problem. You just tell people where to be and get the most out of them, but once things start to change, well, what is this? And once you ask that question, there's a lot of talking, everything being debated to the wire. To people's credit, nobody ever said, 'You're talking shit, I'm outta here.' People in our group are nice and reasonable, and that's a strain. We'd talk and talk and talk, and be reasonable, and then go home and feel like killing ourselves."

Stevie reckons that the main problem was that the group, Stuart David and Isobel in particular, were never really interested in chasing a common goal, that they always had their own interests at heart. This, clearly, does not a happy family make. "Describe the band in one word: dysfunctional," says the guitarist. "You had a situation with all these people getting to know each other, but you also had people who were very ambitious and who took total advantage of the situation. And Stuart just letting it happen, letting people walk all over him. To be fair, Stuart David said at the start, 'I'm always going to be my own man, I'm always going to do my own thing.' But the truth is the band did propel him into being able to do his own thing, but he didn't give us an inch in any respect whatsoever. The meetings were excruciating, nobody wanted to get behind the band, they wanted to get behind their own thing. Chris would come to meeting and just talk about V-Twin. I was like, 'Fuck V-Twin, you're not making any money out of them.' It was just very, very hard to do anything."

"I think I went from being in quite a dysfunctional family into quite a dysfunctional band," says Isobel. "You really take it with you." It's actually not too much of a stretch to cast Belle and Sebastian as a family, dysfunctional or otherwise, with Stuart as the eccentric and unpredictable patriarch, Stevie the long-suffering wife, Richard the bluff and good-natured uncle, Sarah the quiet daughter, Mick the cheeky son, Stuart David the enigmatic elder brother, forever locked away in his room, and Isobel and Chris as the wide-eyed and hyperactive children. The family that plays together stays together . . . after a fashion.

Ever since Stuart and Isobel had become an item, the rest of the group seemed to view them as a power-wielding two-headed beast, someone/thing who would eventually call the tune regardless of the others' wishes. "It used to be a bit of a running joke," says Stevie. "We'd have band meetings where we'd hammer things out, and it'd be excruciatingly painful, but the meeting would end and we'd go, 'Right, Stuart and Isobel are now going to decide what's really going to happen.' It was just very, very insulting and humiliating. It was just one humiliation after another. I was forever on the verge of leaving, but in the end I just switched off and stopped caring. Nothing was happening anyway, we never played live, we never did anything that a band should. So everything was just basically through this Stuart and Isobel filter, and Stuart David was in it for himself, but at least he was honest about it. I think Stuart found Stuart David's attitude quite cute or something, but I found it infuriating. A band can't function like that. Beans was someone else who made everything more difficult. We'd sit and work out where we were going to be touring in October—I remember in 1998 particularly—and a week later my girlfriend has heard from Isobel that actually in October we're going to be making the first Gentle Waves record. And Stuart just took it, and the rest of us had to take it on the chin as well. It was fucking humiliating." Stevie later tempers this outburst, tenderly admitting that "I love those guys," which comes across as completely sincere rather than as an attempt to whitewash his previous proclamations. But one can easily sympathize with his frustrations, and it's clear that these problems hurt him quite a bit, both personally and creatively. "I'm not bitter, and I don't want to complain too much," he protests. "But I got so frustrated, because I knew we could be a great band, an important band, and I just wanted everyone to care as much as I did. I cared so much." And he did, and he was right to, and it must've been a royal pain in the arse.

It seems strange that someone as determined as Stuart should lay down like this, that he should jeopardize the future of his beloved band by acting in such a careless and/or duplicitous manner. It appears that he did genuinely want to turn his one man band into a democratic collective, and yet at the same time he felt that, in the end, he knew best. Was he blinded by his love for Isobel, appeasing her wishes to remain in her good books? Or was he simply too scared to speak his mind, preferring to go behind the group's back rather than admit that his wellintentioned notions of democracy were just impossible to maintain? Either way, it was clearly a battle between remaining loyal to his bandmates, to Isobel, and to his own bloody-minded vision, a feat he could never realistically pull off.

As far as Stuart David was concerned, Stuart should never have relinquished his leadership in the first place. "I always think a group should have a leader, someone whose vision the whole thing is. But Stuart was reluctant to take that role. Even though we all knew that Belle and Sebastian was originally his vision, and one that we admired. It all got a bit muddy when it was supposed to become a shared vision. I always saw my role as helping him out in what he was doing. Before there was anyone else in the band, and Stuart was just putting people together he said, 'I really want to have a defined band, and I want you to be in it.' I said, 'I'll help you out 'til you find the right people, but I don't want to be in it forever.' So as far as I was concerned that was the understanding. I don't know if Stuart remembered that conversation though."

Isobel, for her part, maintains that this presumed Isobel/Stuart axis of power never existed, and that even she was surprised when Stuart would ignore band decisions and go his own way instead. "Everyone would say their piece, and Stuart would sit back in silence, and we'd eventually decide something, but then the next day we'd find out that Stuart had stepped in and totally changed it. He liked to give folk floor space but then he would just do what he was planning anyway. It's terribly psychological, like some political game," she says.

So who to believe? Such was the lack of communication between the group at this time, they're probably all telling their own version of the truth. Amongst the group Stuart is known, with a degree of exasperated affection, as a notoriously fickle and contradictory creature, and while his intentions are always sincere, he may well have drawn up a whole new set of rules within seconds. "He gets very enthusiastic about things," says Sarah. "In fact, he's a bit like Gollum, he goes into a frenzy of self-contradiction. He'll go, 'Right, we need some hits, where are the hits?' And then a couple of seconds later, 'We don't need hits, fuck hits!' What's going on in that head of yours?" she exclaims. As for their not-really-manager, he doesn't seem to agree that this period in the group's story was anywhere near as fraught as they make out. "I don't seriously remember the meetings being that bad," shrugs Neil. Communication breakdown, it's always the same.

"It's Not Fun to Watch the Rust Grow"
Belle and Sebastian began working on their third album straight after the EP sessions, rehearsing and recording in the church hall as they

went. Whereas Stuart had already compiled the first two albums in his mind before they began recording, this time things were far less preordained and therefore less focused. "We really prepared a lot for *Tigermilk,* and *Sinister* was prepared too, but *The Boy with the Arab Strap* wasn't anywhere like as well prepared," admits Chris. "We thought we could just start recording stuff again and it'd be fine."

But it wasn't. Although Stuart had readily encouraged the group to take a more proactive role, it eventually became clear to him that, without someone taking the reins, they tended to procrastinate and wander off in different directions, no one really sure of exactly what it was they were working towards. And yet still he was adamant that he take a less vocal role, keen to let the rest have their voices heard, hoping patiently that something new and fresh would be born from the resulting chatter. Although the group all felt that they had something worthwhile to contribute, had begun to feel more comfortable with themselves in general, they were still nervous of stepping from Stuart's shadow, something he was helplessly aware of. "I think maybe if it had been more democratic at the start, it would've been easier to continue that way, but I think people were a bit reticent about being compared [to me]. It's quite brave, because you're on a hiding to nothing, really," he says. "But I think the songs on that record, the ones that other people wrote, have a lot more vitality, are much fresher." Perhaps. What was clear, however, was that the group were struggling more than they ever had before, with work dragging on far longer than they were used to. Whereas *Tigermilk, Sinister, Lazy Line* and *3 . . . 6 . . . 9* had each been taken care of in a matter of days, the new LP was taking weeks, months, eons. "From the single sessions onwards it was much more of a struggle with the group," Stuart admits. "Because we were changing, people were pulling in different directions, they were getting a lot more confident, and obviously they want to make their mark more and be a proper group. Which is fair enough."

Although they had been more than happy with the recent church hall recordings, the group were still worried about the prospect of recording another album, the sonic disappointment of *Sinister* still ringing in their ears. "After *Sinister* all the records have always been hard to finish," claims Chris. "Because you just worry about what you're going to feel like when it's finished, as we did after *Sinister.*"

Dividing their time between the church hall and Ca Va, Belle and Sebastian plowed on through the winter and into the spring and summer of 1998, increasingly frustrated by their inability to adequately finish the album off. "I can remember it was a grind," Stuart David sighs. "I don't think it bothered me that it took a lot of time, but there seemed to be an awful lot of wasted time." Their lethargic work-rate was hardly helped by the fights Isobel and Stuart were having throughout, their relationship having settled into the bumpy runaway carriage from which it would never escape. Their arguments could hold up work for hours, sometimes wasting entire days in the studio, which hardly endeared them to the rest of the group. "It was a pain in the arse," grumps Stuart David. "It seemed to be at its worst when we were recording in the church hall, and they'd disappear for an hour now and again to argue, and we had to sit about with nothing happening—which was always the thing I couldn't handle anyway. I'd give it a while and then get ready to go home, and then they'd come back, and people would be annoyed at me for almost going home. The way I looked at it, I could have been at home arguing with my own wife, rather than sitting there wasting away."

Amidst all this screaming, ranting, moaning, waiting, and wasting, Belle and Sebastian somehow managed to complete their third album, *The Boy with the Arab Strap*, after nearly a year of fractured work. Things had changed, and not for the better. The bubble had burst, and as the various members hurtled back to Earth with a crash, many began to consider whether it was all really worth it anymore, whether it could ever be fun again. Remarkably, after just over a year together Belle and Sebastian had already become disillusioned with themselves.

In December 1998 Belle and Sebastian finally got around to releasing "This Is Just a Modern Rock Song" as the lead track on an EP also featuring "I Know Where the Summer Goes," the high, fractured lament "Slow Graffiti," and Isobel's "The Gate." A long, languid, aching dirge, "This Is Just a Modern Rock Song" finds the group at their most Velvets-esque, redolent as it is of similarly soporific Lou Reed ballads such as "Ocean" or "I'm Set Free," while "Slow Graffiti's" metronomic Fender chords also sound like a doff of the cap to the Factory's finest. In its faintly musty, mottled fashion, the *This Is Just a Modern Rock Song*

EP marks the end of a chapter for Belle and Sebastian. Rarely would they ever again sound this brittle, this ragged, this bleak. It was time for a polish.

To complement the release of the album, the group embarked on their most concentrated bout of touring to date, with a triplet of U.K. dates followed by a trip to Europe, and then, only a matter of days after they returned to Glasgow, their first tour of the U.S., which would become significant in ways far beyond most bands' usual inaugural Stateside visit. Touring was a novelty for the group, a novelty most of them embraced with excitable curiosity, although for the endlessly overwhelmed Isobel it simply proved to her once and for all that the touring life wasn't a suitable environment for a sensitive soul such as she. "Things weren't very good for Isobel on the European tour, and we supported each other quite a lot," recalls Sarah, who by this time had grown closer to her sole female compatriot after an awkward start. "I think I'm more able to just throw myself into things than she was. She did find it very difficult. She'd not really lived on her own until quite a long way into the band, she'd never lived in shared flats or anything, and she did find it quite wearing getting on the bus with all these . . . I mean, the boys in the band weren't a problem, but I remember on that European tour there were these two French P.A. engineers and one of them was

Stuart David, Chris, and Isobel on tour.
Photo by Stuart Murdoch.

just standing naked in the toilet, hadn't locked the door, and Isobel pushed it open and he went, 'Not bad for thirty-five, huh!?' She was absolutely horrified," she chuckles, mimicking Isobel's seasick groan of disgust.

Stuart David was happy to tour the continent, presumably having few problems with naked thirty-something roadies, although it was clear that he would never really acclimatize to the standard rock band touring schedule, such was their dismay at only having a fortnight off between bouts. "I can remember I enjoyed the European part of it," he says. "But we were relieved to be home, and then a week or something later I remember being on the plane flying out for the American part, and me and Chris couldn't work out why we weren't still at home, 'cause we'd just got home. But a lot of that tour was good too." For Stevie the whole experience was a belated Godsend—touring the States in the footsteps of his idols, hitting the road with the band he'd longed for all his life—a great band, a band who mattered—getting drunk in motels, gazing hungover at endless highways through tour-bus windows; was there anything more beautiful? It was on this tour that he nervously introduced a country-soul number he'd written called "The Wrong Girl," kindova rip from Buffalo Springfield's "Burned" with a little whiff of Glen Campbell and Michael Nesmith, but probably the only song he felt confident enough to rank against Stuart's; they would record it one day and even this most self-critical of songwriters couldn't fail to be pleased with the results.

But then, just three dates into the tour, came Philadelphia, where the kind of freedom Elton sang about was particularly conspicuous by its absence. Isobel got sick, for home, for safety, whatever. Fact was, the girl was stuffed up in bed, weak with a sudden virus which meant that she was unlikely to make the show. The group had been in town for two days, lingering in the carpark around their van, wondering whether they were going to play or not. Stuart was their only link with the sickened Bel, appearing every few hours ashen-faced but boldly optimistic, until the point where he told the group that if the girl wasn't well enough to play then the gig would be off. Belle and Sebastian sans one was not Belle and Sebastian, he argued—if she couldn't play, then he wouldn't, and what was the group without their Prince and Princess Charming? An answer wasn't really necessary. "Isobel had come down with the cold in New York, then she took some pills which didn't really work, so the gig got canceled, but not until the support band had played," remembers Sarah with a sigh. The group mooched around the darkening carpark, waiting more and more impatiently for Stuart's reports, everyone coming to the collective conclusion that if this were the way things were to proceed, then there probably wasn't much point proceeding. "In the history of the world it's a tiny, tiny thing," shrugs Chris. "But we canceled a couple of shows because Isobel wasn't well, and the whole way we went about it was totally ridiculous. Stuart Murdoch was caught between doing the show without Bel and not doing it, and we couldn't come to a decision. That's just an example of the band's dysfunction."

Neil, who had joined them on the tour, admits that the incident was poorly handled. "I had a part in probably not handling that as well as I could've done," he admits. "Basically I told Bel to miss the sound-check, stay in bed, and come for the show, but I never accounted for her getting up before the show and then falling right over again. The doctor came to the hotel and said she couldn't play the show. It was a big show, they'd sold out the Trocadero in Philadelphia, it was possibly the biggest show they'd booked apart from Shepherd's Bush Empire."

Sarah, just six months into her voyage with Belle and Sebastian, was already thinking that her time could perhaps be better spent than loitering in a lonely carpark a million miles from home. "Isobel wouldn't get on the bus, so Stuart said, 'Look, I'll stay with Isobel and we'll fly to Toronto.'" She recalls, smiling with a shake of the head. "I was like, 'Fuck that! I'm not getting on a bus for two days on the off chance that you two decide to fly in for the gig.' A lot of us didn't know if the tour was going to go on, but eventually we headed to Chicago and resumed the tour. When you're thousands of miles from home you have no control over your situation, and I really hated that—Oh God, I just wanted to go home. That was probably the closest I've come to thinking that it's not worth it."

A week later they were home, shaken, bitter, and beaten. At their first meeting Chris was the first to raise his grievances. "I said I wasn't going to tour under those circumstances. I mean, after canceling the show we didn't know if we were going to go home or go on to the next one. And if I hadn't been the one to say that, then Stuart David would have been."

And he would have been. "I think it was the end of something that had been tottering on too long in a lot of ways," says Stuart D. "We had all agreed to go home if Stuart didn't play. We'd spent two days in a carpark in the bus, and it was just so much wasted time. Touring America is hard enough at the best of times, but to have to sit in a bus and then not play was too much for me."

Their first American trip was enough to prove to certain members of the group that they were just too fragile to conceivably leave the sanctity of their backyard; to others it was merely proof that they could never possibly survive without a collective willingness to compromise. To Stuart Murdoch it was just another example of the confusion inherent in his continuing attempt to please all the people all the time.

Almost as soon as they had returned home, the core of the group were back in the studio, this time to record the solo record Isobel had been hankering after ever since the start. Stuart had been understandably encouraging, as had Chris, both of whom sympathized with Isobel's desire to find a forum for her own music, and while the rest were happy enough to play on the record—especially when Isobel announced that she wanted to record it in a week, just like *Tigermilk*—it's clear that they viewed the venture as something of an unnecessary diversion. "I sort of compare it to, like, playing for two football teams," muses Isobel. "In the end, if you're drawn against each other . . . it was tricky. They were kind of supportive but then Stuart was like, 'Why aren't you giving us these songs?' But I wasn't giving them the songs because most people preferred Stuart's songs in the band. I remember being party to times when Sarah and Stevie tore [Stuart David's] 'Paper Boats' to shreds— not that it's my all-time favorite song or anything—but they were like tigers, going, 'Oh, "Lord Anthony" is a much stronger song, but this . . .' God, the most ruthless journalist could learn a lot from Stevie and Sarah, they were just tearing the song to shreds in front of Stuart David. And I remember thinking, fuck, I am not going to let this happen to my children. No fucking way."

"To a certain extent there was a conflict," Chris admits. "Isobel had made an absolutely massive contribution to Belle and Sebstian and deserved to be supported. And we maybe hadn't given her a lot of the support, personally and emotionally, we could've given her as friends through hard times in the band. At least the one thing we could be relied upon was to help her with music. And I suppose it was an acknowledgment that Belle and Sebastian were never going to work in such a way that we could do as much of her music as she was producing. And you didn't want to deny her the opportunity to be making music. She had songs before we started, and if things had worked out differently then maybe we would've been doing her songs right from the start." Did he feel in some way that the group owed her their help? "Not in an obligation way," he counters. "Not in the way that we owed her because she'd done us a favor. We just wouldn't think not to help her, and I love the music that she writes, and I really enjoy working with her in a studio situation. I'll always be happy to go and work with her."

Keen to recapture the freshness she felt the group had lost with *Arab Strap*, Isobel led the group through seven days at Ca Va, utterly in her element. It was like *Tigermilk* all over again, as she wrote in her sleeve-notes for the album. "It involved frantic phone calls and late night laboring, the hiring of transit vans, the 'acquiring' of vibraphones and the kidnapping of friends from their day jobs. Most came from their own free will, whilst others guarded their telephones and recovered from jet lag."

Eventually released in April 1999 (just a month after Stuart David released his first Looper album) under the guise of The Gentle Waves, *The Green Fields of Foreverland . . .* is a sporadically engaging, almost intangibly fragile record, in which Isobel invites the listener into a bucolic twilit world of her own strange imagining, a dark enchanted wood frosted with dirty snow, inhabited by sad and lonely people crying lost under a helpless silver moon. Much of it is quite insufferably twee (sorry, no other word for it), of course—what is a grown woman doing writing a girlish ode to a tree ("Tree Lullaby") for fuck's sake?—and Isobel's halting whisper will always be too weak to sustain an entire album, but there's a dark and unsettling edge to these grim fairy tales which show that there's far more depth to her than her critics often give her credit for. With *The Green Fields of Foreverland . . .* (terrible title) Isobel Campbell managed to create a world just as distinct and fully realized as that of her parent band, and while her subsequent records would prove more varied, she has yet to make a record as honestly enchanting as her debut.

It also proved to Isobel that she could stand on her own two feet without fear of falling. There would be no looking back.

* * *

Back at the church, alone again (or) at the piano, Stuart began Belle and Sebastian's third LP in typically understated style with "It Could Have Been a Brilliant Career," an uncharacteristically sour look at two twenty-something stroke victims, towards whom he seems curiously ambiguous. It is this very ambiguity, however, which prevents the song from sounding mawkish. Whereas one might normally expect him to sympathize with characters such as these, here he almost suggests the boy *"selling lies to the boys with the old Dansettes,"* and the girl whose *"paintings are a sham"* almost deserve their dribbling fate for being such artistic clods. Its cruelty is actually rather refreshing, admirable in its boldness. Here Stuart simmers in a pot of cool black comedy which, although there have been traces of it before and since, is hardly his natural milieu. "Maybe that's because the character isn't a real character," he muses. "It's an imaginary situation, so you can have a bit more of an objective point of view."

The first non-Stuart song on a B&S LP, Isobel's "Is It Wicked Not to Care?" is undoubtedly the finest song she contributed to the group, and the most exquisitely arranged bauble on this here tree. Those who dismiss Bel as a purveyor of flaccid twee-pop, all ladybirds, lollipops, and sexless romance, have obviously never cast much more than a cursory glance over her lyrics, which bristle with a precocious wisdom colored in a deceptively dark hue. *"I know the truth awaits me, but still I hesitate because of fear,"* she trembles, before delivering a possibly self-critical assessment of a girl *"wearing rags to make you pretty by design,"* and fearfully pondering *"Is it wicked when you smile? Even though you feel like crying? Even though you could be sick at any time?"* all of which is wrapped up in her finest ever melody, dressed in delicately sympathetic rags by her bandmates. Stevie's reverb plucked guitar break skips like pebbles cross a pond, becoming all the more effective when doubled up on xylophone to create one of their most irresistible instrumental passages. *"And if there was a sequel,"* she questions, *"Would you love me as an equal? Would you love me till I'm dead? Or is there someone else instead?"* It's a remarkable little song, really, an assured unveiling of Isobel Campbell's talent which announced, quite unexpectedly, that the girl with the cello could pen a tune every bit as good as her feted beau. Indeed, it's one of the best songs on the album, better even than most of Stuart's contributions. Isobel's voice, a breathless, somewhat artless sigh, evidently influenced by the untutored twitterings of her adored '60s Yeah Yeah girls, will always be an acquired taste, and as her solo records attest, is rather too saccharine to stomach in prolonged sittings, but in short bursts like this it's an undeniably affecting tool. In terms of sheer aural pleasure, "Is It Wicked Not to Care?" remains one of Belle and Sebastian's finest recordings.

Stevie Jackson also makes his songwriting debut with "Chickfactor" and "Seymour Stein," which although partly inspired by the Sire man's visit, is more of a yearning love song in the classic blue boy mode. "It's about when you desire something, and you get it, sometimes you're distracted by something else anyway," its author explains. "I'd just split up with my girlfriend, and I had a record contract, all my dreams had come true, but it meant nothing because my girl had gone. You can give me a deal, Seymour, but bring me my girl and I'll be impressed." Stevie came up with the song begrudgingly, of course, and certainly his vocal seems less than certain, straying nervously in and out of tune throughout. It's a shame, as he can sing a lot better than this, and the sad summer groove he'd come up with—like The Young Rascal's "Groovin" by way of "Lay Lady Lay"—is a beauty, with the forlorn Stax-style outro revealing for the first time the classic soul influence which would seep into much of their future work. Although Stuart David claims that Stevie's songs are what made the album interesting for him, there's no denying that his second contribution, "Chickfactor," is one of the most forgettable songs the group have ever recorded, as its ever self-deprecating author is quick to admit. "The difference between 'Seymour Stein' and 'Chickfactor' is that 'Seymour Stein' is pretty good and 'Chickfactor' is atrocious," he states baldly. "With 'Chickfactor' I nicked a chord change from 'Lady Jane' by The Rolling Stones. It's a similar progression.[1] 'Chickfactor' was about going to New York and getting attention. Everyone in Glasgow's in a group, no one's impressed by it, but in New York we were treated differently. People were asking us to hang out and so on."

Stuart David's second spoken-word opus, "A Space Boy Dream," is by far the most incongruous track on the album, a jazzily ambient skank which, as the Space Boy nervously touches down upon his destination,

---

[1] The lyrics also allude to the Stones' "The Spider and the Fly."

rockets off into a full-on jazz funk Hammond freak-out, Chris finally being given a chance to stretch out and flail his funky fingers. Even more so than "A Century of Elvis," this is a clear template for the things Stuart David would achieve with Looper, and as such succeeds on its own bookworm-goes-dub terms, but there's no denying that it sticks out of the album's hide like a brightly feathered arrow. Encouraged by Stuart to contribute, Stuart David opted to tease out the aspects of the group which hadn't as yet been allowed to flourish, allowing them to turn loose on the kind of song Stuart would doubtless never write for them. "I was more interested in using some of the potential that was in the band that didn't get used in Stuart's songs," he explains. "I did stuff that I thought had Belle and Sebastian as a context, rather than just bring in any of my own songs that I was writing. I enjoyed the stuff we did like that, though. It was interesting to see what the group was as an organic group, taken out of the context of playing Stuart's songs, which was what we had come together to do in the first place. I thought it was good to see what we would naturally do as a band, if everyone just inter-acted without a song. So I directed a few improvisations, and then edited them in the computer. 'Space Boy Dream' was one of those." He goes on to tell of a friend who used to tape the album for people leaving off "A Space Boy Dream," which he doesn't imagine was uncommon. "[But] I think it's interesting 'cause it's the sound of all those people playing what they'd play without one of Stuart's songs to define the performance. Stu-art included. I was just interested in seeing another side to the band."

The northern soul influence which Stuart had professed not to care for but, as we have seen, actually coveted for *Sinister,* is given its first full flourish on "Dirty Dream Number Two,"[2] which is also the first time the

---

2 As per norm, no singles would be released from the album, although two promotional videos would be made, one for "Is It Wicked Not to Care?" (as discussed elsewhere) directed by Wee Karn, and another for "Dirty Dream Number Two," which didn't feature Belle and Sebastian at all, starring instead various Belle and Sebastian fans—including members of the Sinister mailing list, the Web's most enduring B&S community—shot in and around the Portland area. The video was directed by U.S. filmmaker Lance Bangs, who would go on to codirect *The Wrong Girl* video with Stevie, and whose other credits include documentaries on the making of Spike Jonze's *Being John Malkovich* and *Adaptation,* plus videos for Moby, Green Day, Pavement, and R.E.M. as well as being responsible, naturally enough, for filming the wedding of Brad Pitt and Jennifer Aniston.

group had worked with a string section. With Richard's solid gutbucket drums lending it an appropriately soulful groove, the song sweeps along sweetly with that same strange air of celebratory melancholy common to most of the great northern soul records, which must've delighted Chris in particular, although he claims not to have had too much of an influence on the song. "I felt I had more to contribute but knew I couldn't write songs the way Stuart did," he says. "So I was really struggling to pull things in a different direction but without having a song to hang it on." Another of Stuart's extrapolations upon the mystery of dreams, this time of the moist kind, "Dirty Dream Number two" is another song which Isobel feels was inspired by her, in particular the line *"dream one you had a whole lot of fun with a comedian,"* which she claims is about a sordid dream she had about British comedian Dennis Pennis. Stuart's response to this is fairly predictable. "A dream Isobel had?" he exclaims, spluttering with surprise. "A dream *she* had?" About Dennis Pennis? "Did she?" he laughs, genuinely tickled. "Well, I'm sure that's right. Cool, well . . . there you go. It must have come from somewhere, so I guess that song's about her then." Glad we got that cleared up.

The undoubted highlight of the album, and indeed one of the imperishable jewels in the entire Belle and Sebastian crown, is "The Boy with the Arab Strap" itself, an utterly captivating pearl of glam-pop boogie which must surely be a contender for their very best-loved song. Built around Chris's rollicking electric piano, Richard's bright 'n' breezy drumming (those fills could have an eye out), and a melody so playground simple it's remarkable that no one has snapped it up before, the song is so joyfully life-affirming the Samaritans should be using it as hold music; surely the recorder solo from "The Boy with the Arab Strap" is enough to convince anyone of the possible joys life can bring? Some happy songs are so ingratiatingly unctuous—"Walking on Sunshine," say, or "Shiny Happy People"—that they achieve the opposite of their desired effect and force the listener into a slough of despair and/or possibly violent retribution, the important difference being "TB-WTAS" doesn't *tell* you to be happy, it just *is*. Plus, the lyrics are caked in cynicism and trenchant detail, such as *"the Asian man with his love/hate affair with his racist clientele,"* or *"you're constantly updating your hit-parade of your ten biggest wanks,"* the kind of lines you'd be loath to find in your average party classic. As noted earlier, the song was inspired by the group's first visit to London, during which they were accompanied by Arab Strap themselves, and, title hook aside, the song does in part address their singer Aidan Moffat with lines such as *"It's something to speak of the way you are feeling/To crowds there assembled/Do you ever feel you have gone too far?"* leading some to conjecture that the song is in some way a put-down of this notoriously candid diarist. "The title certainly refers to Aidan," Stuart admits. "It was around about the time they were playing and staying with us in London. It's about that time, basically." But is it a criticism? "Oh, absolutely not," he offers unequivocally. "If I ever take a seed from a real person it's always done with fondness." Isobel might have grounds to disagree, but no matter. "And I think that's kind of obvious to right-thinking people. I'm not really interested in portraying nasty people, I must say. I like interesting characters, and Aidan certainly was one."

Moffat himself (who mentions Stuart and "the girl who plays the cello" in passing on the Strap's "I Saw You") appeared less than pleased with the reference, however. "I don't give a fuck what people think about me," he protested to *NME*. "But Arab Strap was on the front of their album in bigger letters than Belle and Sebastian, and that isn't fucking cricket. I'm sure they'd be pissed off if we called our next album 'Belle and Sebastian.'" In an interview with Freewilliamsburg.com both Aidan and Malcolm, although maintaining that they were still friends with B&S (Aidan: "They've got a sense of humor"), did complain that "there's a limit to putting someone else's name on an album. They're taking away something from us." It certainly did seem to be source of some irritation for the Falkirk bards, whose patience would be understandably tested by clueless journalists asking them whether they had named themselves after the album.[3] What's more, a good many confused Arab Strap fans—including Helene Christenssen, apparently—ended up buying the album mistaking it for a new release, which, it has to be said, is fairly naïve behavior and can hardly be blamed on Belle and Sebastian (who were probably happy for the royalties, though).

The wonderful title-track aside, Stuart Murdoch's contributions to

---

[3] At an Arab Strap gig in Birmingham shortly after the release of the album, one hilarious wag in the crowd shouted, "Do you like Belle and Sebastian?" to which Aidan replied, with all the malice he could muster, "What, the Boy with the broken face?"

Arab Strap are far from his finest. The quality and quantity of his work up until this point had been quite staggering, of course—two albums and three EPs of near-impeccable delights—but it was clearly only a matter of time before he proved that he was just as fallible as the rest. None of the rest of the songs he wrote for the album—"Ease Your Feet into the Sea," "A Summer Wasting," "Simple Things," "Sleep the Clock Around" (which would always be much, much better live), and "The Rollercoaster Ride" are *bad* exactly, it's just that compared to the brilliance of his previous work, they just seem a little second-hand and generic. Generic within a genre he had himself defined, of course, but this is hardly an excuse. Songs like this are fodder to the group's critics, those who think B&S are nothing more than fey purveyors of wispy indie flummery, which makes the fact that this is still their most widely heard record all the more vexing. As they have shown before and since, Belle and Sebastian are obviously capable of so much more than this kind of prosaic whimsy.

   The Boy with the Arab Strap is a disappointment as a whole, hardly a

An outtake from a cover shoot featuring Bel and Chris. Photo by Stuart Murdoch.

disaster, but an undoubted letdown after the impeccable highs of the first two albums. In encouraging other members to contribute, Stuart should be applauded, for Jackson, Campbell, and David are all clearly talented writers, each with something distinct and worthwhile to contribute, and yet it's this very encouragement of democracy which drags the album down. The differing voices make it a far less cohesive effort than the first two; it's less complete, less assured, more of a patch-quilt than the seamless musical tapestry of *Tigermilk* and *Sinister*. "Electronic Rennaissance" on *Tigermilk* should probably have jarred with the rest of that album, and yet it worked, because despite its electro trappings, it was still clearly a robot cousin to Stuart Murdoch's self-contained musical brethren. But "A Space Boy Dream," for example, no matter how it succeeds on its own merits, just jars with its surroundings, as do both of Stevie's contributions. Plus, Stuart's songs just don't measure up to the heights reached on the albums and EPs so far released. It might be unfair to expect him to consistently come up with such pearls in such a relatively short space of time, but the group set their own work-rate, and the listener can only judge on what they're given. "*Arab Strap* reflects exactly where we were at that time, in a good way," Stuart insists. "It's not my favorite Belles LP, I think it sounds terrible in places, some of the recordings are really poor, but I actually think it does hold together. I just think it feels right."

Today Stevie also feels that it does hold together as an album, although he admits that at the time he thought they'd made a fatal step backwards. "I thought it was a disaster, I thought we'd get buried for it, but we won a Brit Award for it! And it's still our biggest selling album. I thought at the time, in terms of song quality, it was a down step. I thought we didn't sound as good, although I thought *Sinister* sounded like crap as well. I thought overall there weren't enough big songs, like 'Fox in the Snow' or 'State I Am In,' these unbeatable, classic tunes. But in retrospect I think it's the one album where the whole is more than the sum of its parts. It actually makes a lot of sense when you play it in sequence, you get more out of it if you play it from start to finish."

Chris remains philosophical about their achievements. "It got good stuff out of everybody in the band," he says. "*Tigermilk* had a kind of diversity to it, and *Sinister* was just a bit samey, and it was good to get away with that." According to Stuart David, however, this diversity was neither blessing nor curse—the root of the album's trouble lies in the fact that "it's just not all that good." It's hard to disagree.

Released in Britain on September 7, 1998, almost exactly two years after *Sinister, The Boy with the Arab Strap* would eventually go on to become their biggest selling album, a record it still holds to this day. The *NME* were a little too kind in granting it an 8 out of 10 score, praising its "vivid and confident swing"—a description more befitting the title track than the album as a whole. Surprisingly, considering the album's disappointing nature, nearly all of the reviews were similarly positive, most critics welcoming the contributions of the other members, although a good many fans agreed with Stevie that the group should remain a vehicle for Stuart's vision. Unbeknownst to anyone outside their inner circle, however, it looked for a while after the recording of *Arab Strap* that perhaps Belle and Sebastian had given up for good. "I think it was decided that after *Arab Strap* there wouldn't be another album, because it was clear that things were fucked," claims Stuart David, who by this time was busy working on his own solo record. "But then I think we came to a compromise, where we all agreed we'd make one more if it could be made in two weeks. So I recorded for two weeks, but there was no album in sight. . . ."

Stuart Murdoch has only vague recollections of this agreement and doesn't confirm Stuart David's assertion that the group really were on the verge of splitting, although it was clear to him that they had to properly pull together if they were to ever make another album as good, if not better, than their debut. "I probably did agree to that in principle at the time," he eventually concedes. "And I must say I feel a bit sorry for Stuart David now, because it was going to take two weeks. But a band's gotta do what a band's gotta do. . . ."

Belle and Sebastian's fourth album ended up taking longer than two weeks to record. In total it took nearly two years. Two years on the brink and toppling.

Of Bowlies and Brits

In early 1999 Belle and Sebastian discovered that they had been nominated for the Best British Newcomer Award at that year's Brit Awards. On the face of it, they seemed like perfect candidates for the prize; they had only been together for three years and released three albums and three EPs after all. The Brit Awards are basically the equivalent of the American Grammys and as such are entirely meaningless in any true artistic sense, preferring as they do to hand out gongs to acts who have sold the most records and upset the fewest number of apple carts, rather than those who might have made a more substantial contribution to music in the previous year. It is the biggest and most visible yearly example of the music industry congratulating itself on making lots of money, and although it is granted blanket media coverage each year, no one ever pays it that much credence. Or rather, no one with a "serious" love of music pays it that much credence; for one of their acts to win a Brit is sales-manna from Heaven for a record company, and to the mainstream record-buying public it acts as a guide to the records they should be purchasing in the next six months. So it came as great surprise that a group as little-known—in mainstream terms at least—as Belle and Sebastian found themselves nestled in amongst that year's nominees, which included such well-known pop acts as Billie Piper and Steps, the kind of acts who would normally walk away with such an award.

Understandably, the group treated the announcement with a good deal of irreverence, although there's no doubt that they were in some way flattered by the attention, since it was further proof that they had somehow managed to inveigle themselves into the black heart of the music industry without ever having to take anything approaching the accepted route. They had been accepted, and all without asking. Their little group from Glasgow, their little secret world, all of this had somehow blown up into something huge and utterly beyond their expectations; it was all too ridiculous and hilarious to comprehend. Jeepster were probably more excited than the group themselves. They were, after all, a tiny indie label with no track record, a bunch of principled music lovers who had managed to snag a Brit nomination simply by releasing a series of brilliant "proper" records all with the minimum fuss. It was a classic David and Goliath tale; even if they didn't win the award it was proof enough that they'd made their mark. Unfortunately, being such a tiny concern, they didn't have enough money to send the whole office and group down to the event—tickets were pricier than your average music biz lackey's weekly coke bill—so only Mark Jones, Vanessa Sanders, and a couple of B&S representatives would be allowed the trip. Chris sums up the reason why most of the group refused to take up the invitation. "I thought it was hilarious," grins Chris, whose only disappointment at not attending the event was that he didn't get to meet Muhammad Ali, who was sitting at the table next to Jeepster. "I must admit, I enjoyed it much more watching it on TV than if I'd been there. I don't think I could've stood up there and accepted the award." Belle and Sebastian just didn't feel comfortable joining in with such media back-slappery and elected to stay at home, where they were busy trying to knock their fourth album into some kind of workable shape. So it fell to Mick and Richard to man the expensive artistes' table at the event, just in case it transpired that they might actually have to accept the award.

As soon as the nomination was announced, Katrina House had encouraged fans to place their votes via the official Brits Web site, believing that there was little chance that the listeners of Radio One would make much of a case for a band they'd barely heard of. After all, if they'd been nominated they might as well win the damn thing. And so the fans went into overdrive, massing as one to ensure that their beloved Belles wouldn't undergo the indignity of being trounced by some ridiculous pop act. "Their fanbase utilized this new Internet thing," says Stef D'Andrea, who watched the event from a London hotel room with the rest of Jeepster. "And if the other record companies had been more up on it maybe they would've won it, but because Belle and Sebastian fans were very into the Internet they got lots of votes."

Thousands of votes, in fact, many of which came from the same servers in Strathclyde and Glasgow Universities, which could either have been the result of one or two particular committed fans, or the endeavors of a whole sweeping canvas of Belle and Sebastian fans. It's impossible to say. "It was an Internet vote, and a lot of our fans were students, and students were some of the people to have access to the Internet.

Sure, it probably wasn't one member, one vote. . . ." Chris concedes. It wasn't too difficult to fix an Internet vote, of course, but even Neil and Katrina didn't have the patience or means to do such a thing. "I didn't even go at it that hard myself in the office," shrugs Neil. "I was on dial-up at the time, couldn't afford it. I probably only put two or three votes in myself. It still strikes me as pretty complacent on these other people's parts that they don't do the same. It definitely wasn't band led, it was a Jeepster, David Kitchen thing. I hadn't realized that the fans had stirred themselves into action to such a degree."

On the night, televised across the nation, the usual stream of name-less faces and drug-addled mannequins paraded across the stage, picking up their awards and dutifully thanking their record companies before trooping back to their champagne-splattered tables, before it came to the announcement of that year's Best British Newcomer. No one took much notice of the clip of Belle and Sebastian that flashed up across the screens during the nominations. Then, brilliantly, Huey from The Fun Lovin' Criminals opened the envelope and declared in his finest New Yoik drawl, "And the winner is . . . Belle and Sebastian." Suddenly the fragile strains of Isobel singing "Is It Wicked Not to Care?" filled the auditorium, and the barely listening throng suddenly roused themselves from their complacency as two bewildered Glaswegians stumbled their way to the stage. Belle and who? Where was Billie? Where was Steps? Why is there a guy on stage wearing a safari suit? "Err . . . I'm Belle, this is Sebastian," uttered a fazed Richard Colburn. "I'm not sure if this was meant to happen. . . ." And as soon as they'd arrived they were ushered off into a cacophony of flashbulbs and microphones, Richard doing all the talking[1] as a seafood-allergic Mick slowly turned green as a result of the rogue volez-von he'd unwittingly quaffed earlier that night.

Out front, Steps manager Pete Waterman was virtually hemorrhag-ing with rage. He'd had a tip-off that day that his puppets were going to win, and then suddenly there's these two pasty Scottish berks standing up on stage clutching the award he deserved. "Pete Waterman was ag-grieved that the votes of the fans got in the way of what he knew to be the right decision," deadpans Mark Radcliffe, who was present at the

---

1 Quite brilliantly, Scottish television's *Scotland Today* billed Richard as "Nick Cook" the next day. The real Nick Cook looks notably queasy in the footage.

ceremony in his capacity as esteemed Radio One DJ. "There was a genuine sense of disbelief in the hall, and it was the one moment that punctured that sort of vile backslapping thing you get at the Brits. The fact that there was some kind of air of annoyance that Belle and Sebastian had the audacity to encourage their fans to vote for them, which therefore made it the most genuine award of the night, showed it up for the farce that it was." But Waterman wasn't going to take this lying down. Almost as soon as the award had been announced, he was on the phone to his friends in the press. This must've been a fix! Who's ever heard of Bellanne Sebastian?!?! Find out what's going on! And so the very next day, Britain's number one tabloid newspaper, *The Sun,* splashed a typically sensationalistic "exposé" across their front page—*their front page!*—"*Brits Fix Shame!*" The story was that some talentless opportunistic upstarts from Glasgow had unfairly snatched the award from the genuinely popular, genuinely talented acts in their category; it was a scandal and a half. Although most of the group found this coverage hilarious, Stuart failed to see the funny side, seeing it instead as a typically bullying intrusion into the special environment he'd tried so hard to keep separate from the industry. Furious, he first toyed with throwing their award into the River Clyde, then, when particularly wound up, with tossing it through the window of the Brits office. One almost wishes he had: a great punk gesture if ever there was one.

But he didn't. He just fumed and quietly got over it, forgot about it, settled back into the important matter at hand—recording their next album. But to Neil, who still proudly sports an enormous blowup of the *Sun* front cover in his office, the whole debacle was an immense delight. "Getting accused of rigging it was the icing on the cake," he beams. "It was just funny, it was the ultimate in noising folk up. It didn't do much for us in the long run, though, it was a bit of a millstone, probably still is. We never followed it up commercially, and people remember the name from a while ago, that band who won a Brit once. If you speak to Rough Trade now, they'll say that the struggle for the band is to remain current for people who remember us from winning the Brit. There's a great amount of truth to that."

To Jeepster, although they appreciated the punkish triumph of the event, they still encouraged the group to capitalize on the win, to release a single, to play a few dates, to do anything to further the publicity they'd received. Predictably, they refused to do any such thing. "When they won the award we saw the potential that they could sell several hundred thousand albums," says Stef D'Andrea. "But they basically closed up shop and wouldn't leave home, wouldn't release a single, wouldn't tour, wouldn't do interviews. They were in the studio recording their new album, that's the end of that. Most record companies dream of getting this chance and then there's us, this one man and his dog record company, we have an act who win a Brit Award and they don't want to speak to anyone. . . . It was a high and a low simultaneously."

To Stuart Murdoch, the event was everything. Concerts, *gigs,* those were things other more mundane bands bothered themselves with. He wasn't interested in just turning up and churning through the same practiced moves night after night; he wanted memories, magic, fun and games, the kind of all-inclusive event which gave the audience far more than your usual run-of-the-bill gathering.

He'd always been good at organizing events, in fact he'd probably

Picture by Stuart Murdoch and Andrew Symington.

spent more time doing that at university than he had doing actual work, and he was constantly dreaming up wild concert concepts for Belle and Sebastian, including a tour of various British seaside resorts followed by a world tour by boat, ideas which, sadly, never got out off the dock. But the idea of some kind of summer holiday trip was just too good to waste, and together with Neil, Stuart harked back to his days at Butlins and came up with what they considered to be a surefire winner. "Myself and Stuart Murdoch had both been massive Stone Roses fans, and the fact that every gig they'd done had been events," says Neil. "So we thought it would be good to do a tour by boat, but the holiday camp weekend was a substitute for that. And also I knew that these Northern Soul weekenders always worked."

Stuart and Neil, and sometimes Richard, had become used to driving around Britain for days on end in a hired van, personally seeking out suitable and interesting venues (indeed, this is how they came by most of their early gigs), so after deciding to organize a Belle and Sebastian–hosted all-star weekender in a holiday camp, they set off to find a suitably picturesque destination,[2] which they eventually found in the shape of the Camber Sands Holiday Center, a coastal resort in the southeast of England just a pebble's throw away from the white cliffs of Dover. It was almost too perfect. Along with their promoter friend Barry Hogan,[3] Neil and Stuart set about booking their ideal bill, although Stuart was to be disappointed when he discovered that Blondie, Morrissey, and The Velvet Underground were either unavailable, too expensive, or dead, or in some cases a mix of all three. They eventually settled on a bill including the likes of The Flaming Lips, Mercury Rev, Elliott Smith, The Divine Comedy (Stuart's choice), and the expected Glasgow patrol including V-Twin, The Pastels, Mogwai, The Delgados, outright B&S soundalikes Camera Obscura, and Mick's ska band The Amphetameanies. "It was like taking everyone from Nice'n'Sleazy's down to the south coast of England for a weekend," says Neil.

---

2 It would have been all too perfect if they had managed to book Butlins in Ayr, since not only did Stuart once work there but Neil's dad too.

3 Flushed with the success of the Bowlie Weekender, Hogan would carry on with the concept under the banner of All Tomorrow's Parties, which continues to flourish to this day.

The event would take place between April 23 and 25, 1999, with fans and bands staying on site in chalets throughout. But what to call it? Stuart was in little doubt: It would be the Bowlie Weekender. But why? "I must credit the word 'bowlie' to a friend, this guy called Fraser," Stuart explains. "I stayed in a bed-sit just before the band got together, and used to sort of bump into him in the kitchen, and I recognized this guy from the '80s, I used to see him around. He was quite a cool anorak kid, into The Weather Prophets and stuff, and he would talk quite fondly about the bowlie days. He would laugh and say, 'I saw this girl the other day, I can't believe she's still knockin' about. She's a pure bowlie.' It just amused me, and he never really explained what this meant. I don't know if he came up with it himself, or whether it was handed down." One must assume that the term is derived from the bowl haircuts adopted by the majority of indie kids, although its exact provenance will probably never be known.

Clearly the biggest event the group had yet attempted, they were understandably keen to ensure that their headlining performance on the final night didn't disappoint, and so found themselves crawling blearily out of bed first thing that morning to start sound-checking before anyone else awoke. "It was hard work," Sarah complains. "The sound-checks we used to do, these epics . . . it was pretty mad. Neil had told everyone to be up at seven o'clock, but the P.A. didn't get loaded in on time and we finally ended up sound-checking at four in the afternoon. Every time someone asked if they could go back to bed, Neil would say, 'No, we'll be needing you any minute.' It was the last night, and quite a lot of friends had gone down and got drunker than they'd ever been in their lives, but we had to be completely sober and tired, while everybody around you is just ridiculously drunk."

Neil had his own problems, however, with a crew member who "was a bit of a [simulates sniffing coke] troublemaker, and he went AWOL," he says with a shake of the head. "And we all stood there for a couple of hours waiting for him. Apparently he'd been beaten up 'cause he'd been caught shagging someone's girlfriend in a bush. Setting up the night before is supposedly leaving no stone unturned, but it all went wrong anyway. There was no piano there, for one. Barry took the blame for that and he's more than welcome to keep it. Anyway, there was a real panic getting one and we had to pay an obscene amount of money to this really old guy in the middle of nowhere to come tune it, and he said that everything had to be absolute quiet, we couldn't test the lights or anything, and everything was running late, other bands didn't get sound-checks and so on. It was being filmed, which pissed the band off, and the crew needed them to sign a release form, so I got The Delgados to sign it. So they were there filming the sound-check, and Stuart was going, 'Fucking get them out of there.' But I said, [sheepishly] 'Look, you've signed a release form.' Once the sound-check was over a miserable Mick decided to go and drown his sorrows after a recent bust-up with his girlfriend, only for her to discover him later that day entwined with another girl. Bad news. Understandably, he wasn't in the best frame of mind to play a gig, but somehow managed to pull through.

These complications aside, the event was a huge success, attracting thousands of kids from all around the world and turning the site into the teeming bowlie village Stuart had envisioned from the start, with acts and audience joining in the holiday reverie as one. Well, almost. The notoriously somber U.S. post-rockers God Speed You Black Emperor! were, perhaps unsurprisingly, less than enamored with the event, complaining to Neil that it was like an "indie Auschwitz," which forced the harassed manager to retort, "Well, we'll promise not to put you in a room again with people having fun then." But everyone else seemed to throw themselves into the spirit of the thing, be they Elliott Smith dancing ecstatically to DJ Jarvis Cocker spinning "White Lines," or The BMX Bandits' Duglas Stewart dressing up as a camp red-coat and interviewing kids for the BBC. New Jeepster signings Salako held late-night acoustic shows in their chalets, occasionally accompanied by the likes of Stuart David and Cornelius, while Stuart and Stevie entertained fans queuing to get in to see Belle and Sebastian with an impromptu busking performance, including versions of "Rhinestone Cowboy" and "Be My Baby." For the organizers, however, it was an understandably hectic affair. "I was busy all weekend, because I DJed two or three times, and I played with V-Twin as well," remembers Chris. "On the Saturday morning there was a football tournament, and both us and the Fanclub thought we were gonna stroll through and meet in the final, and we both got beaten in the first round." Beaten, he neglects to mention, by some bowlie kids. "It was highs and lows," says Stuart. "It was terrific, but at the same time one of the most stressful weekends I've ever had in my life. It was like running one of these all-night student balls."

For Neil, the day of the Belle and Sebastian show was the most stressful of all, especially in the moments leading up to the performance when he and a herbally assisted Chris looked on in terrified awe as Mercury Rev delivered a particularly showstopping set. "That was a new low for me, I really had a panic attack that day," shudders Neil. "The [Belle and Sebastian] show was amazing, the best they'd done at that point, but the weekend was an obscene hassle. We'd been there for two days and going at it pretty hard. I remember Mercury Rev finishing with this big white noise thing, they were so good that night, and I'd imbibed more than I should've, but I was totally freaked out. We were the hosts that weekend, it was our biggest show, and I kind of lost it, but as soon as they started playing it was great."

Playing before an obviously partisan crowd, Belle and Sebastian rose to the challenge to deliver a particularly buoyant performance, featuring the unveiling of Isobel's delightful girl-group pastiche "Landslide," a song she planned to release as a duet with '60s soul singer Evie Sands—who the group had recently backed at a gig at the church hall alongside legendary songwriter (and brother of Jon Voight) Chip "Wild Thing" Taylor. Sands actually recorded her "Landslide" vocals at Ca Va the day after the gig under the guise of The Maisonettes (i.e. Isobel, Sarah, and their friend Rozanne Suarez; they would be billed as such on the "Legal Man" single), which never got off the ground. The band closed with a raucous and suitably celebratory version of The Who's "The Kids Are Alright." It is unlikely, of course, that the majority of kids were actually alright by that point, but still they ambled back drunk and happy to their chalets, taking with them a weekend memory they would never forget. "We just kind of drifted away at the end," recalls Stuart. "We had to get the train to Dublin. I ended up smashing my guitar in Dublin. I think that was a reflection of how knackered I was."

The Bowlie Weekender and this destructive Dublin gig were to be Belle and Sebastian's only two official appearances in 1999, although unbeknownst to them they were about to find themselves thrust unwittingly into a cruel ampitheater of public glare.

* * *

In 2000, a year after Belle and Sebastian's shocking triumph, Pete Waterman's Steps were handed a specially invented Brit Award for being the biggest selling albums act of 1999, a triumph which will no doubt be remembered long after the name Belle and Sebastian is ground into the sawdust of obscurity.

CHAPTER TWELVE

FOLD YOUR HANDS CHILD, YOU WALK LIKE A PEASANT
I Fought in a War

The Space Boy stared blearily into the mirror, barely recognizing himself. He was sick, poisoned, delirious. He'd been stuck at home for months now, which wasn't in itself that bad; he couldn't think of a place he'd rather be than home, of course. But he'd been too sick to write, to record, to do all the things he'd wanted to do more of ever since the day he ambled out of the church hall for good.

The phone rang intrusively. The Space Boy struggled with the receiver as if it were a barbell. "Hello?" he croaked. It was the curious boy. He wanted to meet, the group wanted to meet, to discuss whatever future they might have. The Space Boy hardly felt like getting out of bed, let alone making his way across town, but something in his friend's querulous tone triggered something within him. He didn't want to let them down and yet . . .

His mission was over. Over and out.

It all meant nothing. The Brit Award, the sales reports, even the reviews. It didn't matter to Stuart Murdoch that his group was selling records, was feted by the press; all he cared about was the quality of the records they made, and what they really meant to those who chose to listen to them. He didn't want to be just another group, releasing just another record, embarking on just another tour; he felt a dull ache in his gut whenever he thought that this might be all his group would ever mean to anyone. No, he had to pull it together, rouse the group from their beaten torpor and make the very best record they could, to pull them somewhere in the vicinity of the greats. He knew they could, was ridiculously certain of it in fact, but he just needed to see it in their eyes again, just needed to know that they were all in it as one again. He'd vaguely assured them that they could record this next album in two weeks, just like *Tigermilk* and *Sinister,* praying that the endless chore of *Arab Strap* could be dismissed forever as a blip on their flight path. But he knew that if they couldn't, if they weren't up to the task, then that would be it for them, dream over, hopes dashed, a horrible, pointless waste.

So in early 1999 Belle and Sebastian trouped into the church hall, where they felt safe, where they'd recorded some of their greatest shining moments, with Tony Doogan's mobile studio parked outside, ready to get back to their raw and honest roots. Hmm, The Beatles had tried this with *Let It Be,* thought Stevie, but half of that was still classic, so what the hell. When you ain't got nothin' you ain't got nothin' to lose. "Obviously I'm always very ambitious for them, and any suggestion that the album wasn't going to be the album they wanted it to be was disappointing," says Neil, who quickly realized along with the rest that their old spark had dulled to the very slightest ember. "There was a lot of vagueness around that time. Me and Beans were living together at the time, Richard would be around a lot, and we were having a pretty good time of it, we went out a lot and what have you, as young boys do. Although the overriding memory is of discomfort and unease, the memories I have aren't of shaking my head going, 'Oh no.' The memories are of hearing 'I Fought in a War' in the studio thinking, fucking hell, that's a really good one, even though it does sound like 'Ordinary World' by Duran Duran. I shouldn't say that, it'll noise up the gaffer. . . ."

Stuart was absolutely dismayed by this general lack of spirit, of course, which only made him more determined to pull things together. "I know people see it a different way, I can only report my personal feelings, but for me that was when things changed," he declares. "There's two periods of this band: everything up to *Fold Your Hands* and everything after that. I think the process changed during *Fold Your Hands.* I was wanting a more officious record with more officious arrangements, I wanted a better sounding record because I was disappointed with the way *Arab Strap* sounded. But it's clear that to get that we were going to have to work, we were going to have to be disciplined, and it became clear that some of the band didn't want to work, weren't interested in this. It was like pulling teeth, basically."

Those who "didn't want to work" almost definitely numbered Isobel and Stuart David, both of whom had more or less decided to flee the coop and concentrate on their own work. Stuart David had seen his first novel, *Nalda Said,* released to great acclaim, and brought out his similarly well-received Looper album, *Up a Tree* (which turned out to be far fresher than *The Boy with the Arab Strap*), just as Belle and Sebastian were toiling in the church hall. It was clearly time for him to relinquish his "favor" to Stuart and branch out on his own. Isobel too was anxious to record another Gentle Waves record, which Stuart agreed to help her with right in the middle of the B&S album sessions, which merely helped to slow down their already sluggish process and fan the flames of old resentments. It was clear after two weeks in the hall that there was no album in sight and so Stuart David packed up his bass and went home. He was done. "He kind of drifted out of the band during the recording of *Fold Your Hands Child*," says Chris. "I think it was after that record that we knew that if we didn't start touring and things, then there probably wouldn't be another record. It was at that point that he left. It wasn't a surprise. The way he conducted himself over the thing was absolutely perfect. Everyone was really sorry to lose him, but could kind of understand why. He felt that there was a lot of unnecessary nonsense to deal with. He's someone who's not going to be dictated to, he knows his own mind."

As far as Stuart David was concerned, he'd settled his part of the bargain, and since it didn't look like it was paying off, he simply retired from the fray. "I just did my two weeks," he shrugs. "That was the agreement, and there was no album after two weeks. So I didn't go back. And then I got poisoned by a duck and I got very ill for a long time. Then when I got better they had an album."

This, it can probably safely be said, is the first claim of retirement by poultry ever recorded in the history of rock 'n' roll. As the months dragged on without Stuart David, Stuart M. phoned him up and invited him to an emergency meeting, the group still far from completing their album. "I was still quite ill, and I'd been at home for three months," Stuart David recalls. "And I was all thin and spooked. The whole band were having a meeting, and I went to that, and I hadn't seen any of them for ages. But I was leaving quite soon for a two-month Looper tour in America, and I knew I'd have to leave B&S at that meeting, 'cause they wanted to get on and do stuff again. It all happened quite easily 'cause Stuart said something like, 'I just realized when I found out your Looper tour was so long that that's probably what you want to do now, and that you're probably not into this anymore.' Something like that. And I said something like, 'That's what I want to do, and waiting about for me is probably holding you back now.' That was all I think. That evening Stevie phoned me and said, 'I was a bit confused in that meeting. Did you leave the band?' And he said he hoped we'd play together again sometime. That was a sweet thing to do." Ever since he'd joined Stuart's group, he had been beset with feelings of uncertainty, anxious that his own creativity was being squandered. "I needed my time back by then," he admits. "I'm very selfish with my time. If that hadn't been the case, I might still have left for other reasons—'cause I felt a lot of the good stuff about the band had had the shit kicked out of it by then. A lot of the irreverence had gone. But even if it had been great I wouldn't have stayed much longer, because of the time."

Neil remembers the Looper's departure slightly differently, however. "I think he put it on the Internet before he told everybody else," he declares, although still he wasn't surprised or particularly hurt by his exit. "He still came and did the photo-shoot afterwards, it wasn't like he stormed out and never spoke to us again. It was a gradual wind down." Stuart Murdoch, it seems, was similarly unsurprised, realizing that his friend simply wasn't up to the task of recording the classic record he had in mind. "Stuart just wasn't prepared to work any harder, wasn't prepared to change," he says. "But I had to make the record I wanted. When it comes down to it, the record's everything, it's the blood in your veins."

But still they had to admit to themselves that nothing was working. Nothing they had come up with inspired them in any way, they were just going through the motions, utterly listless and despondent. "I remember listening to the recording of 'The Model' we did in the church hall, and it just sounded really tired," says Isobel, who was far more excited by her solo record, meaning that she barely turned up to any of the B&S sessions. Having already lost Stuart David, this just seemed to the group that they were falling apart. At the same time as they were struggling with the record, Stuart was busy remastering *Tigermilk,* which they had finally decided to release on CD. After eons spent struggling on their new record, he was shocked, saddened, and yet inspired by the music they had made just three years before. "I was mastering *Tigermilk* for CD, and also I was listening a lot to a group called Camera Obscura,[1] who had just started rehearsing at the church hall," he recalls. "And the combination of seeing them being just brilliantly fresh and easygoing, with these beautiful songs, and then hearing *Tigermilk.* Compared to this shit that we'd come up with, *Tigermilk* was fresh and hard-sounding." He was similarly inspired by the working practices of Isobel, ironic considering the lack of interest she had shown in Belle and Sebastian of late. "I must say that Isobel was quite influential for me having this change of heart, because I was helping her record her own music around the same time, which as you can imagine wasn't that much fun, because your loyalties are split, blah-de-blah," he says dismissively. "But at the same time she was very forthcoming and knew exactly what she wanted in her solo records, and I thought, how come she can do that for her record, whereas I have to lay down like a doormat and put up with the shit I'm getting from some of the group, and putting up with this crappy sound that people aren't interested in—what is the difference? So I thought, fuck that. I listened to that garbage and knew we had to start again."

After scrapping virtually all of their work so far, the group started from scratch with a fresh and slightly desperate sense of purpose, fearfully realizing that this could well be a last-ditch opportunity. "Stuart left and Isobel wasn't around, and that's when we got on with it," remembers Stuart M. "The rest of the group pulled together. Bel occasionally came in to play her parts. And we got there. That's when I started writing string arrangements, we worked hard on the production. The result was that *Fold Your Hands* was a salvage job, and overall it's a weak LP, but there's nice things about it, and I'm still very fond of that record, because we pulled it together. We could've put out this crap, this garbage,

---

1 Stuart would go on to produce their single "Eighties Fan" at Ca Va.

but we didn't. With *Fold Your Hands* it changed, where I'd learned to calm down a wee bit, stand back and say, 'Right, let's make the production better.' That's when I started looking to and referencing older records. Let's fucking make these records, then, let's make a record that sounds as good as *Some Velvet Morning*. It meant people were going to have to work a lot harder, stand back from the process when it needed something else. This is tough to take for instrumentalists in the group, but in a sense it had to be, because seven people getting together and just making the first noise that comes into their head around a certain chord sequence isn't going to produce *Be My Baby*."

With a string section camped upstairs at Ca Va the album that would eventually be released under the rather unwieldy title of *Fold Your Hands Child, You Walk Like a Peasant*—a title stolen from some graffiti Stuart had spied while sitting on a toilet at Glasgow University—gradually began to mold itself into some kind of workable shape, although not without some cost to its harried director. Desperately intent on salvaging the record, Stuart spent hours, days, and nights slumped over the mixing desk with Tony Doogan, as the months and expenses rolled ever on. But he wasn't alone in the task, as Chris explains. "Mick and Stevie had a massive amount of input into the record, they worked massively on the string arrangements. It started out sparser, just with the band, and they pushed the strings. Mick works so fast. He'll get three parts down in the time I come up with one."

As for Jeepster, they could only bite their nails in London and peer nervously over the parapets as their biggest investment lurched slowly and expensively towards their goal. "With *Tigermilk* they had three thousand pounds and they recorded it in a few days," says Stef D'Andrea. "*Sinister* they recorded in two weeks and it cost us about ten thousand pounds, *Arab Strap* took a few months to record and cost about sixty thousand pounds. We thought we'd got the balance right with that one, and then with *Fold Your Hands* all of a sudden it took one to two years and the budget went on and on, doubling and tripling, and ended up spiraling well over 120,000 pounds. It was becoming more difficult as time goes by."

To Stevie Jackson, all he could see as the months dragged on were his rock 'n' roll dreams dribbling through his fingers. "I think *Fold Your Hands Child* was probably the worst period of all," he sighs. "No one was communicating at all, and I wish I'd spoken up more at the time, because I thought the album was completely misconceived. Conceptually it was like, that album took so long, let's do one quickly. But the songs weren't there. There was a track-list of ten songs, two of which were Stuart David numbers. He had a concept of sampling us all, which is an interesting idea, but there was no way of knowing whether that would work. On the original sheet there was 'I Fought in a War,' 'The Model,' 'Women's Realm,' 'Family Tree.' I remember thinking track for track that's the weakest collection of songs I've yet seen, so I couldn't get too excited about it. It was just back to the same old thing. We didn't rehearse them, there were no demos. And then I find out from Stuart that actually it was Isobel who wanted to make the album, but she wasn't bringing any songs. And then our sessions stop so Stuart can go and work on her second album. This is a low point. I kind of thought it was the end."

Intent on completing her own record, Isobel—who only offered the briefest of cameos at the *Fold Your Hands* sessions—felt that "We should have—and this is completely naïve, I know—but we should have taken a holiday and gone back to the drawing board. But I appreciate that money had been spent on it and the wheels were in motion, but at the time I didn't. At the end of the day the buck stopped with Stuart, and he was under a lot of pressure, and he probably really had to deliver that album." Although Stuart admits that he did momentarily feel like giving up ("I'm talking about hours rather than months"), he was far too proud to ever release a record without any real worth, and eventually, in late 1999, he decided that finally they had done all they could feasibly do. Belle and Sebastian had done their very best, worked harder and more intently than they ever had, and now all they could do was set their record free and pray for its welfare.

Neil was right. "I Fought in a War," the opening track on *Fold Your Hands Child, You Walk Like a Peasant,* does bear an undeniable similarity to Duran Duran mid-1990s comeback hit "Ordinary World," but even this can't puncture its baroque beauty. A traditional B&S song in terms of its Stuart vocal and fragile group performance, it's lent added breadth by the dusty canyon string arrangement that swoops in melodramatically halfway through, the first sign on the album that Belle and

Sebastian had found a string section and weren't afraid to use it. The sound is big, cavernous almost, rich and wide, a sweeping, encouraging breeze of an opener, which immediately suggested that the deficiencies of *Arab Strap* would have no home here. But alas 'twas not to be. If the best thing you can say about an album is that it has uniformly pleasant string arrangements, then chances are that album is far less than the sum of its parts. Those lush, buoyant strings are everywhere on the record, on "The Model," which they had worked so hard on but would never be happy with until its later live incarnation, on Stevie's great "The Wrong Girl," on the magnificent "Don't Leave the Light On, Baby"—a sultry soul groover, Davis Axelrod producing Isaac Hayes, proof of the incredible heights this group could still attain when inspiration struck— and on the faux–Northern Soul knockoffs "Woman's Realm" and "There's Too Much Love," which are basically the same song, and not a particularly memorable song at that. Sarah makes her songwriting debut with the spectrally pretty if naggingly insubstantial "Waiting for the Moon to Rise," unveiling a voice as breathy and slight as Isobel's, whose own "Beyond the Sunrise" should probably never have been included on the record. A blatant Lee and Nancy pastiche, the song features an embarrassingly lugubrious faux-Hazelwood vocal from Stevie, who sounds like he's taking the piss, frankly. "That should probably have been better off on a Gentle Waves album," Isobel concedes. "Not every Belle and Sebastian fan is going to like my stuff, and vice versa." Placed just three tracks in, and followed by Sarah's less than essential effort, it kills the album dead before it's had a chance to breathe. *"Fold Your Hands Child* doesn't really work, I think it's the wrong sequence. It's a disaster," admits Stevie.

The one undoubted stroke of genius on the record is, ironically, the recording with the least adornment. "Chalet Lines," the song Stuart wrote about the rape of his Butlins workmate, is an unbearably chilling thing, so naked and stark it almost feels prurient to eavesdrop upon it. Lyrically, Stuart takes a dangerous gamble, placing himself into the mindset of the victim, an approach which could so easily have ended up sounding gauche, mawkish, or just plain offensive, but hearing that sad and weary angel's sigh singing lines like *"I missed my time/I don't think I could stand to take the test/I'm feeling sick/Fuck this, I've felt like this for a week,"* the effect is both disarming and utterly convincing, the lyrical details just right, sparing, unexploitative, the androgynous vocal lending it a slight but necessary distance in perspective; were "Chalet Lines" actually sung by a woman, it would be far too raw for comfort. Sung by a man it's distressing enough as it is. "I remember thinking it was satisfying to write, it felt good from start to finish," says its author. "It didn't need an arrangement, because it was just a story to be told. That was recorded in the church hall, and that's the way we should've been recording, with that nice acoustic sound, creaky floors and stuff." "Chalet Lines" remains one of Belle and Sebastian's most powerful and finely judged recordings. But *Fold Your Hands Child, You Walk Like a Peasant* as a whole does not.

Released in the U.K. on June 5—with a cover starring Gyda and Kristin Valtysdottor from sleepy Icelandic soothe-poppers Mum, who the group had been friendly with since Bowlie—Belle and Sebastian's fourth album wasn't the bold step forward they or their fans had hoped for. It was all right. It was decent. By most other people's standard it was probably very decent. But Belle and Sebastian had set themselves such giddily high standards, this album, the one with the title no one could quite remember, just seemed tired, complacent, too much of the same ol' same ol'. Despite the strings, the sporadic splashes of soul, the teasing hints of old brilliance, it all seemed a little stale, repetitive, far less magical. The group just didn't seem special anymore. One of the few bands who mattered seemed to have slunk into the kind of drab fug of complacency you expected of most of the bands you'd foolishly invested your faith into. But not Belle and Sebastian—surely they were different? "As an album it just doesn't work," Stevie admits. " 'I Fought in a War,' 'The Model,' 'Waiting for the Moon to Rise,' and 'Don't Leave the Light On, Baby' are all great. 'The Wrong Girl' is all right, 'Chalet Lines' is pretty amazing. So you'd think it was a great album, but when you actually play it it's not." The errant Stuart David was both disappointed and confused. "I couldn't really work out what the record was for. I couldn't work out why it had a song about fighting in a war or being raped in a holiday park on it," he frowns, even though he is alluding to two of the best songs on the record.

Fold Your Hands Child, You Walk Like a Peasant is the sustained

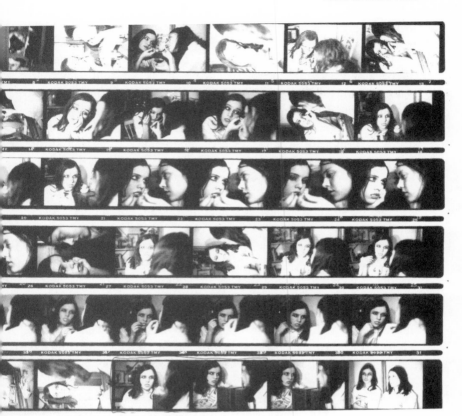

ttakes from *Fold Your Hands Child, You Walk Like a Peasant* cover shoot.
otos by Stuart Murdoch.

sound of a band treading water, one long unsteady tinkle of uncertainty. "I think it's really good to have a sense of style, and I like continuity, but you've got to evolve," complains Isobel, who couldn't deny that the group were starting to repeat themselves. "Maybe it was more knowing and cynical by that point." Chris is more pragmatic. "We could make an album of pure Detroit techno and someone somewhere would say we were treading water," he says dryly. "I knew it didn't sound as good as it should. As much as I'd have loved to have put out records quicker than we did, I knew we had to keep going. There were a lot of points where maybe you could've gone, 'Ah, fuck it,' and put it out, but I think that probably would have ended the band. If we hadn't kept

197

going and got some kind of satisfaction out of it, then that might have been it."

So Belle and Sebastian decided to write themselves a hit single. It was something they'd always craved, after all, a proper copper-bottomed hit, something to be sung and slung around playgrounds and adored not only by their core audience but also by the man on the street; a song to define the summer. Isobel had just seen and been bewitched by a recent Glasgow appearance of the Reverend Al Green, whose "L.O.V.E Love" had been reverberating around her head right up until the morning Stevie Jackson unfurled his new sitar/guitar sound upon the group. Stevie had dug the sound from afar ever since he'd heard it on those old Boxtops and Elvis's American sessions from 1969, with guitarist Reggie Young waxing lithe and funky with quasi-Eastern soul. "I love that sound, it's a very '60s soul sound," Stevie enthuses. "So this guy made me one. I played it at rehearsal and we thought, well let's write a song around that. And it was the first time the whole band sat around and wrote a song. It's funny, I usually get the credit for writing it, but that's not the case. We're sitting in the room above the church hall and I played an Eastern scale backwards, which is the "Legal Man" riff, and Isobel just went 'L-o-v-e love, it's coming back, it's coming back.' I thought that was fantastic, even though it was an obvious Al Green/Orange Juice reference. So we need a tune for the verse, and Stuart vaguely sang one, and then I said, 'Right, what's the song about?' And the day before we'd been visited by Robert White,[2] our lawyer, so Sarah suggested we write a song about him. And I went, 'Legal Man?' The inspiration for the song is a song by The Pointer Sisters called 'Don't Try to Take the Fifth,' which is a love song in legalese. It's a good format, so I just got the Jeepster contract and just took out legal terms. It took about fifteen minutes. And then Chris wrote the coda and, bang, that was it." Although Chris did feel that it should've been taken at a less frenetic, funkier pace, and Stuart too was initially less than enamored with the result. "I thought it could've been better as a collaborative effort," he complains. "But it was a departure because other people were at the helm, not me, and I think that's a good thing."

---

2 A picture of White nestles next to Katrina House on the back cover of the "Legal Man" single.

Released in the U.K. on May 22 just a few weeks ahead of the album, "Legal Man" became the hit they'd hoped for, peaking at number 15, and bagging them a slot on BBC1's legendary weekly music show *Top of the Pops*. "Being a '70s boy I grew up with *Top of the Pops*," says Stevie. "I used to get sent to bed at seven o'clock when I was really young, but Thursday night when *Top of the Pops* was on was the one night I was encouraged to stay up, so it really meant a lot to me personally. My two dreams were

Stuart in front of *Top of the Pops*, before the mischief began. Photo by Mark Trayner.

playing *Top of the Pops* and playing [famed Glasgow venue] the Barrowlands."

Joining them on the trip to London to record the show was Tony Doogan, who would invade their performance halfway through dressed as a "monkey cavalier"—Chris's description—perhaps as a nod to Stuart David's monkey-suited appearance on the *Fold Your Hands* sleeve. Doogan's unscripted appearance was just one of the many "incidents" to pepper this suitably high-spirited excursion. "My wife says it was the best day of that year," declares Neil. "And we got married a month later."

Stevie can only chuckle conspiratorially at the memory. "It was hilarious, it was a highlight," he smiles, while Stuart claims it was "bad behavior all round. Kids in a toyshop." During a break in the long day of filming, the group took a wander around the BBC studios, eventually stumbling onto the supposedly impenetrable set of the hugely popular soap opera *Eastenders*. Somehow managing to breach security, they scampered merrily around the set for at least twenty minutes until security arrived on the scene. "Stuart was in the [famed *Eastenders* pub] Queen Vic, pulling a pint, when security came in," recalls Chris. "They took us to this security chalet, called the cops. We said, 'Look, mate, we've just been on *Top of the Pops*, lighten up a bit.' Neil and Richard managed to sneak off when they came along and arrested us, but Neil came over eventually—and everyone fully knows that he was in [*East-*

enders'] Albert Square five minutes before—and he goes, 'I *told* you not to go anywhere near it!' "

Neil and Richard had actually been emptying their bladders in a BBC bush at the time of Chris and co's incarceration; no doubt a serious offense in television circles, so it's probably just as well they weren't caught. "When I got there I was going, 'What did I fucking tell you?!?' " says Neil, grinning at his duplicity. "I was saying to the security guards, 'I'm really sorry about this, they're in a lot of trouble.' But they weren't buying it and they phoned the police. I gave them a verbal bollocking, and they're all trying to keep a straight face. *The Sun* reported that '[*Eastenders* stars] Barbara Windsor and Tamsin Outhwaite Looked On in Horror,' and they weren't even fucking there!" As soon as Stuart saw security arrive on set he did what anybody would do in such a situation. He ran away. "Aw, c'mon, it was a break for freedom!" he laughs. "It was me that went and got [*TOTP* host] Jamie Theakston." Fortunately, Theakston eventually managed to smooth things over with security, and the group were released. "Theakston's word is gospel at the BBC," deadpans Chris. "It's a shame he's not the world ambassador he deserves to be."

Once they'd enthusiastically mimed to their smash hit platter in front of a robotically baying audience, most of whom probably had no idea who Belle and Sebastian were—"I sort of felt like you could have put a steaming poo on the stage and the audience still would've gone, 'Waaaaaaaahhh!!!' " posits Isobel cynically—with Snow Patrol's Johnny Quinn on bongos (sadly he didn't end up exposing himself as he'd promised before the taping), the B&S party repaired to the BBC bar and proceeded to knock themselves into a celebratory state of disarray. "We were sitting in the BBC bar skinning up, us and the Doves, and my wife, Gemma, went up to Chrissie Hynde and asked her to sit with us," remembers Neil. "Then we got the guitar out and Chrissie started playing, and my wife, God love her, is tone deaf but she sang a duet with her."

"Chrissie Hynde kept saying to us, 'Are you guys aliens?' " Isobel recalls. "She was playing air guitar, pulling flying-V shapes and kicking off her shoes, and she had ladders in her tights," she says, sounding genuinely appalled. "We actually had to get rid of [Hynde] in the end," claims Neil. "It was another messy day. I was so out of it that I started crying during [manufactured pop muppets] S Club 7 singing 'Reach for the Stars,' I thought it was the best thing I'd ever heard."

But despite these antics, to one member of Belle and Sebastian the whole experience was just another in a series of lifelong disappointments. "I was really nervous, but afterwards I just felt a bit of a slump," moans Isobel. "It's like that Peggy Lee song, 'Is That All There Is?' That is the story of my life: Is that all there is to fire, is that all there is to love, is that all there is to the circus?"

For Stuart Murdoch, Belle and Sebastian's BBC adventure would be the last burst of activity he would undertake for over a year. Already exhausted by the trials of *Fold Your Hands,* he had begun to display creeping symptoms of the M.E. which he hoped, prayed, he had left behind for good. "He was borderline . . . I dunno, he'd probably been drinking more than was good for him," says Chris cagily. "And he'd picked up a flu-ey virus which he'd struggled to shake off. He's had years and years of M.E., and I think he realized he needed to turn things around. As far as I'm aware the main reason why we completely disappeared was due to Stuart's health. It's hard to picture him as someone who needs to worry about his health, because he is one of the most energetic, active, fit people I know."

"I was struggling at that point, because I was beginning to feel unwell, and I remember thinking that this was the last thing I was going to do," remembers Stuart. "I went straight to San Francisco by myself, virtually the day after *Top of the Pops.* In recent years if the tour's going anywhere near San Francisco, I'll go there and take a few days by myself. I love it there." For someone with such a precarious medical history, it was clearly unwise for him to have put himself under such overwhelming pressure, and sure enough his workaholism had finally taken its toll. "He was spending ridiculous amounts of hours in the studio, because he took it all on himself," says Stef D'Andrea. "He's a typical Virgo, a bit of a control freak, wants hands on everything, so he was never able very much to delegate work to anybody else. But I think after that album he realized that he had to. It was a big thing for him to do, to let go of the production to a professional producer."

And so another missed opportunity. When Belle and Sebastian should have been capitalizing on the success of "Legal Man" and promoting the follow-up to their Brit-winning album—which reached a respectable 10 in the U.K., 80 in the U.S.—they disappeared without trace. "Personally that's when a big change came, because I thought I was completely better," says Stuart. "And I'd just been going, going, going with the band, taking all this pressure—and I'm not saying I'm the only one—taking all this crap all the way through *Fold Your Hands,* and then I got sick. It was frightening for me, because I thought I was completely over it." The rest of the group were concerned for their friend, of course, but still they were hugely disappointed by this enforced retirement. "Stuart getting ill, you can't blame anyone for that, but it didn't help the fact that a lot of people sat twiddling their thumbs getting quite frustrated," says Mick. "I thought about jacking it in several times, probably more around *Fold Your Hands* time than any other," he admits. "It was pretty hard for everyone, and then afterwards when we didn't tour I think a lot of us felt like quitting. I know Stevie and Richard felt the same. We'd been through all that to record a record and we didn't even tour it." Understandably, Jeepster were similarly dismayed, only being told about the situation just before the group were meant to be embarking upon the biggest and most expensive press campaign of their career. "We were just getting into this big album push which we'd waited all this time for and spent all this money on, and he said, 'I'm not up to it,'" recalls Stef D'Andrea sorrowfully. "We knew he'd been an M.S. [sic] sufferer in the past, we were empathetic towards that, but obviously it came as a bit of a shock to us because we realized that this was going to be the fourth album that's not going to be promoted. In the beginning, perhaps *Sinister* represented the thirty-thousand-pound investment, but by the time we got to *Fold Your Hands* the whole caboodle represented 300,000 pounds. The stakes were getting higher for us, and although their attitude had changed—they were definitely becoming more serious—it became more obvious to us what the problems were: Stuart's health, his relationship with Isobel, and Stuart David wanting to go and do his own thing. All the things that were going on behind the scenes became more obvious to us."

With an uncertain future hanging over them, the members of Belle and Sebastian spent 2000 busying themselves with various extracurricular musical activities—including Richard and Mick with Gary Lightbody's

Glasgow "supergroup" The Reindeer Section, which also starred one Bob Kildea—as Stuart holed himself up at the church hall trying to recuperate. "We'd never lost touch," he says. "I told the group that I'd have to do things at my own speed, and they were really gracious about it. In that time I wrote songs and we would occasionally record."[3]

Fortunately, by the end of the year his health had begun to recover, his enforced sabbatical only serving to make him more adamant that the B&S show must go on. He'd had a lot of time to think over the past year, and had come to several unimpeachable conclusions, principal amongst them being that Belle and Sebastian were far too precious a commodity to just let wither away like this, therefore they had to return to the battlefield with a firm and collective sense of commitment. There would be proper touring, proper promotion, the group finally working together as one to achieve a common goal. He knew they wanted it, had always really wanted it. They deserved this, they owed it to themselves, they owed it to their fans. A lot of faith had been invested into them, and Stuart Murdoch is a man who places great stead in faith. Isobel wouldn't be happy, of course, but Isobel, Stuart had eventually realized, would never be happy existing on anything other than her own terms. No, he had to stop worrying about Isobel. Stop caring. He had work to do.

The long cold winter fell and melted away, the blossom on the trees springing forth and hopeful. The curious boy took a run through town, a determined flash of ruddy aching health, lost in flight and thought.

---

3 They recorded "Take Your Carriage Clock and Shove It" and a version of the carol "O Come O Come Emmanuel" for indie station XFM's *Cool Cool Christmas* compilation released through Jeepster in December that year.

CHAPTER THIRTEEN

BOBBY KILDEA

The Denim Hard Riff of the Irish Troubadour

Belfast snuggled deep beneath his mound of duvet, luxuriating in the life of leisure he had half-built for himself.

The needle had been running round the outer groove of Sticky Fingers *for about ten minutes now, but it was just too snug and warm under here to bother stumbling across the room to flip it over. In any case he liked that sound, that zip and crackle. It felt warm, like oozing in static.*

After a few more minutes of this, Belfast suddenly became sleepily aware of some familiar sounds emanating from the next room; the thump of a bass drum, the rattle of a snare, guitars being tuned up through recalcitrant amps. But that didn't bother him either. This just meant it was time to get up and join the band. And surely that must be the only real reason to ever get up at all?

Since pretty much everyone who knows him refers to Robert Kildea as Belfast it would not be entirely beyond the realms of reasonable thought to assume that he was, in fact, born in Belfast. It is therefore something of a surprise to discover that he actually hails from Bangor, a town on the east coast of Northern Ireland a good twelve miles from the nation's capital. Belfast, then, is presumably considered far more rock 'n' roll a nickname than Bangor. And a boy like Bobby deserves a good rock 'n' roll nickname.

He was a spring baby, in bloom March 1972 at the height or thereabouts of glam. With the nation quaking to the glitter-beat fantasia of T-Rex and Slade, Bobby slipped out unnoticed; but already, one imagines, he was taking notes. His dad worked in the civil service, his mum—born and raised in the Scottish town of Lenzie—busying herself with whatever odd jobs she could find. It was, he says with typical understatement, "just a regular childhood—two parents, one brother, a dog . . ." Preternaturally laid-back from birth, Bobby rarely broke into a sweat over life, content to amble by and let fate lead the way. As long as it didn't drag him too forcibly. "I was terrible at school, awful," he admits. "Didn't study, had no interest whatsoever. At the end of first year they put me on a weekly report, where I'd have to get my teachers to mark my application and behavior, A, B, C, D, at the end of each week. I got off that in second year, but went back on it in third year. I wasn't the greatest at school. It wasn't for me."

Music, however, was. He was eleven when he first heard The Beatles, on a tape made by his auntie, with *With the Beatles* on one side and *Sgt. Pepper's* on the other—did the kid even realize they were the same band?—and off he went, swept up immediately by the all-conquering tsunami of rock from which he would never, could never, escape. "From the first track on *With the Beatles,* 'I Won't Be Long,' I'd never heard anything like it. Before that I was listening to Two-Tone stuff, but I was hooked on The Beatles, The Stones, Status Quo."

He had to have a piece of this. Up until his teens he'd had absolutely no ambitions whatsoever, but now it was clear to him what he had to do: He had to learn guitar. The only instrument he could actually play at this point was the trumpet, which he played from the age of seven to eighteen, eventually giving up because he "didn't have the puff for it anymore. I had this bad technique of instead of using your diaphragm to get the high notes, I used to push really hard into the mouthpiece, so I'd be walking about with big swollen lips. But I managed to get to grade five or six."

But it was unlikely that the trumpet was ever going to carry him aloft towards the mystical portals of rock Valhalla, which were his natural destiny, and so he swapped swollen lips for swollen fingers, doggedly practicing on his axe (oh, he knew all the proper terms already), an old Vox electric gifted to him by his uncle. He and a similarly minded rock buddy would bunk off classes and secret themselves in the music room jamming Guns'n'Roses covers; probably not the kind of education his parents wished for him, but still the only one Bobby really cared for. He was a naturally bright kid, anyway, and he had the smarts to achieve something if he really wanted to. He just didn't really want to. *"Schooool's out faw evah . . ."*

Having left school as soon as he could, Bobby soon became bored with his aimless lifestyle. Most of his friends had already left home, and he felt left behind, trapped in the town he had lived in all his life. "I knew I had to move on. And I was getting on my mum and dad's tits, just the usual stuff," he shrugs. And so at the age of twenty-one he decided to sail across the Irish sea towards Scotland. Glasgow to be exact, a town he had visited every Halloween in his youth, when the family Kildea would holiday with his grandmother. "We'd come over to Glasgow, and I'd love it, although I wouldn't know what it was." A common quandary. But the main reason for the move was Glasgow's torrentially thriving and unimpeachably cool music scene. And if anyone was born to hang in Nice'n'Sleazy's, supping a pint and playing pool with the hipster cognoscenti, it was Bobby Kildea. He was just that kinda guy: louche, relaxed, self-deprecating, easygoing, and funny. He was very Glasgow. He would do well here.

Unfortunately, he first ended up in Greenock, a small town just outside of Glasgow, dropped off by his dad with just a couple of bags, an acoustic guitar, and a stack of LPs to his name. It was official: He was now a rock 'n' roll drifter. So off he drifted into James Watt College, where he enrolled in a communications course, purely, of course, for the student grant. How else was he going to live? He lived above a pub called the Dugout, run by Scottish football legend Archie Gemmell, basically in a room with three beds which he shared with two other drifters, one from the Highlands, the other a speed freak. This, thought Bobby, is how one pays one's dues.

Only carrying out the barest minimum of college work needed to get by, he left the pub loft behind and moved to Glasgow, where he got a job in the Western Infirmary cleaning the pathology labs—"five 'til eight, Monday to Friday, an extra fifty quid on top of your giro"—and set about finding him some musicians to play with. He soon became a regular face on the scene, eventually joining a garage band called The Ducks led by Warren Macintyre also of The Moondials (you're no one in Glasgow unless you're in at least nine bands), and he also played with perennial Scot-pop legend Eugene Kelly, ex of Kurt Cobain faves The Vaselines.

It was in 1996, however, that Bobby started playing with V-Twin alongside Chris, and it was through the band's leader, Jason MacPhail (him again) that he first met Sarah, MacPhail's then flatmate. When she moved out in late 1996 Bobby moved in, turning the place into a wholly V-Twin-centric base of operations. He had become an accomplished guitarist—MacPhail nicknamed him The Human Metronome—having soaked up all the best licks—maybe every single one of them in fact—from all the best sources. He didn't pick up the bass, however, until MacPhail asked him to play on an album he and members of Teenage Fanclub were making at Ca Va with Stephen Burns of cult '70s power-pop band The Scruffs. Burns came over to Glasgow from Memphis with his friend, the legendary Big Star frontman Alex Chilton, but sans bassist. So Belfast Bobby stepped up to the plate. "I'd never played bass, but I thought, how hard can it be?" He got the gig. In fact he ended up flying over to Memphis to finish the album, memorably driving alone with Burns to New Orleans for Mardi Gras, living out his *Easy Rider* fantasies.

Yes, things hadn't turned out too badly for the boy from Bangor.

Belfast loved the group, he really did. Great band, great tunes, kinda punk, kinda blue, kinda cool. He was in their circle from the start, from the moment the tiger was milked, an affable and reliable staple of the happily incestuous world in which they all lived.

So when they asked him to parlay his Belfast charms on their new single, he was, as ever, only too happy to comply. Just another fun diversion, he smiled, as he flipped over the record and let the needle strike the groove.

Murdoch for President

Even though he'd actually stopped studying there in the mid-'90s, Glasgow University had continued to play a part in Stuart's life, principally by virtue of its complimentary launderette facilities. Complimentary, that is, for students, not thirty-something jobbing pop 'n' rollers, but that hadn't stopped Stuart taking advantage of their amenities. As he's often been quoted as saying, being in a band has given him the enviable opportunity to carry on with a free and easy student lifestyle well past the point where he should by rights be settling down into some form of respectable adult life.

His continuing affair with the university took a surreally unexpected turn in early 2001 when he was flattered to discover that a group of students had nominated him for the position of university rector. Although basically an honorary position, traditionally given to Scottish celebrities, from the great and the good to, in tiresomely time-honored ironic student–fashion, low-rent soap stars and comedians, those chosen can still take the role as seriously as they like. "Basically it was to represent the students before the high council, the dean and the principal and all the high-falutin' people with money," Stuart explains. "And although it's an honorary post, you are a figurehead in a way. You get an office, and you can do as much as you want."

Initially, he considered it just a bit of fun, something which, after his long year of illness, he could happily throw himself into before he reconvened with the group, but after meeting with the students, he realized that he was in a position to make some changes for the good, and set about forming his manifesto. "I was trying to stop the development of the student halls, which were being sold to private investors. And the new sports development, which was already two thirds of the way there, I was very behind that. I actually went round all the departments meeting students, and that's when I formed my manifesto. But before that I thought, this is great, I'll be able to use the university laundry forever now without feeling guilty. I use the university more than I did when I was there," he sheepishly admits.

In an attempt to publicize his campaign, he and the group played a "secret" gig at the university's John MacIntyre Hall in February, a low-key affair with a rather subdued Stuart, dressed plainly in gray shirt and trousers, making a tentative return to the stage after more than a year away. But despite his better efforts, he—and Teenage Fanclub's Norman Blake—was eventually still beaten in the race by Scottish comedian Greg Hemphill, who was probably a more recognizable face to the majority of students, as well as being someone who the university board would consider a more palatable incumbent than some scruffy pop star they'd never heard of. As an incorrigibly competitive sort, the defeat probably caused Stuart some irritation, but the whole episode was still comparatively trivial compared to the adventure on which he was about to embark.

CHAPTER FOURTEEN

STORYTELLING

Are You Sick? Are You Crippled? Insane?

Belle and Sebastian were, of course, only too happy to welcome their be-leaguered bard back into the fold, happier still to hear of his newfound desire to hit the road like a battering ram (on a silver black phantom bike if necessary). The time, it seems, had come to start doing things properly, to start doing some of the things that other bands do. This involved assembling a proper road crew around them for the first time, something they would absolutely require if they were ever to be-come a proper working live band. Isobel had never made any secret of her hatred of touring, but Stuart had by now given up on trying to appease her, having belatedly realized that he had to take into account the desires of the rest of the group, himself included. "Suddenly any-thing was possible," he says. "I don't want to sound too cruel, but we'd stopped listening to Bel, I stopped feeling that I had to kowtow to her. I just thought, bugger it. We suddenly had this organization around us which made it a lot more possible for us to concentrate on the show."

Led by friend and tour manager Stevie Dreads, one cannot underes-timate the positive impact the Belle and Sebastian road crew have had on the group over the last three years. The well-meant if impractical

Stuart with road manager and friend Stevie Dreads.
Photo by Mark Trayner.

DIY ethics of the first few years had seriously hampered the group's live abilities and reputation, but with the assistance of these noble knights of the road, they gradually turned into some-thing most people, the group included, thought they could never become—a tight, engaging, and—despite the rather dubious connotations of the word—professional live band. What's more, in an attempt to accurately recreate their increasingly expansive sound, the group took the costly if artistically correct decision of taking a large orchestra section out on tour with them. Goodbye shambles, hello showbiz.

So it was decided that the group should dip their frozen live toes into these unfamiliar waters via a six-date tour of Scotland in June, starting with a show at Dunoon on the west coast and ending with two dates back home at legendary live mecca, the Barrowlands. These last dates seemed like a deliberate announcement that the group were no longer interested in playing sporadic gigs in libraries and theaters, that they had now, Pinnochio-style, transformed into a "real" group. To Stevie in particular, to whom the group's unwillingness to play live had been a constant thorn of contention, this was a chance to sweep away the cobwebs of the last few years and begin with a renewed and much needed sense of purpose. "Bands should play, and we're capable of playing, people want to see us, so we play," he states, matter of factly. "It's the simplest thing in the world, it's just communication. That whole period was fairly positive. Not everybody liked the session players being there. I don't think Sarah was that keen on it, which is understandable, her being the fiddle player, but there were a lot of strings on the previous album so it just made sense. I think Sarah seems a lot happier now. I think it was hard for her because she had to run around the stage a lot picking up bits and pieces. But Sarah's got all her instruments around her now; it's a fundamental psychological thing, she's at home now. She's quite rightly insisted on that."

Surprisingly, to all concerned, this renewed activity didn't result in the expected protestations from Isobel. In fact, she seemed just as enthused as the rest about their imminent return to action. Perhaps the long sabbatical had reminded her of how much she actually enjoyed playing with the group, or maybe she just needed something to take her mind off the troubles at home, since her parents were then in the middle of a divorce. Not that her relationship with Stuart had improved any. In fact, they had pretty much stopped communicating altogether by 2000 and barely spoke a word to each other from then on, which actually appeared to make the situation much easier to deal with for everyone. If they weren't talking, then they weren't fighting, meaning the group could actually get some work done. With both sides worn out by their endlessly combative relationship, it seems neither had the energy to sort out their grievances in person. Stuart, for one, obviously felt that he could no longer communicate with Isobel in any other way than song, penning the bitter and quite obviously autobiographical single "I'm Waking Up to Us" (recorded in January with a working title of "The Season Has Arrived" and eventually released in November that year) as a kind of musical farewell note. The lyrics are some of his most candid and emotionally unambiguous, basically a pained outpouring of confusion, vindictiveness, and regret: yer average breakup spat, in other words. *"I need someone to take some joy in something I do,"* he croons, somewhat affectedly, his voice caked in a woody richness which, despite its contrivance, rather suits the emotional undertow of the material. *"You need a man who's either rich or losing a screw,"* before delivering as fine a piece of character assassination as you'll find in the great breakup annals of pop:

> *I think you never liked me anyway,*
> *You like yourself and you like*
> *Men to kiss your arse*
> *Expensive clothes,*

Please stop me there
I think I'm waking up to us,
We're a disaster

Hardly a Hallmark greeting. Throughout Stuart is at pains to remind his subject that he loved her—*"you were the one love of my life"*—and that all he wanted was to care for and adore her, were it not for the fact that she just wouldn't let him, which certainly isn't the way Isobel sees it, but since when have two acrimonious ex-lovers ever seen things the same way? But to say that Isobel comes off badly in the song is an understatement of almost comical proportions. If we are to take the song as complete autobiography—pause to let Stuart barge in with his "all art is abstract" argument—the picture he basically paints here is of a superficial, neurotic, and spoiled woman who took all the love and lessons he gave her (and there is a rather patronizing implication of some kind of Henry Higgins/Eliza Doolittle relationship here) and used them to her own advantage. That she agreed to perform on the song is quite staggering, frankly, but she seemed to accept the

d Isobel in happier times. Photo by Sarah Martin.

attack with a measure of quiet dignity that the subject of the song apparently appears incapable of. Just how did it make her feel? "It made me feel a wee bit sad, to have to sit and play on it, especially when my parents were getting divorced," she says, with an almost tangible sorrow. "That's the thing with people, though, isn't it? You never know the full story, it's so hard to judge people and say, 'Oh, they're this and they're that.' You never really know what's going on with them. The song sounds a bit like me, but I couldn't really say."

213

And since she and Stuart weren't speaking, she never asked him about it. "I didn't ask him, because I never spoke to him at that point. There was another one, 'Take Your Carriage Clock,' which I think was even worse. God, I take after my granny, I'm a bit of an old fighter, I just fight my way through things, I'm quite a feisty one. It wasn't lovely, but he . . . he wrote nice songs about me as well. The full spectrum!"

By its very nature, the song can't help but seem one-sided, and Stuart perhaps unfairly paints himself as the saga's sole victim, which is presumably why when the group performed the song on BBC2's flagship music show *Later . . . with Jools Holland* in late 2001, Isobel was allowed to rebuke Stuart's tirade with a suitably bitter spoken-word interjection of her own. *"And I'll meet someone else/And he'll be fine/Because he won't be you,"* she sighs, with the same air of pissed-off disinterest familiar to anyone who saw her perform with the group in those last couple of years, although to be fair, the fact that she's standing there on national television as her ex berates her in the harshest and most personal terms could hardly have lent her much cheer. The last word goes to Stuart himself, who when asked whether the song is actually about Isobel, can only offer a smile and the most self-consciously diplomatic response he can muster. "I'm going to answer like a politician: You can take a person, a seed of an idea, and turn them into something. But I must say that song is more about a person than any other song I've ever written, and that person is Bel. But it's not all Bel. It's a bit about how I feel about Bel, but it's also about trying to get a big '60s-sounding dramatic voice, trying to over-egg it a bit. In the end it's a fiction, but it is more about a specific person than any other song I've written."

The actual details of Stuart and Isobel's relationship will only ever be known to them, of course, but it's clear that for a time the two were very much in love, which makes the fact that the relationship ended up with them unable to even communicate other than through music—through the very thing which united them in the first place—all the more poignant. Lyrics aside, the song itself is a passable success, a suitably sonorous and autumnal sweep of baroque melodrama lent a pleasingly emotive bassoon, piccolo, and string arrangement by Mike Hurst, the first producer the group had ever worked with, primarily chosen by these inveterate '60s-philes for his work on Petula Clark's classic "Downtown." Stuart would claim to be mildly unhappy with Hurst's work here, and this would remain their only collaboration, but "I'm Waking Up to Us" remains one of the most dramatic Belle and Sebastian recordings and announced with some assurance that the group responsible for the underwhelming *Fold Your Hands* album were far from burned out yet.

The *Waking Up* sessions, which also begat the bumptuous throwaway "I Love My Car" (a tribute to Stuart's trusty automobile, Max, and featuring Dixieland jazz trimmings from The Uptown Shufflers, who would join the group throughout the Scottish tour), saw longtime friend Bob Kildea fattening up the mix Spector-style on rhythm guitar, alongside guests Francis MacDonald and John Hogarty from the BMX Bandits. Like most of the group's circle, Bob had long been aware of Stuart and Isobel's problems, so he wasn't surprised to witness one of their regular bust-ups in the studio. "At the 'I Love My Car' session I remember an argument going on, but because we were all friends, it wasn't like Billy Preston joining The Beatles, where everyone's on their best behavior. They obviously felt comfortable enough to have an argument in front of everyone," Bob notes wryly. The year off had obviously done nothing to stave off their personal differences, and it wouldn't be long until the two would decide to ignore each other altogether lest the group finally crumble under the weight of their dispute. But although Bob doesn't claim to have introduced any kind of stabilizing influence, his easygoing presence and impressive musical chops were a welcome addition to the group, and so it was decided that the laconic Irishman should play a part in their forthcoming live plans, fluctuating between bass and a guitar when required, upping both the group's rock and eye-candy factors in the process. "It wasn't that I personally wanted another Rolling Stones fanatic around me," Stevie explains. "It just immediately overall made us stronger. Bob's got that ability that Mick's got, just to play anything. Jason from V-Twin calls him a human metronome, very tight. It really helped as well because he's just so nice and easy to be around." Sarah is similarly complimentary: "He's just so easygoing, he just turns up and plays solos, and goes away again. And he's always up for anything. It definitely gave us a shot in the arm, having someone new, especially Bob. He's just a lovely guy."

Before the Dunoon show on Saturday, June 9, as an army of Belle-starved fans and journalists sailed excitedly across the summer-specked

Atlantic towards the picturesque west coast town in specially hired Cal-Mac ferries—some of which probably dated from Robert Murdoch's time with the firm[1]—nerves in the B&S camp were running understandably high. Although the group had been rehearsing diligently for the first six months of 2001—having whittled their catalogue down to around twenty songs that would sustain them throughout the tour—and despite the fun they'd had at the Socialist Party show, they were still worried about falling on their ass. Stevie, for one, was worried that Stuart would persist with the onstage aloofness which had blighted many of their past performances, drunkenly pleading with him a few days before the show to rediscover the confidence he had shown early on. "I said, 'You were the best fucking talker on stage, so why did you clam up?' And he said, 'Nah, it'll be cool.' And sure enough it was."

Opening, as they did on every show on the tour, with "Le Pastie de la Bourgeoisie," the group immediately put their qualms to one side, appearing confident from the off, and when the string section joined them for "There's Too Much Love," lending them a weight and richness they could never previously attain: The disparity between the sound on stage and that commonly parlayed by the pre-2000 group couldn't have been greater. Gone were the awkward silences and lengthy between-song tune-ups, replaced by smooth segues and relaxed banter between Stuart and Stevie, who had suddenly developed into an amusing and likeable double-act. The biggest change, however, was in Stuart. Whether chatting amiably to the crowd or dancing freely across the stage with his, in Stuart David's memorable description, "mad early-eighties hybrid half punk, half Jane Fonda jogging," it was a revelatory performance, announcing at last the emergence of Stuart Murdoch as a fully charismatic frontman. If he had previously preferred to present himself as just another member of the group, he had now come to terms with his role in the spotlight, freeing and energizing the group in the process. The tour also showed that the group had finally worked out how to structure a

---

[1] "I enjoy sea travel, very much more than plane travel," says the seaman's son. "I'm very much drawn to Caledonian MacBrae ferries; must be something in the blood. One of the happiest experiences of my life was the three days of so-called working we spent in Dunoon before our Scottish tour. We spent three days of production rehearsing with the core of our crew and session musicians, and we traveled every day by ferry, and I insisted we took a Cal-Mac one, even though they're more expensive."

properly dynamic show, and while they would always remain slightly rough around the edges—thankfully, as that is undoubtedly part of their charm—they still possess a rare ability to engage a crowd no matter how large. Belle and Sebastian at their live best can create an inclusive party atmosphere capable of turning gigs into genuinely celebratory events. From Dunoon onwards the group's priority was simply to have fun, dragging fans up on stage to sing or dance or both, or speckling their sets with unlikely but usually wonderfully realized cover versions.[2] Often they will ask the audience what they would like to hear, with predictably comic results, as the group attempt to vamp their way through the likes of Europe's "The Final Countdown" proved. A virtual human jukebox, the enormous variety of covers chosen over the years offer a fairly representative cross-section of their influences, numbering the likes of Elvis, The Beatles, The Mamas and the Papas, Love, The Zombies (their version of "Time of the Season" is remarkably faithful), Serge Gainsbourg, Sly and the Family Stone, and The Byrds, to name but eight.[3] On the last night of their U.K. tour in summer 2001, they even closed the show with a hectic version of Queen's "Don't Stop Me Now," with Stuart as Freddie Mercury, shirtless and crowned, a square of black Gaffa tape stuck under his nose, strutting the stage like the camp rock God he was clearly born to be. Such shameless behavior would be unthinkable of the B&S of yore, but that group was gone, replaced by a vibrant, unpredictable pop colossus who more than ever before wanted to gift their fans—and themselves—with the kind of live event they would never forget.

In the early stages of the tour the group introduced a new song to their repertoire, "Jonathan David," the lead track on an EP released in the U.K. on June 18. Featuring Stevie on slightly strained lead vocals ("I recorded the lead vocal with a bit of a cold, so it annoys me when I hear it") and a slightly discordant tack piano riff, it seemed like a curious choice of single at the time, especially after such a lengthy absence from

---

2 See "Official Releases" in the back for a comprehensive list of covers.
3 The tour would also introduce a couple of new songs, namely "(My Girl's Got) Miraculous Technique" and a great Day-Glo west coast pop tune called "The Magic of a Kind Word," a collaboration between Stevie, Stuart, and Isobel which, although a live favorite, would never make it to record, although the group would record both these songs for a John Peel session in 2001.

the charts, but it remains one of the group's favorite recordings. Like "Legal Man," the song was born naturally from an original rehearsal room idea of Stevie's, with Stuart adding the biblically metaphorical lyric—Jonathan being the loyal yet marginalized mate of David, of David and Goliath fame—after Stevie described the love triangle scenario he wanted to get across. Mick then assisted with the arrangement—including the great Zombies-style *"visions of love"* harmony breakdown towards the end—with the rest of the group building their parts from the ground up. Considering the tortuous gestation of much of *Fold Your Hands,* it is easy to understand why the group found working on this song so refreshing. Thanks to this organic way of working the song sounds a lot more live and spontaneous than most of *Fold Your Hands,* closer in spirit to their earlier recordings, although the song itself, as good as it is, can't compare to the best of 1996–99. "I thought the song was a positive step," says Stevie. "I didn't think for a minute that it was as good as 'The State I Am In' or anything off the second album, but sonically it was a step in the right direction. I enjoyed the harmony thing, which we've been developing ever since. Isobel played keyboards on it, but it was Sarah coming to the fore, and she's got a real talent for harmonies. I think that song was a big breakthrough for her. It was the first song for a three-part harmony part. I thought it was maybe the best co-idea I'd come up with."

The video is one of the group's best, a '60s/'70s homage featuring a black-and-white thread starring Stuart and Stevie as the titular characters, gamboling around a monochrome Glasgow like the stars of some Richard Lester '60s knockabout, and a colorful '70s segment featuring the whole group—Mick and Bob dressed in the togas they sport on the EP cover—and Stevie, the ultimate '70s troubadour in feather boa and porn-tache, crooning sincerely at a white grand piano. Best of all, though, is Stuart, who makes for a disconcertingly pretty street mime. The whole thing was, you won't be surprised to hear, entirely his idea.

The other tracks on the EP are the charmingly titled "Take Your Carriage Clock and Shove It" and longtime live staple "The Loneliness of a Middle Distance Runner," which the group had finally managed to record to their satisfaction. "Carriage Clock" is another example of Stuart melding a rancorous lyric with an offsettingly pretty tune.

Unfortunately, it is the tune to Charlene's MOR classic "Never Been

To Me," something Stuart has no choice but to admit. "It's a shame that's such a rip of another song, because I actually think it's one of the group's best performances," he laments. "I love the arrangement and it has a really good sound." Considering what we know about their relationship and the way it affected the group, it is virtually impossible to believe that Stuart didn't write this about Isobel. Isobel certainly thinks he did, although when asked, Stuart exclaims, "Why is that about Isobel?" with an air of amused surprise which may well be disingenuous.

> *Honor forbids me but honor be damned*
> *You have whined till you got what you want*
> *I did the work and when things were going badly*
> *You left us to rot*

It is possible to read too much into these things, of course, but . . .

> *Night after day after night I've been working*
> *Despite of you fucking us all*
> *Now I'm going to die I don't care if you cry*
> *Just please leave me alone*
> *And spare your tears from yourself*
> *We've had those till we're sick*
> *You should leave while you still have the chance*

Hmm, on second thoughts, it doesn't really stand up, does it?

If we are to assume that the song does address Isobel—and it's not really that much of a leap of faith, let's be honest—then it shows in no uncertain terms that Stuart had come to the end of his tether and that he had neither the energy or inclination to kowtow to her demands any longer. In fact, so disgusted was he with her behavior, he couldn't even be bothered to write her an original tune.

The long-serving "The Loneliness of a Middle Distance Runner"[4] could, of course, also be considered somewhat self-referential but perhaps more in regard to its title than the specific content of the lyrics

---

[4] The title is a play on the great novel and film, *The Loneliness of the Long Distance Runner,* but you already knew that, of course.

(which are fairly abstract). Based around a chunky, funky, almost Hendrix-like groove—offering Stevie the chance to reel off a neat and dextrous little guitar solo—it's one of Belle and Sebastian's slinkiest offerings. The *Belle and Sebastian Sing . . . Jonathan David* EP certainly wasn't the stellar comeback many had hoped for, but for most it was simply good enough that the group were back at all.

Early in 2001, U.S. indie director Todd Solondz, then riding on a critical crest thanks to his blackly comic films *Welcome to the Dollhouse* and *Happiness,* contacted the group with a view to them recording some music for his next film, *Storytelling.* Fans of Solondz's work, both Stuart and Stevie agreed to fly over to New York to discuss the project with the mordantly idiosyncratic auteur. In its rough cut form the film was a sprawling four-hour epic which, although messy, was inspired enough to convince the boys that this was too good an opportunity to pass up. "When we first watched it we thought it was all over the place, but we liked that, being fans of Robert Altman," asserts Stevie. Solondz had conceived the film as a three-act anthology centered around the themes of Fiction, Non-Fiction, and Autobiography, requesting that Belle and Sebastian write music for the second segment, which concerned the efforts of a pretentious documentary filmmaker and his misguided attempts to sculpt poetry from the life of an uber-blank high school student. The rest of the score would be taken care of by Shudder to Think's Nathan Larson, and Nina Persson of The Cardigans. So far so funky. But as soon as the group arrived in New York in February to begin recording for the first time outside of Ca Va or the church hall, they immediately became aware that all was not well on Planet Solondz. Warners had, somewhat unsurprisingly, ordered him to cut the film substantially, eventually forcing him to cut the Autobiography segment entirely, allegedly because it contained graphic scenes of clean-cut *Dawson's Creek* star James Van Der Beek receiving sexual gratification in the most vivid manner imaginable. Understandably preoccupied with these problems, the director had very little time to discuss the soundtrack with the group, leaving them to flounder in a directionless gulf of uncertainty. When Solondz did come down to the studio, however, his directions were so vague—asking the group to pen a tune evocative of a housewife stroking her favorite box of detergent, for example—and his opinions of their ideas so dismissive, that they were left in an even greater sense of confusion than before. As Mick notes in the sleeve notes for the album they would eventually salvage, "Todd kept saying, 'I love it all, but it's not right for the movie.' We just didn't know what was right for the movie."

"That was a really bad thing," winces Neil, who had come along for the ride, but probably wishes he hadn't. "Todd was having such a hard time with the film, it rubbed off on us. I developed such a relationship with the travel agent. Every night at six o'clock I'd phone the hotel and find out if we could go home yet, and then I'd phone this woman and change the tickets again. I had to do this every day. Then we'd hear that Todd was going to come down and hear what they'd done, and he just never came. I'm not dissing him, because I know he was having such a hard time, but it certainly left us completely out on a limb. And when he did come down he wouldn't like anything." He can hardly contain his despair, hissing, "Write it yourself, then!" at an imaginary Solondz with such vanquished desperation, you really do feel for him.

"For instance," continues Stuart, who seemed happy to let the group spread their compositional wings on this one, content merely to contribute the odd idea while he sat back engrossed in a copy of Ian MacDonald's seminal Beatles book *Revolution in the Head*, "Todd wanted a song for the end, and we gave him three. Sarah wrote 'Storytelling,' I wrote the words to 'Big John Shaft'—although the music came from Chris and Bel—and Stevie had 'Wandering Alone.' Sarah wrote the words for 'Storytelling,' which was based on what she thought was going on with Todd. The theme of his film was what he was going through as well, so we were kinda looking at Todd and writing about him. And he didn't like it. He heard 'Big John Shaft' and just shook his head. He didn't like the lyrics at all. It was bad for him but good for me. I thought it captured something, and I'm glad we put it on the record." Stuart's lyrics are rife with such artistic disillusionment and self-abasement that they probably proved too close to the bone for the harried director, and when Sarah—who according to Chris related to Solondz far more successfully than the rest—sings with characteristic lyrical exactitude that *"In directions, actions and words, cause and effect, you need consistency,"* she's not only chiding the fictional director in the movie, but also the director who had made the last three weeks so vexing for them. This was probably another barb too far,[5] although Solondz did end up using the song on the closing credits, which suggests either last-minute desperation on his part or an eventual change of heart. But no matter what he thought of their material, his occasionally ungracious behavior towards the group hardly did anything to dispel the atmosphere in the studio, as Neil recalls. "On the last day, we had these three songs for the end credits and we gave him a lyric sheet and about ten seconds in he just shook his head and threw it away. I'm going, 'Mate, I know you're having a hard time, but show some fucking respect.' He'd dragged us over from Scotland to sit and treat us like that. Hardly any of us could wait to get home quick enough. As soon as we got home we thought, let's try and make a good wee album. And I think it's pretty good for what it is. I never even went to see the film. I'm very sensitive about these things." He does admit, however, that Solondz and the group still have a friendly relationship, and have even discussed the prospect of making a film together. "But that'll probably never happen," shrugs Neil, ever the realist.

Stuart admits that despite the director's occasional truculence, they "loved hanging out with Todd. You've got to respect that he's an auteur, a man with a vision. This time the vision was his. It was maybe a taste of my own medicine," he muses. "Maybe this is how Stuart and Bel felt when I said *Fold Your Hands* would take two weeks and then threw everything away."

On the day Neil told the travel agent that, yes, he would in fact be needing those nine one-way tickets back to Glasgow, the group resolved to rise above this disappointing experience and salvage something from the work they had already done, most of which they loved, even if Solondz didn't want it for his movie. As it transpired, when the film was finally released later that year, the director had only used a total of six minutes of their work on his butchered eighty-seven-minute final cut, which rather undermined their ambition to create a soundtrack as essential to the accompanying film as Simon and Garfunkel's *The Graduate* or Bob Dylan's *Pat Garret & Billy the Kid*. "I was less annoyed by the

---

5 What Solondz himself actually does think about any of this is anyone's guess, sadly, since his management consistently failed to reply to any of the messages I left for him, meaning that the whole *Storytelling* saga is presented here in an unavoidably one-sided form.

amount of our stuff that was used than by the amount of scenes that had been cut from the film," Sarah claims graciously. "At one point I thought it was an absolute masterpiece, but I was disappointed when it came out. If it had all the music we'd recorded and all the scenes that had originally been there, it would be brilliant." Maybe, but as it stands, *Storytelling* the movie is a hugely disappointing effort. Although Solondz had always dealt in the depressingly unpleasant underside of human behavior, he had always managed to temper it with a curiously poetic, albeit refreshingly unsentimental, humanity. But *Storytelling* is just cold, a black mass of cruelty for the sake of cruelty, and the director commits the unforgivable sin of thinking he's far cleverer and funnier than he actually is, offering up a smug, venal, and aimless piece of work which ultimately falls far short of whatever it was trying to achieve in the first place. If the group's claims of early cuts of genius are to be believed, then it must surely stand as one of the most sorry compromises in recent movie history. And that really is saying something.

Asked whether he thinks the film worked better in its original cut, Stevie has no doubts: "Yes, yes, *yes,*" he insists. But would more of the group's music have made it had Solondz not been forced to compromise his original vision? Stevie thinks not. "Looking back, we misjudged it," he concedes. "We probably shouldn't have done it. It was the wrong film for us to do. Me and Stuart went to meet Todd initially, and we should've sussed that. At that time we'd just come out of the *Fold Your Hands* period, and it looked like something to start again on—and ultimately it was—but it was the wrong film. We weren't up for tinkering about, we're a big group and we have a lot of talent, we can orchestrate, Mick, Beans, Sarah, and Stuart can all score. It's kinda heartbreaking, but we should've accepted a movie where they wanted music," he admits, not unreasonably. "Ultimately Todd didn't want that much, but we were so intoxicated by the idea. But when it came down to it we didn't have anything. It was a mistake, but a good mistake. There should be more mistakes like that."

This is not Belle and Sebastian's only foray into the celluloid jungle, of course. Apart from contributing "Slow Graffiti" to the *Acid House* soundtrack, they have also agreed to allow their music to be used in Sean Meadow's *A Room for Romeo Brass* and the Farrelly Brothers' typically

facile *Shallow Hal,* a choice they made after regretting turning the Far-
rellys down when they asked them to contribute to *There's Something
About Mary* (this was before the involvement of Jonathan Richman).
Their most famous appearance in a film is undoubtedly in *High Fidelity,*
where "Seymour Stein" is used as an example of the kind of sensitive
student-rock so loathed by obstinate record shop employee Jack Black
(coincidentally, the star of *Shallow Hal*). The group were rather ad-
mirably willing to have themselves sent up in this way, although they
could argue that, since Black's character is meant to be a buffoon, it
doesn't really matter what he thinks, and that the whole point of the
scene, really, is that John Cusack's character—the main character, no
less—is urbane, intelligent, and sensitive enough to recognize the quality of Belle and Sebastian's work. You *could* argue that. Also, the movie
was a hit and regardless of how negatively the group are depicted, it was
the first time a lot of people had heard of, let alone heard, the group,
which was no bad thing, although this didn't stop them from—with
typical inconsistency—refusing to allow the song's use on the soundtrack.

Following the disappointment of *Fold Your Hands,* there was just no
way that Belle and Sebastian were going to let this one get away from
them, and once back at Ca Va with Tony Doogan, they set about making a record less about the *Storytelling* movie and more about their experiences of working in New York: a soundtrack to the making of a
soundtrack of the original motion picture (twice removed). "To the
group's credit, that was a more democratic record than any of them,"
says Stuart. "I just sat back and listened to them, going, 'That's good.' It
was a really nice record to make. We came home and rerecorded pretty
much everything we gave to Todd, and made it into the mostly instrumental LP we'd had in our minds beforehand."

Sarah, Stevie, and Mick in particular began to shape the proceedings
in a way they never had before, contributing most of the album's musical themes, although the standout instrumental, titled, with typical per-
versity, "Fuck This Shit," actually arose from an initial idea of Stuart's
ultimately fleshed out by Stevie and Chris. A wonderfully melancholic
Western-style lament carried by sunny canyon strings and Stevie's
achingly lovely chromatic harmonica lead, the influence of John Barry's

classic *Midnight Cowboy* theme can hardly be denied, but in an ideal world it would be as familiar a piece of music as any in the film score canon. The title probably doesn't help, mind.

"Fiction" is the album's prevailing theme, a nocturnal piano instrumental of the kind of delicate melodic prettiness at which Belle and Sebastian excel. This, along with the similarly brittle "Freak," shows just how unobtrusively effective the group could be as soundtrack composers, making it all the more disappointing that Solondz used so little of their material. "Storytelling" itself remains Sarah's strongest contribution to the group so far, a catchy skip of gossamer pop which sums up rather neatly, from the group's point of view at least, the working mind of Todd Solondz, while posing him a few pertinent moral questions such as *"Have you considered the way/People might react to all the things that your characters say?/And are their actions hand in hand/with what you want to portray?"* before asking, not entirely unreasonably, *"Are you sick?/Are you crippled?/Insane?/Expressing the desires that daren't speak their name?/Are you the one to blame?"* questions which initially seemed to offend the unashamedly sick director, although since he eventually used the song over the end credits, we might assume that his ego was eventually piqued by the notion of these hip indie minstrels writing a song about him, even if it does worry aloud for his mental health. Stevie's "Scooby Driver" is one of the few songs here capable of a life outside the album, a rattling, harmony-gilded blast of garage-pop and undoubtedly the most "American"-sounding recording they had made to date, while the Spanish-flavored "Wandering Alone," another showcase for Stevie's increasingly confident croon, became something of a live favorite, although probably only because it gives the crowd a chance to supply massed bolero handclaps, since its unfortunate but wholly inescapable similarity to The Mavericks' MOR wedding staple, "Dance the Night Away," means that one can't listen to it without thinking of drunk aunties frugging with five-year-olds. Stevie concedes the similarity, but claims it is entirely unintentional, his intention being merely to write a kind of Spanish bandit hoedown. "Stuart wrote the words to a tune I had for a long time," he explains. "That happens quite a lot—I get credit for writing songs I didn't write myself. But since 2001 there have been a lot of collaborative things going on. For that song he scribbled all these words and I took what I wanted from them."

By its very nature, *Storytelling* remains Belle and Sebastian's least essential record,[6] and yet it is somehow more admirable than *Fold Your Hands* in that it succeeds entirely on its own terms and works as a consistent whole. It is an album intended to be listened to from start to finish, and as such works perfectly as a suite of beautifully arranged chamber pop, although the dialogue clips—a standard soundtrack device used ever since the success of Tarantino's *Reservoir Dogs* and *Pulp Fiction* collections—do seem a little redundant and obtrusive here. That aside, the music has a lightness and sparkle about it sorely lacking on their previous LP, with the group sounding increasingly confident in their ability to realize both their ambition and their individual strengths. With *Storytelling* Belle and Sebastian sound free and inspired, and considering the essentially compromised nature of the project, it works remarkably well. A necessarily transitional record, it lightly brushes off the disappointments of the past and sets its sights on visions of the future.

The Scottish tour had fulfilled its intention of convincing the group that they had a future (Chris: "The tour of Scotland was great. The weather was nice, fantastic venues, and the whole thing did feel like becoming a proper band"), which is just as well, seeing as they had agreed to tour most of the rest of the world that year. "I had a fear of flying around that time," Stuart remembers, "looking at fucking London on a map going, 'We're going to have to go twelve hours there and back, twelve hours there and back, in the space of a couple of months. Better get some valium and booze.' " Suitably numbed, Stuart and group immediately followed the Scottish tour with a jaunt around the rest of the U.K., once again with Bob in tow who, following a meeting at—where else?—The Grosvenor Café, had been only too happy to accept their offer to join full-time. "I'd been working in pubs for four years," he explains, so was

---

6 The cover stars are Sarah and Liz Liew dressed in the kind of Japanese regalia which so impressed Stuart on his day in Harajuku at the end of their Japanese tour. The feet they are acupuncturing belong to Mark Jones. Stuart originally intended to include Todd Solondz on the cover but got fed up with the director's procrastination. "Somehow it feels more appropriate that the sleeve was unrelated to the movie now," he muses. "We really recorded all the music as a separate entity for the record."

understandably keen to get back out on the road. "It felt very natural, because I'd known everybody for so long, it was very relaxed. Stuart David had been out of the band for a couple of years so it wasn't like I was taking somebody's place."

The highlight of the tour, at least in terms of prestige, was the performance at the Royal Albert Hall on June 29, usually the live preserve of bland rock patriarchs like Eric Clapton, but here transformed into the world's most cavernous indie disco. Infamous for its troublesome acoustics, pulling off such a gig was never going to be easy, and one shudders to think of how the B&S of yore would've made their presence felt in such a hall, but fortunately the new model managed to escape intact. "We had to pull our socks up quick for that," Stuart admits. "A year and a half before we'd never have got away with it. But we got this crew in place, and everything seemed more simple. And Bob joined the group, which was fantastic, because you've got someone in the group [Isobel] who's not keen and enthusiastic, and then this new guy comes in who's *completely* keen and enthusiastic, and you can't believe the shot in the arm that gives you. Everything was suddenly forward-looking." The group weren't the only ones welcoming Bob on stage. Up in the royal box his dad, seeing his son perform live for the first time, was so overcome with pride he supplied one of the concert highlights when he bellowed "That's ma boy!" like a Celtic Spike from Tom and Jerry. "It was the first time they thought, 'So you're not wasting your fucking life,'" smiles Bob. The group also weren't beyond staging a bit of rock theater, recruiting the help of Glasgow DJ Andrew Divine and Sarah's boyfriend Sean Hamilton who secreted themselves in the royal box dressed as Muppet Show curmudgeons Statler and Waldorf, raining insults down onto the stage. Hardly Alice Cooper, perhaps, but a clear intention of their desire to inject a few more surprises into proceedings.

Despite all this tomfoolery, the old disillusionment had returned for Isobel. Her initial enthusiasm for the group's return had quickly waned once the reality of their touring schedule had hit home. "I was realizing at that time that the tire was going flat for me, even when we played the Albert Hall," she admits. "Richard and I had stayed up until six in the morning the day of the show, so my hangover was kicking in when we went on stage. But, y'know, Dylan played here and he was on fire!" she says, her expectations of the group's performance being perhaps a little unrealistic. "And I was totally Peggy Lee again: Is that all there is?"

She did manage to enjoy some of the group's European tour, however, having been allowed to open each show with a solo set accompanied by experimental jazz musician Bill Wells. The skeletal, downbeat torch songs with which they regaled the audience each night were a far cry from the headline act, their performances seemingly designed to show the fans just how little Bel and the Belles now had in common. She also admits that there was fun to be had on the autumn tour of the West Coast and Canada, although not particularly because of the shows themselves. "I think I was smoking quite a lot of marijuana," she giggles. "But I don't think I travel very well," she frowns, suddenly changing tack, before offering one of the most ridiculously trivial reasons for touring aversion ever heard in the history of rock. "You're always fishing around for things in your suitcase, it hurts your back." As an excuse it beats fear of flying, I suppose. Spurious reasoning aside, Isobel had always been almost pathologically uncomfortable in the spotlight, and more than any other member of the group was particularly distressed by the attentions of their often fanatical following. "I was really uncomfortable with fans' reactions, people knowing things about you is quite weird. I met some people in a dress shop in Virginia recently," she says by way of genuinely disturbed explanation. "People I'd never met before, and they were like, 'Oh, it's so nice to meet you, and if you want to go out, please let us know.' Well, it would be nice to go out with people but it's going to be awkward."

The group had invited mercurial indie godfather Jonathan Richman, then undergoing something of a renaissance thanks to his appearance in *There's Something About Mary,* as tour support. "I keep thinking I'm going to turn up at the venue each day to be told that we're supporting him instead of the other way around," Stuart told the audience at the Orpheum in Vancouver. But Richman, not one to hand out praise unduly, reciprocated this respect, and continues to list the group as one of his few favored contemporary acts. For many American and Canadian fans, this was their first chance to see Belle and Sebastian in action, and the group, sailing on their newfound high—the sight of Stuart roaring on stage on a motorbike during a cover of The Shangri-Las' "Leader of the Pack" in San Francisco, for example, is not one even the most open-minded fan could ever have feasibly expected to witness—sent most of them home bedazzled and, one would hope, perhaps a little bemused.

On their first visit to L.A., Belle and Sebastian gained perhaps the ultimate proof that they were now swimming with the proverbial big boys, when the makers of *The Simpsons,* hearing that their fave-rave Scottish indie combo were in town, got in touch and asked them whether they would like to come down to the studio and sit in on a read-through—in exchange for free passes to the gig, of course. Even before the receiver hit the cradle, the group were riding at high speed through the Fox lot, swerving urgently through the set of *NYPD Blue* before arriving excitably at the real-life home of *The Simpsons.* "It was an amazing experience," grins Mick. "We arrived at the room where the read-through was taking place. It was a pretty small room, and we had to squeeze in round the outside of this huge table. All the main actors were there, with the exception of Marge, who was on speaker phone. Dan Castellaneta and Nancy Cartwright were particularly impressive with the sheer number of voices they do, and how quickly they could switch between the voices." After this fascinating and slightly surreal experience, they were then ushered out to meet the show's creator, Matt Groening,[7] who gave them each a signed copy of the script. A few hours later they were on stage at the Wiltern Theatre singing with Evie Sands before around 2,000 devotional Los Angelenos. Life had become very odd of late. But oddness, they must have thought, is definitely where it's at.

Between their U.K. and U.S. tours, the group made their first visit to Spain's Benicassim festival, an occasion most groups treat as much a holiday destination as simply another summer commitment. Based in a small Spanish tourist resort south of Barcelona, the sun-blessed fest today attracts most of the world's fave rave acts, but at the time Belle and Sebastian played there, it was only just becoming familiar to English-speaking audiences, mostly through starry-eyed recommendations from sunburned indie stars, to whom the backstage swimming pools and go-cart tracks obviously made a welcome change from the rain-drenched

---

7 Two years later Groening would, by curious coincidence, curate All Tomorrow's Parties Festival at Long Beach, California. He didn't invite Belle and Sebastian.

airstrips common to your average European festival. Neil had cased the joint the year before when, in the middle of the group's annus miserablis and in dire need of a break, he took up an offer he couldn't refuse. "I went out for a pint with Arab Strap in Nice'n'Sleazy's and ended up in Barcelona. That was a big night," he says mock-understatedly. "I was well due a holiday, and this was before Katrina started to help, and I think I was on the verge of a nervous breakdown. So they were going over to Barcelona and I just went with them. We drove for two days and got to Benicassim at midnight on the Friday night, and there were Mogwai running around in their underpants." A powerful image. "You can get up to a lot of mischief at Benicassim," laughs Bob knowingly.

Around half an hour before the group are due to take the Viaje a los Suenos Polares stage, the crowd swells to such an extent that the sides of the tent have to be removed to make room. With such support, they could hardly fail, and in the Mediterranean evening blue, Belle and Sebastian, dressed for the beach in T-shirts and sun hats, attempted to lasso the sun and squeeze it across the throng like orange juice. It was a perfect setting for their newfound sparkle, most agreeing it was one of the highlights of the festival, proving that these whey-faced Scots were more than capable of satisfying a festival crowd, something they themselves had never been sure about.

They had also never been sure whether they could sustain themselves over a lengthy tour, but as tiring as it could often be, they were—with one obvious exception—having a globe-trotting ball. Stevie in particular was delighted that the group were finally beginning to live up to the stature he'd always known they deserved. For him, it wasn't enough that their records sold and that the critics loved them; he wanted to reach out to the people, to get on and off planes in exotic cities, meet some pretty girls, get some pretty drunk, play some rock 'n' roll, and have fun in the sun with his friends. Sometimes, when the group were ferried from airport to hotel to be greeted by a phalanx of eager fans in the foyer, Stevie almost felt like one of his beloved Beatles, but never more so than when the group touched down in Rio de Janeiro to be greeted with scenes which, if you were feeling particularly charitable and moved by the incident, could feasibly be described as Bellemania. Having discovered that they had built up a rather sizeable fanbase in South America, it seemed only polite for the group to pay them a visit, but—much as the Beatles were surprised by the reception at JFK in 1964, if you want to stretch the comparison—they couldn't quite believe the reception which greeted them. Flashbulbs, autographs, "Steeeeeeewerrrrrt!!!," the works. "Brazil was nuts," says Sarah with a shake of the head. "People with cameras at the airport. We thought the people of Brazil would have better things to do than come and see us." The surreal nature of the trip was compounded by an unlikely and excruciatingly entertaining appearance on Jô Soares's top-rated talk show, in which the rotund host—displaying that mix of sarcasm and smarm which is evidently endemic to talk show hosts around the world—clearly having no idea who the group are, asks such probing questions as "Aren't Scottish the nicest people?" and "Who here is the best cook?" (Chris, apparently), with Stevie basically being forced to sing in Portuguese ("Fantastic!" Soares exclaims, turning like a fat viper. "You sing in Portuguese—and no one understands a fucking word you say!") and Chris's sexual proclivity being brought into question based not unreasonably on the fact that he happens to be a vegetarian. After all that, their version of "Wandering Alone"—bemused audience dutifully clapping along—can't help but be a let down. "Basically," Neil explains. "We got asked to do it, and we thought, 'When else are we ever going to get the chance to go on a Brazilian chat show?' So we just did it for the experience." The appearance is historic for another reason, as it is undoubtedly the only time anyone has ever appeared on Brazilian television wearing a *Perthshire Advertiser* T-shirt. Richard Colburn, you are a credit to your nation.

Before they'd even had a chance to wipe the sunscreen from their brows, the group found themselves in the alien and, if anything, even more fanatically devotional cityscapes of Japan, a nation renowned for its adoration of all things Scottish rock. And while being "big in Japan" has long been a rock 'n' roll euphemism for complete lack of success anywhere else in the breathing world, it would be remiss to begrudge a global sensation such as Belle and Sebastian their success in what uninspired travel writers still like to call the Land of the Rising Sun. "I think there's an audience for anybody in Japan. If they're into something they go all the way. It's a collector mentality," muses Bob, who had actually toured the country a month prior to the group's arrival, playing guitar with cult Scruffs singer Steven Burns.

The gracious devotion of Japanese fans is a well-known phenomenon, but for a group such as Belle and Sebastian, who inspire reverence wherever they go, one can only imagine the treatment they receive over there. "They usually want to meet Stuart anyway," says Bob. "And God love him, he deals with them. After a show we'll be having a few drinks and he'll be out there meeting people, he always makes the effort." Even when he's at home, Stuart can't escape his Japanese apostles, many of whom used to turn up, nervous and awed, at the church hall. Such is the price of having such a well-publicized address. Still, appreciating the ridiculous lengths these kids had gone to find him, he couldn't help but invite them in, make them a cup of tea, and hope to God they spoke English. And if they want to solicit his advice, just as he had on that doomed yet fateful trip to seek out Lawrence? "I just meet them halfway and give them some practical advice. If they're talented they'll make it, and if they're not they'll still have good fun failing. I was a rabid fan when I was younger, so I think I'd outdo any of the fans for unctuousness," he smiles. "I can accept a lot, 'cause I know I was worse." So he's fairly comfortable with his indie godfather status? "I'll bless any indie kids within my reach," he laughs. "Just so long as I don't have to remember their birthdays."

Meanwhile, back in the real world . . .

Suffice to say, the girl wasn't happy. She'd spent most of the year living out of a suitcase, doing something she didn't enjoy doing in places she didn't enjoy being, and since the ever more curious boy was no longer interested in acceding to her complaints—fuck, he wouldn't even look her in the eye anymore—she'd pretty much decided that she was going to jump this seasick ship for good. She really meant it this time. No, really, she did. She would show him.

"My heart wasn't in it anymore." Photo by Stuart Murdoch.

Isobel Adieu

"My heart wasn't in it anymore, because there was so much disrespect and craziness," Isobel despairs, mulling over a coffee in Glasgow's Grassroots Café just over two years after she bid the Belles adieu. Although she admits that the whole affair—with Stuart, with the group—took a long time to get over, she seems to have put most of her grief behind her, frothing with an endearing excitement over the possibilities of the solo career which she probably should have begun years ago. When she talks about her traumas she does so with a laugh pitched somewhere between incredulity and mild hysteria, as if she can't quite believe that any of it really happened. "It was a neurotic setup—and everyone's pretty neurotic in the band."

The heavy touring schedule of 2001 clearly took its toll on this most unwilling of pop starlets, who by her own admittance was overwhelmed and uncomfortable with the whole situation from the *Tigermilk* launch onwards, and who, quite clearly, was never cut out for the rock 'n' roll life from the off. Her onstage sullenness could often seem like an irritatingly self-conscious attempt at ice-queen cool—Nico in pop-socks—but as it turns out, her aloofness actually masked a genuine anxiety. "I didn't look at the audience for the first four years," she says. "It just freaked me out, made me want to run away. I think I was just overwhelmed." The word "overwhelmed" is a recurrent motif in Isobel's recollections of her time with Belle and Sebastian; the image which lingers is of a rabbit with headlights a speeding inch from its face.

Asked whether, away from the stage, she actually enjoyed her time with B&S, she more or less admits that she was always far too headstrong to ever be much use in a group. "I liked aspects of it, but it was like dancing to someone else's tune, and I'm quite a determined wee bugger, so sometimes I'd get pissed off a wee bit."

Basically, Isobel always wanted to do her own sweet thing and just couldn't stomach the idea of being told what to do, which was always going to be a problem in a supposedly democratic cabal such as this. This, matched with her prolonged and destructive relationship with Stuart, obviously meant that, for the most part, her time with the group was a tortuous morass of heartache, frustration, and resentment.[1] "Our relationship was a mess and coming to an end, so this was kind of cathartic for me, doing my own thing. Plus I'd grown up, and I didn't want to be singing about school when I was thirty," she says waspishly. She thought it was curious that Stuart should write so much about school? "I thought it was a bit disturbing, yeah." To be fair, it's no more disturbing than Isobel actually *dressing* as a schoolgirl, as she often did, or talking like a twelve-year-old in the *Don't Look Down* clip, which unavoidably brings up one of those pot/kettle hypocrisy interface incidents which so often occur between exes.

---

[1] And Stuart would doubtless claim the same thing. Take away the heartache, and the rest of the group probably would too.

Since 2002 looked like being another busy year of touring, Isobel could hardly rouse herself into action, so tired was she of the whole endless affair. She had threatened to leave the group so many times now that people had stopped paying her any heed, so when she complained to Neil that she wasn't willing to go along with their planned two-month U.K., Europe, and U.S. tour, Neil merely encouraged her to stick it out as he had always done. Spitting out the bullet and biting her lip, she acquiesced, traipsing solemnly through a couple of dates apiece in Denmark and Sweden, before packing her suitcase—the one which caused her so much pain to fish things from, remember—and setting out reluctantly on another bout with the globe. "Neil was trying his best to keep her in the band until the tours that had been committed to had been completed," says Sarah. "I was thinking, bloody hell, if I was Isobel—given that touring is the bit I hate the most—I would just want to get out now. I felt that if she'd already decided to quit then it was very noble of her to continue with the tour as her last thing, something she really couldn't be arsed with at all." It is clear that after their initial aloofness, Isobel and Sarah had bonded over the years, and that along with Chris and Richard—and her departed ally Stuart David—Sarah had come to sympathize with Isobel's awkward plight. The two would always share a room on tour—although Sarah does complain that Isobel's extraordinarily light sleeping patterns would often cause her a good deal of irritation—and, being the only two females in a primarily male touring party meant that they couldn't help but sympathize with each other.

Isobel had felt for so long that the rest of the group held her responsible for their general malaise, she couldn't bear the paranoia anymore. "Sometimes I felt vilified, and sometimes being female wasn't really taken into consideration," she complains. "Being female is so different to being a guy on tour. Basically, I think I had quite a tough time of it because of this crazy relationship, and I've heard through other people that the others felt sorry for me and they knew what was happening, but they didn't do anything. Maybe I was looking to be nurtured a little bit more, I could've done with a bit of support. But it was quite a crazy time, and we were all reacting to different things, different situations."

Adrift and confused in both her familial and professional relationships, Isobel stuck it out for as many dates as she could—seventeen to be exact—before she decided she'd just had enough. "I was having my mini–Judy Garland moments, crying in hotel rooms, and I thought, this is not the life I want for myself," she recalls, evidently feeling that the group she'd joined had morphed into something far beyond her realms of tolerance. "I thought that I was going to become a crazy alcoholic or some druggie. It had come so far away from what it was, it had become about all these crazy things which I wasn't comfortable with. It was about how many records we were going to be selling, it had become about drugs, about groupies. I mean, Chris used to bring cakes to rehearsals, and that was my kind of thing, really. And I think I knew that Jeepster weren't going to be anymore, so I thought, shit, the next step is going to be major-league, I'll definitely have to give more than my pound of flesh for the next album." Plus, she felt that she had moved beyond the group's field of reference into a world she could never possibly explore with them. "I'd started to feel that my own artistic preferences and ideas were moving away from the band. I was getting really into The Bad Seeds, and listening to Cole Porter and Tom Waits, and I was hanging out with Bill [Wells]. I liked risky music, and I didn't want to be doing *that* anymore." She gags on "that" as if it were the sourest candy in the pack, suggesting that the artistic gulf between her and the group was so great she just couldn't bear to play on Stuart's songs anymore, although it has to be said that most of her solo output deserves the "twee" criticism more than anything Belle and Sebastian have ever released. "It wasn't as creative a time anymore for me, and in the studio it was really tough, because it was impossible to get things mixed, because everyone was pulling in different directions." Or maybe they were just pulling in a different direction to the one she wanted to explore, since the rest of the group agree that from the start of 2001 a greater sense of unity prevailed, and that, as *Storytelling* had shown, they were more than capable of pulling together and getting some work done. Isobel, clearly, just didn't want to be in Belle and Sebastian anymore.

Finishing up in Milan, the last venue they played on their spring European tour had the unfortunate name of Alcatraz, the stifling connotations of which couldn't have been lost on Isobel. Once back home in Glasgow, with just over a week until they embarked upon their U.S. tour, a tired and despondent Isobel realized that she really couldn't take any more. So she called up Neil and told him that she wouldn't—couldn't—get on the plane for the upcoming dates, including an appearance at the Californian desert festival Coachella. Neil, as he had done so many times in the past, pleaded with her to reconsider, and after much uneasy argument, it was decided that she would join the tour once Coachella and the first couple of tour dates were taken care of. In retrospect, Neil wishes he hadn't pressured Isobel into taking the trip. "I persuaded her to stay for this tour, which was probably a mistake. I shouldn't have made that happen."

When Isobel and cello finally dragged themselves to the airport, bad omens dogged them from the off. "It took me and this other flute player three days to get to Boston because of hassles with getting the cello on the plane," she recalls despairingly. "Air stewards just hate cellos, they give you so much grief. When it used to go on a seat next to me, they'd hate it. So it was a hassle getting there and I was just kind of at my wits' end. And my parents had just got divorced, which was a great source of . . . it was really awful for me."

When she did finally make it to Boston, Stuart—although he and Isobel were barely glancing, let alone speaking—sounded genuinely relieved when he declared to all that it was nice to have everyone together again. Although their relationship was in ruins, Stuart still felt that Isobel was an essential part of the group, still an important aspect of the magic they were capable of; an original member, there before the real world so rudely butted in, a beautiful remnant of an innocent past which reminded him of the special thing he'd started the morning after the New Year's night before, when he met the drunken girl in the queue for the toilets, the girl he would eventually love and despair of in almost equal measure. "I tried my best," he sighs, his body almost crumpling in defeat. You tried because you cared? "Of course!" he exclaims, probably rightly astonished by the question. "I *tried* to speak to Bel, and she wasn't having it," he shrugs, "She might say otherwise, but she knew from a certain point around 2000/2001 that the band wasn't gonna go at her pace, we weren't gonna lie down and have her walk all over us. And she knew from that point that she was always gonna leave. But I didn't care anymore."

And he was right not to care. If Isobel didn't want to be in the group anymore, then she should fuck right off. *But still he wished she would stay.*

So Isobel joined them in Boston, a damn good show she thought, and followed them for two shows at the Hammerstein Ballroom in New York, both of which let her down. "The crowd seemed really far away, it was one of those air hangar places, so the atmosphere was a bit flat," she says. "I remember on my day off Stuart told me to go and learn 'It Had to Be You,' because we were in New York so he thought I should sing *Annie Hall*. I was like, 'Aww, fuck, it's my day off.' I was wrapped up in my bed. He was like, 'C'mon Isobel!' But I said, 'No.' And I thought, if he doesn't get off my case, then I've had it. Then we did another show, and I wasn't that into it. Then we got to Montreal and we were all just really tired, because touring is just exhausting. And when we came off stage Stevie and Stuart were really agitated because they were like, 'We were really shit.' And I didn't actually think so. And he started flaking out in front of the session musicians." She says this as if recalling an incident in which the father of the family insults the mother in front of the serving staff. "No, that's not good!" she declares, her voice cracking with disbelief. "You get them out of the room, and *then* all hell can break loose. And also the more session musicians got involved, they're kind of wheedling their way in; it's all politics, completely. So I'd had enough. And I had a friend in Toronto[2] so I went to stay with her. So Montreal was the last straw for me . . . in front of session players. In the end it was a kind of snappy decision."

"The reason why the discussion came up in the first place was that at the end of the last song Isobel and Sarah just ran off," Stevie insists. "Stuart was like, 'Are we doing an encore, what are we doing? This isn't good enough.'" The guitarist refutes Isobel's accusation that he was picking on her, although he'd clearly had enough of her attitude. "She was just never interested in being in a band, and she was just so mollycoddled by Stuart," he complains. "When the actual real world kicked in it was just inevitable that she would go." When asked whether his backstage outburst may have hurt her feelings, Stevie is regretful yet unrepentant. "I don't think I did anything wrong, but if she was here I would apologize. I don't want to make anyone feel bad. When you have these discussions, it's not to my advantage to belittle or insult anyone. I was asking, 'Who wants to be here, who doesn't? Who's interested,

---

2 Fiona, the friend she used to do the summer concerts with as a child.

who's not?' I remember Stuart saying, 'If you're not interested, go away.' I was just asking questions, but I made it very general, I never picked on Isobel. I was saying, 'A friend saw us in New York and said that we just looked bored up there, what's happening to us?' But she took it totally personally. And so she should have done, because she was definitely the worst culprit. But I never picked on her, and I know Sarah thinks I did. But I don't care—I didn't."

So on May 9, 2001, the day after a show at the Kool Haus in Toronto, Isobel Campbell decided that she wasn't going to take the bus. Ever again. That morning, before they took off for Detroit, Isobel told Sarah in their room that this was really the end. As the group assembled on the bus, Stuart received a call in reception which he'd expected yet dreaded for years. "Sarah knew, because she had similar grievances," Isobel recalls. "And Richard and Chris came to my door in the morning and said, 'Take care and see you later.' And Stuart phoned me from the foyer going, 'Do you know what this means, do you know what this means?' And I was like, [feigning disinterest] 'Yep . . . yep . . . yep.' I was a wee bit shitting it, but I listened to him."

"I remember thinking she was really brave," says Sarah, who got on the bus numb and surprised, miles before Stevie even realized that Isobel wasn't even there. When he did eventually realize, he remembers, "No one was shocked or upset. I seem to remember, actually, that I was the only one who said, 'This is terrible.' Everybody else accepted it: 'Now we can get on with our job.'" Stevie's dismay remains as double-edged as Stuart's. Although sorry to lose a friend—and despite their differences, there always was affection there—the guitarist was still as incensed as anybody at her frustrating inconsistency. "All I know is that when we started touring again in 2001, for the first six months Isobel was great, it was a happy time," he says. "We were playing live and she was really on the ball, but when we started again in 2002, it was just hell, she didn't want to be there at all, she was difficult, it was no use. She'd do maddeningly unprofessional things like agreeing to do a tour then three days before saying, 'I don't want to go for three weeks, I want to go for two.' Isobel always had this thing, 'Well, no one told me.' But she did always know."

Sarah, though, staring out the bus window at the Canadian landscape rolling before them, still couldn't quite believe that the girl was gone. "I was quite gutted when she left," she says. "It all seemed to come to a head over such a silly thing. People were saying me and her should brighten up, should start moving around and dancing. Fuck that, we're not dancing girls." To Isobel and Sarah it seemed like the band's problems were being blamed solely on the fact that they didn't want to dance around, which to Isobel in particular was the last straw, especially since she didn't even want to be there in the first place. "I don't think it was meant to be insulting," Sarah concedes. "Stuart knew that Isobel didn't want to be there and wasn't participating, and once people have got an idea in their head it's sometimes a bit hard to shake. I was quite upset when she left. I do kind of wish Isobel was still there. Stuart had always given the impression that the band were really important and that there was no point continuing if Stuart or Isobel left . . . but here we still are."

As the bus heaved out of Montreal, Stuart sat dazed but not entirely amazed. He knew it was only a matter of time, and despite his desperate subservient efforts, he knew that there was no way that he or the group could survive if they continued to tiptoe around Isobel's desires. "There was nothing I could do, believe me," he pleads. "I tried everything to accommodate Bel, to make her happy. I tried to the detriment of my health, to the detriment of the band, to the detriment of the quality of the records, and to the detriment of the quality of the performance. I wanted her to be happy, but she had to realize that there were four thousand people out there, and we had to concentrate on the people out front rather than the one person on stage. So I'm sorry if she was unhappy, but . . ." And he shrugs, sad, and sighs, tired of the subject and lost for something to add, apart from: "In a sense she had virtually left around *Fold Your Hands*. It was tougher before that because that's when we were still trying to get on, jostling and negotiating, just basically fucking arguing the thing into the bloody ground."

"I tried every approach," argues Isobel, almost parroting Stuart to the letter. "I tried to go at it from many different angles, but no matter what I tried it wasn't right. I just followed my heart in the end. I found that false democracy really difficult, it just seemed like a bit of a sham."

As for the departed Stuart David, he feels that "along with Chris, Isobel was the person I was closest to in B&S. She's been one of my main friends outside the band at different times too. She's very funny and very smart, and I don't think she gets the credit she deserves as a songwriter. Sometimes she gets weird friends though," he adds with a frown. "Sometimes she took up with weird hangers-on of the band and stuff. You would say to her, 'That person's an arsehole.' And she would say, 'No they're not, you're just cynical and full of shit.' And then a few years later she would quite often go, 'That person's an arsehole.' Unless you were wrong and just being cynical and full of shit. . . ."

Shit, cynicism, arseholes, whatever—Stuart just wanted his group to stay together, a hope that was probably rather unrealistic considering the internal disputes they had wrestled with for so long. But still he was aware of the interminably fracturing nature of the spell he had originally attempted to weave. "Maybe she should've left sooner," he muses. "But I didn't want to push her, I didn't want her to go. And I didn't want Stuart to leave. I practically spent the first two or three years trying to keep the group together. That was my mantra: *keep the group together.* Because I know what happens when somebody leaves a group. I always like the first lineup of a group. The magic goes, things change, and I am admitting that some of the magic went—it did—but I don't regret it, because we could live our lives again. I've had the best years of my life since that time, definitely. We've managed to play to thousands of people who we'd never played to before, and make really satisfying records. I know it's different, I know that some of the magic might've gone, but fuck it, you've got to move on."

Left alone in her room, buzzing with adrenaline, both fearful and excited, Isobel threw apart the drapes and winced into the sunlight. Time for a swim, she thought. "Once they were on their way I got my swimming costume on and went to the pool, doing roly-polies off the diving board. Freedom! I was like, fuck, I don't know what's going to happen, but I've followed my heart."

And with an uncertain splash she was gone.

It is early autumn 2003, and Stuart Murdoch is sitting in the Grassroots Café in Glasgow, one of his favored west end haunts since the sad demise of the Grosvenor, the "celestial café" where so many of his plans and songs had been hatched. The day before, at her suggestion, I met Isobel Campbell in exactly the same place, which rather suggests that the estranged couple continue to share at least some things in common, even if it is only a fondness for bijou Glasgow eateries. Towards the end of each interview I ask both of them the same question: Are you proud of your achievements with Belle and Sebastian? "I've loved it," he says in an instant. "Some of it," he counters, in another. "It's a constant spur, though, your failures. I think we've had some good ideas. I think you've just got to keep the standards high, you've just got to go for that quality every time."

Isobel muses over the word "proud," eventually conceding that she "learned so much in so many ways." In particular? "I liken it to being down the pit, down the mines, there's no daylight. That's what an engineer's lot is." So it was purely a practical education? Nothing more? "I look back on some really great times," she relents. "And Stuart and I shared a lot. We were awful to each other but he was a great companion in many ways. In these kind of extreme situations, you see the extremes of human kindness, you see everything. My mum often says to me, 'You don't need to do anything else in your life, you've already done a lot more than a lot of people.' And I find that quite hard to believe. I took quite a lot of it for granted, and I think I was really spoiled because we got everything our own way, people really loved us, and now, of course, I realize a lot of bands have to pay their dues for so long without even getting anywhere."

Aside from a brief encounter at the Banchory Christmas party in 2003, I wonder whether she has heard from Stuart since the split. "He e-mailed me around about the time my last album came out, but I couldn't really reply," she says sadly. "For the last two years I was in the band I found it almost impossible to speak to him. And the first six months after I left the group I saw him in a shop and I wanted to run away. But recently I bumped into him outside the rehearsal studios and we chatted; he looked me in the eye," she adds pointedly. "Sometimes it upsets me because it was such a huge part of my life and I think about him a lot, and I'm sure he probably still thinks about me, but there's still a lot of water under the bridge there."

Across town, Stevie Jackson sneaks a guilty cigarette, a necessary prop for one waxing philosophical. "Everything happens for a reason," he puffs. "And it's been proved time and time again where something bad happens there's a reason, because something better comes along. And I sometimes think that if things had happened the way I'd wanted them to, we'd maybe be split up by now. We had a few difficult years, but since Bob joined the band and we started playing again it's been up all the way."

It is no surprise to discover that Stevie and Isobel, never the bosomest of buddies, don't really stay in touch anymore, but he remains respectful of her talent and, in retrospect, sympathetic of her position within the group. "From what I'm told, Isobel is much happier. She's doing what she's good at, which is actually being in control of her own destiny," he notes adroitly. "She's just not any good in groups, she's just not a team player. I think *Amorino*[3] is just a fantastic record, I'm so proud of her, I think she's a great talent. I do miss her. When we were putting the session record together, both Stuart and I said, 'God, it's really great hearing Isobel's voice.' For the last few months on stage we were getting into a groove with the four voices, it was getting quite powerful, and I miss that."

There are things, no doubt, that Isobel misses. But there seems so much more that she wants. Ms. Campbell is certainly not one for looking back, possibly fearful that it might hurt her neck. "I've got so much fire left in me, creatively," she enthuses. "There's so many things I'd love to do." But no matter what she achieves in her solo career, Isobel will always be associated with Belle and Sebastian, something she has no choice but to accept, even if it does clearly irritate her. "My boyfriend and I went up for a walk in the Appalachian mountains to watch the sunset," she reminisces, painting a romantic picture soon to be destroyed by the rude intrusion of her past. "And we met a Belle and Sebastian fan at the top." They get everywhere, these people. "And she was singing Belle and Sebastian songs to me all the way down, and I was like, 'D'you know what? I'd rather have sung Carter family songs to myself.' But years ago I would've ran a mile from that person, but now it's fine. I can see what it was, although I still find some of the fans quite scary, but I'm not quite so devastated by it all. I suppose I'm always looking forward, but what has gone has been really valuable. And awful." She winces, smiles. "But amazing as well."

---

3 Isobel's third album, released in 2003, and the first to be released under her own name.

CHAPTER FIFTEEN
DEAR CATASTROPHE WAITRESS

Like a Fresh Manifestation of a New Phenomenon

It was a shame that Isobel missed Coachella. Taking to the stage just as the Californian sky lazily arranged itself into a languid wash of purple and blue, the kind of sky Scottish people can only ever imagine seeing in their most clichéd dreams—or on front of an Eagles LP, as Stuart noted on stage—Belle and Sebastian played their first ever outdoor show, braving the heat and unfurling their picnic blanket of pop for all assembled. The sight of the group, Isobel or no, stirred this crowd into a whooping state of glee. Irresistibly incongruous and triumphant, it would make the perfect denouement to any underdog-made-good Hollywood flick. The group were so at ease and loose—Stuart kicked footballs into the crowd à la Rod Stewart[1]—the audience couldn't help but follow suit, and when Stuart improvized the last few lines of "Arab Strap," acknowledging the sound of Foo Fighters playing across the site and admitting *"I know it's not summer/But it feels like summer to us,"* and Stevie launched unrehearsed into a mock-rock-God coda, the audience adulation was so genuinely warm it could melt the thickest of Alaskan 'bergs.

---

[1] "Since 2002 Stuart has reverted to his old self on stage, only it's quadrupled, he's Mr. Showman, a brilliant, brilliant performer," Stevie enthuses.

Richard at Coachella. Photo by Sarah Martin.

Backstage that day, the group found themselves chatting to a friendly if somewhat overbearing woman responsible for dressing the artists' caravans and who, she revealed to some surprise, also happened to be the housekeeper for legendary U.K. record producer Trevor Horn. "She told us that her boss was a fan of the band, as was her five-year-old kid," Mick recalls. "She was saying, 'How would you feel about working with him?' And we just thought she was this mad woman ranting on, she was quite eccentric, but we did say it would be great to work with him." Following the *Fold Your Hands* disappointment, the group had decided that it was imperative that they work with a producer next time round, someone to harness their indulgences and lead the way. But who? Fatefully, the decision was made for them a few months after their Coachella encounter, when the self-same Mr. Horn got in touch with them out of the blue. "He just happened to get in touch at the right time," says Mick. "We thought it would be an interesting collaboration because we were interested in making a proper pop record, we wanted to shake off the indie production ethics of the past, which is what we did." Fresh from his success with self-consciously controversial "lesbian" girl duo t.A.T.u., Horn appeared, on the face of it, an incredibly unlikely choice of producer. Renowned for his slickly bombastic work with the likes of '80s pop behemoths such as ABC and Frankie Goes to Hollywood, or MOR dullards such as Seal and Celine Dion, Horn's methods seemed to be vastly ill-attuned to Belle and Sebastian's far more low-key and organic approach. So when it was announced in 2002 that Horn would indeed be at the helm of the group's sixth long-playing opus, the collective shudder of surprise almost set the world of pop spiraling off its axis. Almost. A great many fans gnashed their teeth to stumps in dismay, fearful that their beloved Belles would be fatally neutered by this slick establishment producer, who couldn't possibly understand their precious and magical ways. Could he?

What the doubters failed to note about Horn is that he is actually a multifaceted pop craftsman capable of honing his talents to whatever artist he happens to be working with, even if the majority of those artists happen to be utter shit. In any case, after talking with Horn over the phone, Stuart was certainly left in no doubt of his suitability for the job. The fact that he'd been in Yes—albeit briefly and at a point when they were long past their prime—probably didn't harm his chances, either.

And so it was that in the autumn of 2002 Belle and Sebastian moved into Horn's Sarm Hook End mansion to record their first album for their new label, Rough Trade, who had stepped into the fray once the group's six-year affair with Jeepster finally came to an end. Mark Jones had long been frustrated by the group's unwillingness to tour and properly promote themselves, not to mention their generally problematic nature, which caused him no amount of headaches, and it was becoming increasingly clear that he'd become tired of dealing with the group. "Mark got very, very frustrated," claims Stef D'Andrea. "I wouldn't say he'd given up on them, but he'd become quite cynical and sarcastic about the whole thing. Big opportunities had been missed and it was too little too late. He has a very good ear for music, Mark, and I think he found it a massive stressful strain that we had this great songwriter on our label but nothing was being done by the artist himself. It was a big frustration for him and really depressed him at times."

It's impossible not to sympathize with Jones and Jeepster, although the group do protest that they had never made any secret of their desires to do things at their own speed. "One of the things they made clear to Mark from the start was that they weren't going to do things the usual way," says Katrina House. "And he accepted that initially, but I don't think it's any secret that he was very frustrated with them. But even though they went about things differently, it worked. Stuart has always wanted to give the fans something special, something to remember which they could feel a part of, and it's always worked. So while that could be frustrating as an employee, I just think it's very commendable that they do that. There aren't many bands who go to that kind of trouble for their fans."

In retrospect, D'Andrea feels that the group exploited the label's liberal attitudes. "We were really into the music ourselves, and were really into the idea of letting artists do what they want to a very large extent," he says. "But perhaps not to the extent that Belle and Sebastian took it, which was basically just recording a record and putting it in the post. We were very laissez-faire, laid-back, and relaxed—tell us what you want to do and we'll make it happen. We wanted them to feel that the whole thing was their creative project, which it was. So we feel that we gave a lot in terms of freedom and trust and money, which is why Mark got very frustrated, because he felt he wasn't getting any cooperation. All the ideas that Mark would come up with, all the opinions he had about the technical side of things, most of them fell on deaf ears. A, because Stuart had such a concrete vision of how he wanted to do things, and secondly because there were so many opinions in the band, we were classed as the people who didn't know anything."

Stuart, for his part, did have some sympathy for Jones's plight. "The thing with Mark is that he tried so hard for so long to make us a proper working band, and in those early days we didn't want to be," he says. "We wanted the band to be a reflection of our lives, because we were scared it was going to take over and spoil the magic. Mark wanted us out there gigging and promo-ing, like any record company would. I mean, we made money for him all the way, we did well for Jeepster, but it got to a point where he started getting fed up with us, losing interest." Which is rather ironic, considering the fact that, since 2001, the group had finally begun touring in earnest, and were certainly more visible and media cooperative than they had ever been, a fact not lost on Stuart. "I realized at that point that we could become a proper working band, and I wanted to, but at that stage Mark had already turned off," he says. "It's such a shame. I kept telling him to hold on, good things are coming, the personnel problems are sorting themselves out, the band's working great together. But I think the whole epiphany was round about 2001, starting with the Dunoon gig, that was when everything turned around, where we got this great crew together, and they were like the rock upon which the live performances were built, and I couldn't convince Mark that things had changed, and I think he'd already made his mind up to let us go." Although Neil claims the split was amicable, he does admit that Jones was maybe less than happy with the way things had ended up. "We don't really have any contact with them now," he says.

Once it was announced in early 2002 that Belle and Sebastian were free agents, Neil found himself fielding the expected overtures from interested parties, although not as many as one might expect for such an established act. On one telling and somewhat sobering occasion Neil phoned up the Independiente label, asking to speak to their M.D., but the receptionist had never heard of Belle and Sebastian and, despite his protestations—"We won a Brit Award!"—she told him to send in a demo like any other unsigned hopeful. "We realized how much ground we'd lost with *Fold Your Hands* and *Storytelling*," he says. "We hadn't realized this because we really started touring at that time and we were playing the same venues as people who sell five times as many records as us, but that was because there was a whole backlog of hundreds of thousands of people who had never seen us over five years of record-buying. But people had gone off us because of a couple of dodgy records."

Sad but true. Thus it was decided that with the next record—and the next label—the group would resolve for the first time to promote themselves in the established rock biz fashion. In truth, as Stuart has noted, they had already begun behaving like a "proper" group in their last year with Jeepster, but next time, if they were to sell as many records as they wanted—and make no mistake, Belle and Sebastian have always craved popular success—they would have to embark on something which would've been laughably unimaginable in days of yore—a press campaign. "The whole we don't do press thing was fun for years," says Neil. "And everyone had their own reasons for doing things, but I was so bored with that I'm really happy that now we do more, it's better fun. It got really boring being belligerent and obstinate. We were in an indie ghetto, as Stuart said, and being known more for what you don't do than what you do do is very boring, so we thought, fuck it, let's be a pop band now."

Suitably chastened by the realization that their moment might have passed, the group were lent some much needed cheer by the attentions of Rough Trade, the seminal "indie" label formed in 1978 by London record store owner Geoff Travis. The label lent musical succor to a whole generation of post-punk listeners in the '80s, Stuart Murdoch amongst them, via releases from the likes of Galaxie 500, The Fall, The Sundays, The Go-Betweens, and their greatest success, The Smiths, and although subject to the kind of fluctuating fortunes common to such comparatively small music biz concerns—including a brief loss of ownership in the '90s—Travis's label of love has endured long after nearly all of its contemporaries. Considering the acts he had signed in the past, it's no surprise that Travis was a Belle and Sebastian fan, but the group were still surprised when he requested a meeting. "Geoff just phoned up," Neil recalls. "Our options were pretty much Rough Trade, Matador, and Island." The latter, although initially enthusiastic, abruptly decided to pass after witnessing a particularly bad gig at the Brixton Academy in London. "In the first meeting you'd have thought they wanted to marry us all, but they soon stopped returning our calls. But everyone wanted to go with Geoff. We found him quite inspirational, he asked all the right questions like, 'Is your best work behind you?' No. 'Good.' And we set up the deal," said Neil.

Travis was immediately pleased to discover that the group were willing to promote their first Rough Trade album properly, and after some debate, he also managed to convince them to release singles from an album for the first time. "They asked us when we first met them what we felt about releasing singles off albums," Mick recalls. "And we said we could be persuaded. And we ended up releasing three. We released one, and then Rough Trade said, 'Well, what about another one?' And we said, OK. And they said, 'Oh, that one went so well, what about another one?' I do miss the days when singles were their own entities, there's something pretty special about that," he adds wistfully. These changes, along with the recruitment of Trevor Horn, quite predictably set the group's more puritanical fans into an outrage, although this kind of inverted indie snobbery, which places doing things such as selling records and being interviewed in the *NME* on a par with horse-molestation, should never be given any heed. Belle and Sebastian had always unashamedly classed themselves as a pop group—pop meaning "popular"—a fact which has always seemed lost on most of their hardcore followers, whose unwillingness to share the group with anyone outside of their exclusive cabal often borders on the pathological. "I think getting Trevor Horn in, even if it's only to shake up people who think they know exactly what Belle and Sebastian are all about, is worth doing exactly for that reason," notes Mark Radcliffe.

On December 18, 2002, the group took a festive break from recording and traveled to John Peel's country home—affectionately known as Peel Acres—to record a live session primarily consisting of a Santa's sack–full of Christmas covers. Taking over most of the show, the group—backed by a particularly rowdy choir—jingled merrily through the traditional likes of "O Come All Ye Faithful" and "Silent Night" as well as another take on "O Come, O Come Emmanuel" (with Isobel's part being taken by Tracyanne Campbell from Camera Obscura), climaxing with a genuinely funny and anarchic take on "The Twelve Days of Christmas," with Richard supplying some impressively convincing bird noises. In between they tackled The Sonics' "Santa Claus," which almost manages to out-fuzzbox the original, a convincingly funky version of James Brown's "Santa Claus, Go Straight to the Ghetto," featuring funk fanatic Chris on vocals (the thought of this bespectacled—and very white—beanpole taking on Soul Brother Number One is a charmingly incongruous delight), and Stevie in his chocolatey element on a bouncy take on Elvis's "Santa Bring My Baby Back to Me," and, best of all, a cool jazz jaunt through "O Little Town of Bethlehem," with Stuart introducing the group one by one in time-honored hep cat style ("Jackson, play some festive guitar") and cracking up at Mick's ridiculously groovy bass line. It's definitely the most entertaining session the group have yet recorded, and remains a fitting epitaph for the mutual affection betwixt Belle and Sebastian and the late lamented Peel.

Back at the mansion, work on the album continued in a more controlled and swiftly productive manner than the group had managed since *Sinister,* albeit using the kind of ridiculously expensive computer equipment one would expect from a millionaire record producer with Rod Stewart on speed-dial. Horn and his disciplined team of engineers proved to be incredibly copacetic and helpful collaborators, allowing the group to arrange as they always had, only stepping in to offer their professional assistance when the need arose. The only songs Horn had any hands-on involvement with were "Step into My Office, Baby"—whose arrangement he worked on considerably—and the horn arrangement for "Roy Walker." The group were becoming increasingly ambitious with their vocal arrangements; in particular, Sarah, Stevie, and Stuart discovered that their varying vocal timbres combined to create a rather fetching whole, and the Horn squad spent a great deal of studio time coaxing the finest vocal performance from each. "Trevor's guys were great," Sarah recalls admiringly. "They would spend loads of time with you to help you get whatever sound you wanted. I loved working in that way, you really felt that you were doing the very best work you could." After a month at Sarm Hook End, work continued at Horn's Sarm West studios in London, the former Island studios above which Bob Marley once lived. With Rough Trade breathing down their necks for an autumn release, the group were up against the clock as work continued apace into the summer, Stuart ending up recording some last minute takes in his pajamas. "The rest of the group had gone back to Glasgow," he explains. "And I was meant to be going with them, I'd sent my clothes up, but Trevor's going, 'We just have to finish this off, hang around.' So I just had my pajamas and my toothbrush, walking down to the studio from the flat." Must've turned some heads. "Well, it's London. There's a lot weirder stuff going on."

Once work was completed, Stuart and his pajamas returned to Glasgow, and, following a spot of remixing with Tony Doogan at Ca Va, Belle and Sebastian submitted the tapes of their Horn-produced meisterwork to Rough Trade, who, to the relief of all concerned, loved what they heard. And what wasn't there to love? The fear that Horn might homogenize their sound turned out be entirely unfounded, as the finished album—although laced with an undeniable sheen—proved that the veteran producer had simply buffed up the group's sound to a level entirely befitting the zesty pop spark their new material required. Horn's production is commendably unobtrusive, his role instead being as creative motivator and guide, lending these beautifully arranged and performed songs a warmth and crispness which the group probably would have struggled to achieve themselves.

Dear Catastrophe Waitress is Belle and Sebastian in Technicolor, the funky, chewy splurge of bubblegum for the brain they'd obviously always had in them but were never confident nor unified enough to create. More cohesive than both *Arab Strap* and *Fold Your Hands,* it was their most consistently excellent record since *Sinister.* While the songs may, with the exception of "Piazza, New York Catcher" and the ancient "Lord Anthony," lack the dew-dropped elegance which made their other albums so uniquely affecting, *Waitress* still buzzed with that confident sense of eccentricity, intelligence, and loving attention to detail which defined the group's very best work. Two not entirely unlikely antecedents, in terms of their colorful scope and surprisingly cohesive eclecticism, are The Beatles' (overrated) *Sgt. Pepper's Lonely Hearts Club Band* and The Monkees' (underrated) *Pisces, Aquarius, Capricorn and Jones Ltd,* two records positively bursting at the seams with their delight in the possibilities of the pop form. Throw in the best of 10cc, The Left Banke,[2] Kassenatz-Katz, ELO, XTC, and the group's own *Tigermilk,* and you have a template for a pop LP of endlessly repeatable pleasures.

It is ironic, then, that the album's opening gambit and leadoff single, the Stevie/Stuart/Horn co-creation[3] "Step Into My Office, Baby" actually turned out to be one of its least successful tracks. There isn't anything particularly wrong with the song—it does have a likeably, groovily lascivious charm—but although an attempt to vary the tone is attempted via unexpected shifts in tempo and the inclusion of their most complex vocal harmonies to date—shades of Brian Wilson's in his *SMiLE* sandpit—the song's essentially repetitive nature wears out its welcome long before the end. Though Stuart's unabashedly priapic lyrics—basically one long list of office-based double entendre: *"She gave me some dictation/But my strength is in administration/I took down all she said/I even took down her little red dress"*—are amusing enough, the song

---

2 Whose timeless "Walk Away Renee" is name-checked in "Piazza, New York Catcher." Their compilation *There's Gonna Be a Storm: Complete Recordings 1966–1969* is a good place to start if you haven't already.

3 "It's basically Stevie's song," Stuart explains. "He had the music and the tune. It's quite a nice thing that's happened recently, Stevie would get to this stage and then come to me and we'd talk through the scenario, the idea, and I would go away and write all or most of the words, and what I find quite easy to do is come up with a bridge section or a bit of a chorus to finish the song off. So that's a typical collaboration, a good collaboration."

merely sounds like a playground joke stretched too far.[4] But in opening an album for the first time without Stuart's hushed tones, opting instead for a pop-glam Garry Glitter–style stomp, the group was clearly attempting to unveil their newly revitalized colors from the off. Certainly, if you played "Office" side by side with, say, "The State I Am In," it could almost be the work of a different group, and while this does show an admirable desire to expand their horizons, here they seem to be moving too far from the things which made them so great in the first place.

The title-track, which lyrically also deals with work-related mishaps, dates as far back as 1995 and was actually first attempted at the *Fold Your Hands* sessions. It was, therefore, a more traditional Belle and Sebastian song, albeit one lent a new lease of life by a suitably expansive string arrangement and production. In it Stuart relays the tale of a hapless café waitress beset by a bullying boss and—in time-honored Murdochian fashion—her uncomprehending peers, who could never possibly understand her cool and sensitive ways. *"You'll blow them all to the wall/When they realize what you've been working for,"* he counsels, never realizing what that goal might actually be. Not having cans of Coke thrown at her in a café, quite possibly. Like so many in his canon, the song was inspired by a real life character, a put-upon waitress Stuart glimpsed one busy Saturday afternoon in his beloved Grosvenor Café, and for whom he left a sympathetic—and romantically intended—note. "It was verbatim the first verse of the song. It's quite a cringy thing to do," he cringes. "I was breaking my own rules of going to the Grosvenor on a Saturday, when it's full of families. She had just started, and I noticed her, and she walked down the aisle with a big tray of soup and tea and everything, and she dropped it with a huge smash, people shrieking. She left the next day, I never saw her again."

The silky soul-tinged "If She Wants Me" is another song from 1995, one only resurrected by the group after Stevie found Stuart's lost lyrics one day after they had reminisced about the song. "I keep everything he ever gave me," he reveals. "I think the first song we actually rehearsed

---

4 The video—directed by *Father Ted* co-creator Graham Linehan—makes the roots of the song explicit, being an affectionate and fairly amusing tribute to the notorious *Confessions Of . . .* series of '70s sex comedies, with the ever game Richard scuttling around in his underpants as a harassed and unlikely sex-magnet.

was 'If She Wants Me.' The only reason that turns up at all is Stuart said, 'I don't have the words to that anymore.' And I found them, because back then we tried doing it in the style of The Left Banke, which was a band we had in common. We also both admired 'The Wild Ones' by Suede, and when he first played the song I was trying to play the guitar in the style of Bernard Butler, which didn't work out too well."

Partly dedicated to Jo (the titular "she"), the song appears to elucidate upon the uncertain period in Stuart's life just before the release of *Tigermilk,* as he posits aloud *"If I could do just one near perfect thing I'd be happy/They'd write it on my grave, or when they scattered my ashes,"* hinting at his desires to create something lasting and substantial, something artistically worthwhile to give his life meaning. "I felt a feeling of such nice achievement with *Tigermilk,* making our first record," he beams. "And that certainly answered and satisfied the line in that song." He also alludes to a John Peel competition he once entered, in which the veteran DJ asked listeners to send in something special in an envelope. Thus, Stuart wrote him a song called "Something Special in an Envelope." It didn't win.

And far away somebody read the letter
He condescends to read the words I wrote about him
And if he smiles, it's no more than a genius deserves
For all his curious nerve and his passion

"Piazza, New York Catcher," is like Robert Altman gone folk, intertwining myriad story threads—including an abstract tribute to "not gay" baseball legend Mike Piazza—into the most traditionally recognizable B&S song on the album, its acoustic skip and lovingly tended prose bearing more in common with the kind of music with which they made their name. Featuring just voice and guitar (played by Bob), its unadorned nature was deemed so perfect by Horn that it was decided that any additional arrangement would detract from the song's not inconsiderable charms. Melodically redolent of The Beatles' similarly folk-tinged "I've Just Seen a Face," the song finds Stuart at his most nakedly emotive and lyrically precise:

I love you I've a drowning grip on your adoring face
I love you my responsibility has found a place

Beside you and strong warnings in the guise of gentle words
Come wave upon me from the wider family net absurd

It's difficult to imagine any other contemporary songwriter pitching lines such as these. "Piazza, New York Catcher" is not really about the baseball star at all, of course, beyond the singer asking, *"Piazza, New York Catcher/Are you straight or are you gay?"* the kind of unexpectedly blatant line Stuart likes to throw into his songs like a grenade into a ball swamp. It's as dazzling a lyric as anything from the writer's early period, and a timely reminder of Stuart Murdoch's distinct song writing brilliance.[5]

This unreconstructed heavy-metal guru exercises his passion for Thin Lizzy on "I'm a Cuckoo," one of the album's highlights, and one soul-assuaging blast of FM pop to boot (whatever that actually means). Boasting the immortal line, *"I'd rather be in Toky-o/I'd rather listen to Thin Lizzy-o"* the song might musically pay tribute to one of Stuart's heroes, but lyrically it is one of Stuart's most straightforwardly autobiographical songs, touching on the joys of touring (*"Scary moments, loving every moment/I was high from playing shows"*) as well as the breakup of a relationship, although, contrary to what most people have assumed, not that of Stuart and Isobel. With lines like *"We lost the singer to her clothes,"* it's once again not entirely unreasonable to assume that the song is about her, but when asked Stuart is as apparently shocked by the question as he is whenever it arises. "No!" he exclaims. "Isobel? It's nothing to do with Isobel—I've had other more substantial relationships since then. Allow me to have a life outside the band," he laughs, obviously somewhat affronted by the assumption that every bitter/bittersweet song he's written since 2002 should be a specific reference to his relationship with Isobel. In case we're left in any doubt, he goes on to explain the precise genesis of the song. "On the last day in Japan I was hanging out by myself in an area called Harajuku [*"watch the Sunday gang in Harajuku"*] which was near the hotel, and it was real freak show. It was almost like the Camden of Tokyo, with these kids in bizarre costumes, which I tried to recreate for the cover of *Storytelling*, almost like Victorian maid costumes, with completely white faces, like a Gothic

---

sadistic house-maiden. It was bizarre but great. And I happened to be listening to Thin Lizzy as well, just having a great time to myself, which happens quite a lot in this privileged life. And the song just arrived one day when I came back, I was locked out of the church hall, I'd had a really shitty day and I was breaking up with someone. And the girl guides had been locked out as well, so we were all waiting for the guide leader to turn up, and one of the guides was a kid from my youth club and we were just chatting about her day at school, and, I dunno, it just took me out of myself for a bit. So I went upstairs and got it out my system."

Hence the second verse:

> *Glad to see you*
> *I'm outside the house*
> *I'm not thinking well today*
> *I've got no energy*
> *I'm glad that you are waiting with me*
> *Tell me all about your day*

The remainder of the lyrics poignantly capture that sense of bittersweet breakup bemusement most listeners can doubtless empathize with, Stuart lying on his *"empty bed"* feeling shaken and sorry for himself, his girl *"staying with your friends tonight,"* although she might just as well be in Harajuku for all the distance he feels between them. Like the similarly themed "I'm Waking Up to Us," Stuart casts himself here firmly in the victim role, the wounded lover who *"counted on your company,"* the *"little lost sheep,"* in desperate need of his long gone shepherd. It's a song entrenched in ennui, and yet the arrangement is so joyous—Horn's horns blaring like a Vegas show-band on vacation—the mood seems valedictory rather than vanquished, displaying the kind of incongruity betwixt lyric and tune which Belle and Sebastian have turned into something of a trademark. The slightly edited single version managed to reach number 14 in the U.K. charts upon its release in February 2004, the group's biggest hit since "Legal Man," thanks to an encouragingly greater amount of radio play than they were used to.

The single offered another first—something most people thought they'd never see on a Belle and Sebastian release—namely a celebrity remix, further confirming their commitment to more conventional group practices. Remixed by Australia's big beat surrealists The Avalanches, it is at least a little more inventive than most, boiling the song down to its riff played on a patina of flutes, around which a cacophony of bongos battle with the unfettered wailings of the Southern Sudanese Choir to create something which, though it might sound brilliant on paper, in actuality sounds very annoying indeed. Also featured was Stevie's "(I Believe in) Travellin' Light," which was produced by Horn but left off the album at its author's own insistence; Stevie has always been very pragmatic when it comes to his own material.

The third and final single from the album, "Wrapped Up in Books" (another respectable U.K. hit, reaching number 20 in June 2004), was, fittingly enough, textbook B&S. From its title downwards it conforms unashamedly to the group's firmly established aesthetic—confused boys and girls, coy sexual references (*"our inclinations are hidden in looks"*), and the escapist sanctity of literature (*"our aspirations are wrapped up in books"*), with a cursory reference to prayer thrown in to complete the set. And while this could easily result in the kind of self-parody which sunk most of *Fold Your Hands,* here it seemed more like an almost nostalgic reassertion of the group's core appeal.

Although they'd been playing it live for years, the group had never managed to nail a satisfactory version of Stuart's "Lord Anthony," another remnant from the class of '95. Although they'd gotten close during the *Fold Your Hands* sessions, they still weren't quite satisfied. Clearly deeming it too good to go to waste, they returned to it for *Waitress,* and finally managed to come up with a definitive reading. As rendered, "Lord Anthony" was the heavy heart of the album, a pathos-ridden account of a smart misfit bullied at school who, in a typically audacious twist in the final verse, eventually finds some kind of personal happiness by becoming a transvestite in his adult life (with, strangely, a Toblerone under his dress; some kind of Marianne Faithful–inspired confectionary-as-phallus reference, one presumes). In Stuart Murdoch's world, the most personal and unlikely forms of redemption are always the most poignant. "It's one of these typical storylines: a loser made good in his secret world," he admits, almost sheepishly, as if acknowledging that this is a theme which has sustained him long throughout his career. "Again it's a snapshot of a person; this is me looking back at this fella who turned up in the school one day, came from another school. He dressed kind of different and I could see he was going to have a hard time, he was a bit of a misfit, but in retrospect I tend to admire these figures more than I did at the time. I used to run with the pack at the time, just like any other boy. If you're a songwriter or a storyteller you tend to pick up a detail and run with it. It interests me, that side of things. It interests me to get inside that sort of character." There is undoubtedly something slightly voyeuristic, almost obsessive, about Stuart's fascination with characters like this, but he writes about them so beautifully, and with such genuine empathy, he succeeds where other writers might sound exploitative.

"When You Find Yourself Caught in Love" is the most overt statement of faith Stuart has ever made in song. Previously, his religious allusions have been used as mere details and narrative conceits (cf. "Jonathan David"), but here he virtually throws himself onto his knees in joyous subservience to *the man above.* Whereas in "If You're Feeling Sinister" he suggests that you might very well be better off having a wank than seeking out religious counsel, here he declares emphatically that prayer is our only answer. "I found that song quite fun to write," he says. "Because as you go along, get a bit older, you become more aware about songwriting. This can be a good thing and a bad thing. There's something about the discovery process of writing that's very nice and lends itself to poetry, just the way something comes out when you're discovering it for the first time, it comes out unformed, and this is nice for songs. But when you get older, you can stand back a bit and consider what you're writing about to an extent. But you have to be wary. In this case it was quite a nice thing. I may have thought for a second, what am I writing about here? But then I thought, why not? I had a good feeling, it's almost like [feeling] bolshie, it's almost as missionary as I ever could be. But it's fine, it's fitting, because it's in the midst of this up song. Why not have a bit of gospel zeal? It's quite nice because I think that if the song's any good, then for complete agnostics, it won't stick in their throats." Just be thankful they didn't hire a gospel choir.

Stuart explains one of the most surprising and un–Belle and Sebastian songs the group have ever recorded, the Madness/Stiff-like "Stay Loose," as "another song I just woke up which I could hear completely.

With the group I said, 'This might seem a bit strange, but I'm going to sing in quite an affected way.' And that's the great thing about the group recently, because they're so confident and versatile in what they can play, and I'm so comfortable with them, I can come up with these songs and feel like a different person. I can see what David Bowie was about when he disappeared into his different personas, you just feel much more comfortable, you can howl, you can pretend you're Smokey Robinson—and fail miserably—you can pretend you're anyone."

Dear Catastrophe Waitress became the album *Fold Your Hands* should have been, a rich summation of the group's various influences and strengths coalescing into one symbiotic whole. But whereas that album stalled as a result of weak material, a piecemeal recording process, and, ultimately, a basic inability to properly realize their ambition, *Dear Catastrophe Waitress* thrived on its combined sense of purpose, with the group clearly energized by working with a confident and professional collaborator such as Horn. Belle and Sebastian knew that after the combined disappointments of their last two albums, they had no choice but to pull out all the stops with this one, and while they couldn't help but lack the magical mystery which made their early records so special, it remains commendably fresh and inspired for a group eight years and six albums into their career.

Although the group found working with Trevor Horn an immensely satisfying experience, they doubt that they will be reunited anytime soon. "Trevor basically produced us for free," Sarah revealed. "It was done more or less as a favor, he didn't make any money out of it, and I don't think his wife—who's also his manager—will let him do that again. But I think we'd all love to work with him again if possible." Still, they did collaborate with him one more time, when he performed his Buggles classic "Video Killed the Radio Star" live with them at their sellout show at the Greek in L.A. in August 2003. Did he have to be forced into this at the group's behest, one wonders? "He couldn't wait!" laughs Mick, whose idea it in fact was. "He said to me that whenever we played in L.A. he wanted to do the song with us," he recalls, before adding conspiratorially, "there is an effect on his voice in the record, but that actually is the way he sings."

* * *

Released in the U.K. on October 6, 2003, the album—with a cover featuring the whole group for the first time[6]—eventually titled *Dear Catastrophe Waitress,* would reach 21 in the homegrown album charts, and a fairly respectable 84 in the U.S. It also received some of the most positive reviews the group had received in a long time, with the *NME* for one praising the group's "newly found confidence that points to a great future." As promised, Belle and Sebastian embarked upon a promotional campaign which, while hardly aggressive, was certainly more sustained than anything they had previously attempted. Stuart in particular seemed unable or unwilling to turn down any request, be it writing about his favorite albums for *The Guardian* newspaper, or presenting the aural equivalent on BBC Radio 2. "The person who was most dead against playing the game was Stuart," says Mick. "But he's definitely a lot more relaxed about it these days. He's really into the idea of being in a popular band."

Interviews and features appeared in virtually all of the world's major rock journals, the harried group dutifully answering those probing "Why did you decide to work with Trevor Horn" questions with the kind of practiced tolerance your average pop star has to perfect in such circumstances.[7] When not fielding the inquiries of studious Scandinavian journalists or Mediterranean radio hosts, the group could be found a-rockin' all over the world for the rest of 2003 and most of 2004, spending two prolonged bouts in Canada and the States—playing to around 8,000 people a night at three sold-out outdoor shows in Brooklyn, Berkeley, and L.A.—plus return trips to Japan and Europe, and their first ever visit to Australia in July 2004. They took in as many festivals as they could, with appearances at Coachella, Benicassim (where they placated Morrissey fans disappointed by their idol's no-show

---

6 Plus Shantha Roberts, who would also appear on the *I'm a Cuckoo* cover and accompanying video, as the eponymous food and beverage operative.

7 Although they weren't beyond poking fun at their sudden willingness to play the game. Speaking to Lauren Laverne on London indie station XFM in 2003, Stevie claimed, not entirely satirically, that "I'd love to prostitute myself, if only I could work out how, y'know? I just never works out that way. Selling out's hard—Christ, I wish I could work it out . . ."

with a version of "The Boy with the Thorn in His Side"), Glastonbury, Eurorockeennes in France, the charmingly named Chicobum in Italy, Piazza Castello/Indipendiente and Central Del Tennis/Cornetto-freemusic (the only known ice cream–sponsored festival in the world?) in Italy, Oxygen in Ireland, and the famous Fuji Rock Festival in Japan. They even made a highly incongruous appearance at the Trevor Horn Prince's Trust benefit at the cavernous Wembley Arena in London in November 2004, slotted in amongst fellow Horn-produced luminaries such as Seal, Pet Shop Boys, Lisa Stansfield, The Art of Noise, and Stuart's beloved Yes.

But what, in the end, did all of this activity really achieve? "It hasn't made all that much difference, really," sighs Mick. "*The Boy with the Arab Strap* is still our biggest selling album. So that was our moment in the media spotlight, and I think we blew it really. I think on the back of the Brits a lot of bands would've capitalized on that, because it was a big deal, but we missed that boat. We were always pretty precious about what we did and didn't do, but real pop bands—The Beatles, Franz Ferdinand," he explains, unabashedly uttering the two in the same breath, "go out and push themselves. It's not just the music you make, it's the way you portray yourself, and we've never quite got that sorted out. Even if we wanted to now we wouldn't be able to, because the interest has to be there in the first place."

Katrina House is more pragmatic: "I don't think it was too much. It certainly wasn't as intense as the kind of campaign most bands go on. They did it out of respect for Geoff, and I thought they did really well, they never complained, they did everything they had to do. And the album went gold, so it wasn't as if it was all for nothing."

And yet Sarah certainly feels that the campaign was unnecessarily time-consuming and creatively stifling. "I think we've gone too far in the wrong direction," she states. "In the last year since *Waitress,* we've recorded one new song, and that's terrible! I mean, what the hell are we in it for? We're meant to be coming up with interesting new stuff, not just cramming out the same old stuff. It's not got boring, but it's teetered on the edge. I think it was good to do the year's touring, but I don't think we should do it at that kind of level for . . . the rest of time, really."

* * *

The one song Sarah exasperatedly refers to is "Your Cover's Blown," a six minute art-funk epic which continues the group's exploratory trip into the outer reaches of their record collections. And if it's an only partially successful mission, it at least confirms that they have no intention of resting on their creative laurels. "The main instrumental idea, it was me on guitar, Mick on drums, and Bob on bass," explains Stevie. "Bob had the bass line and I tried to do a kind of Keith Richards disco thing over it, like 'Miss You'—it was called 'Stoned Disco' on the demo. Stuart and I tried to write it together, he came round to my place and he had the bit in the middle where it speeds up. This is crazy, how's this going to fit in? But it fits in because we say it does."

Well, maybe. The sudden shift from slick chic groove to unexpected gypsy gallop after three and a half minutes of funky mood setting just seems unnecessarily incongruous, and if the song is supposed to be the ultimate realization of Stuart and Stevie's desire to create the perfect song to dance to, then that intrusive middle section shoots 'em right in their dancing feet. Still, the rest remains seductively groovy, and there's a cool maturity and looseness about Stuart's delivery that is almost, but not quite, impossible to equate with wan and lisping choirboy of yore. The song eventually ended up as the lead track on the aforementioned *Books* EP,[8] alongside "Wrapped Up in Books, Cover (Version)," Chris's fine funked-up remix of the main track, and "Your Secrets," a catchy old song of Stuart's based around a shimmering Stone Roses–like guitar groove; summer pop for people *"introverted to a fault."*

Having spent so much of the last two years away from Glasgow, the group decided in early 2004 to bring it all back home with a special free summer jamboree in the city's vast and fecund Botanic Gardens. After the cancelation of the Kelvingrove Park show in 1998, they had always vowed to organize another outdoor show in their backyard (literally, if need be), but now they set about the job in earnest. Understandably keen to stage the show during the summer, Neil got in touch with the organizers of Glasgow's annual West End Festival, who eventually

---

8 Cover star Alexandra Klobouk, who also stars in the Blair Young/Stuart Murdoch–directed video, appropriately shot on location in Caledonian Books in Glasgow.

agreed to stage "School's Out with Belle and Sebastian and Friends" on Saturday, June 12. The "friends," it was soon revealed, were V-Twin (of course), Camera Obscura (natch), The James Orr Complex, Mother and the Addicts, and veteran Glasgow janglers The Trashcan Sinatras, with our gracious hosts topping the bill. Afterwards there would be "Stay Loose," a charity disco at the Queen Margaret Union with proceeds going to Friends of the Earth Scotland. Oh, what a day it would be. If Glasgow's notoriously unforgiving weather decided to cheer up for once, that is.

In the weeks prior to the gig, the well-drilled Belle and Sebastian organizational machine set briskly into motion, with Stuart setting about his duties with the kind of enthusiastic perspicacity with which he'd organized those university balls and discos all those years ago. He was all over the local press that month, encouraging dogs and grannies alike to come down and rub shoulders with the expected throng of bowlie kids. It was to be a true family event, totally inclusive, power to the people, right on. Despite the insular nature they had displayed in the early days, Belle and Sebastian had undoubtedly grown into a community-galvanizing bastion of true old socialist values. "We wanted to set Glasgow on fire," glints Neil with typical ambition. "Not literally, of course."

And so, on the morning of June 12, 2004, the sun braised down on Glasgow town, a quite remarkable stroke of luck considering the decidedly average weather in the days leading up to the event. All along Byres Road, hundreds of bowlie kids massed in giggling gaggles, trooping towards the Botanics, the mood on the grass playful and calm, exactly the sort of summer holiday atmosphere the group had hoped for. There were children, there were dads, there were grannies, and there were dogs, just as Stuart had hoped, and by the time the group took to the stage at eight o'clock that evening, the crowd was around twelve thousand strong.

"The sun came out that day, but it didn't the week before, it didn't the week after," Stevie says, still amazed by this phenomenon. "It was beautiful. After all the touring it was nice to get back to a more personal idea, which was about our own town, about the people of Glasgow."

"It was a warm feeling," beams Stuart, who was on hand throughout the day to give out crowd announcements and introduce the acts. "It was a cross between the physical environment we were surrounded by and the feeling that was going on. It did lift you into a different place. I'd never done hallucinogenic drugs, but the way the sun was blasting the stage—we were facing out towards it—and the strangeness of seeing the park full of people . . . I was absolutely on a high."

It didn't matter that the show wasn't one of their best ("I was drunk," admits Mick), everyone assembled still had a whale of a time. Belle and Sebastian lifted the spirits of thousands that day, the sun at their command, hometown at their feet, the uncertain trajectory of an eight-year voyage coming momentarily to a halt on a joyous and benevolent island of celebration. For one voyager at least, the curiously ageless thirty-five-year-old Stuart Murdoch, it was a quietly triumphant occasion, a sunny vindication of all those years of sickness and struggle, courage and confusion. As he squinted out across the vast blanket of bodies before him, the group he'd always dreamed of playing tenderly around him, he couldn't help but marvel at the way fate had led his hand. He thought of all the friends he'd made and those that he had lost. He thought of Isobel, and wondered if she might be out there somewhere, maybe giggling under a tree with Stuart David, neither really paying much attention to what was happening onstage. He looked around at Stevie, at Sarah, at Chris and Richard, Bob and Mick, and thought about the old church hall, about the beaches of Brazil, the streets of San Francisco, about the town of Ayr and his mother's piano and the strange places it had taken him, and the stranger places yet to come.

"I Never Really Thought It Would Be Like This, I Know It's Kind of Hard, But I'm Glad That It Is, I'm Glad"

So where to next? "It's the beginning of a new chapter and it's quite exciting," Stevie enthuses, still the greatest fan the group could ask for. "I've never felt happier in a sense. The band have become the band I always knew we could be. Everybody's grown up, me included." As for what actually will happen, Stuart talks about taking a break and a backseat, about "doing something else musically," which at the time of writing he's not prepared to reveal. The thought of Stuart, the group's creative visionary—the incredibly gifted individual responsible for all of their greatest songs—taking a backseat immediately fills one with concern, but the group have undoubtedly proven their collective worth in recent years, so maybe it's not the harbinger of disappointment it might initially seem. "When we finished the touring for the *Waitress* LP," he explains, "we'd done something which Stevie and Richard and everybody wanted to do for ages, which was to make an LP which we were satisfied with and do proper tours. And when we did that I had a sense of, well that's finished, let's do something different. The last thing I want to do is go back and present the group with a whole load of new songs, we've gotta do something new, fresh. I think new B&S stuff will come from a new direction, from other people. We'll continue this progressive approach."[9]

As for Belle and Sebastian's ever loyal manager, the eternally pragmatic Neil Robertson, he could only grant the group a metaphorical pat on the back, justifiably proud of the fact that they remain creatively vibrant and true to themselves after eight years spent in such a depressingly transitory business. "It's fairly easy," he says of shepherding his wayward charges. "A few headaches maybe. There's too many people, it's way too expensive. But I'm very proud that eight years later they're still making records. We're not millionaires, but we do all right. I've no regrets, we've all avoided getting real jobs for a long time, we get to travel the world. It's not bad."

Asked to muse upon the group's appeal, Monica Queen, Belle and Sebastian's soul sister number one, can only prostrate herself in awe. "I think what Belle and Sebastian give that a lot of other artists don't give is lots of very special moments, both lyrically—particularly from Stuart—and melodically. He kind of sweeps you along with him. He creates a whole picture for you to be involved with and be a part of, and filmmakers these days don't create enough of that. It's very emotive, and I think that whole spiritual connection is something that I feel very comfortable with. And they're just a kerrazy bunch of guys—

---

9 He presumably doesn't mean "progressive" in the Yes-sense, although in his online diary Stuart does mention a proposed concept album on mathematicians and philosophers which, although meant as a joke, could very well be the way forward. . . .

they can rock 'n' roll with the best of them. They're powerful, they're mighty, they're beautiful, they're gentle. Just beautiful melodies, beautiful lyrics."

"There's a lack of artifice about what they do," posits Mark Radcliffe, the DJ who offered them their first platform on national radio. "Their performances are very honest, his voice is very bare, the emotions are very bare. When you see them live they're not trying to look cool, the guitar straps are not put on just so, there's no need for any macho bullshit. They've become quite a big band without ever having become part of the music biz establishment. And it's a feeling that it's somehow a club, a private members club, and to feel really at home there you have to know everything that was going on. Which doesn't mean that we don't want it to be the biggest possible private members club. And I think Belle and Sebastian and their fans deliberately or by chance engendered that feeling, that the band is ours, and we'll never release it to the mainstream, and the band have a personal affection for the fans."

The boy who opened the doors to the club in the first place can only offer a surprised if satisfied smile and quietly marvel at the delightful unlikeliness of its success. "I've been told that we're the biggest indie band in the world, in a sense, which is hilarious because every person in the band at various stages has railed furiously at that title, 'indie.' But it must mean something, otherwise people wouldn't use it. The more you fight it the more you're stuck with it." Has it lived up to his expectations, his pop star dreams? "I must say I didn't really have that many fantasies of being a pop star," he claims. "And I never thought I'd be a working musician, even when the group got formed, but to my everlasting pleasure, from the Dunoon show onwards, that's when the band became a real pleasure, and it hasn't let up. I feel so lucky. It's amazingly comfortable, considering what we go through and what we've gone through. I think it's down to people being so gentle and accommodating. And, of course, a sense of humor. We've been laughing since we started." Quickly realizing how much this makes him sound like a rose-tinted octogenarian celebrating his golden wedding anniversary, he adds with mock nostalgia, "*Laugh?* Oh, we've laughed 'til we've cried . . ."

It was one of those late summer nights, warm and cool, the city streets stretching out contentedly like a cat on the hearth. The curious boy took a

walk through the park, past the joggers, the dog walkers, the bowlie kids ly-
ing in the dawning shadows, the gentle evening breezes cooling their tans
and blisters. He let his feet take him unconsciously through the paths he'd
walked so many times before, a new song floating serenely around his head.
It was a song about a girl, of course, a curious girl at that, a friend for Lazy
Jane and Mary Jo, for Lisa, Chelsea, Jonathan and David, for Judy and her
dream of horses. For Belle and the boy Sebastian.

But just as he was deciding upon the fate of the girl in the song, an idea
suddenly flashed across his brain, interrupting him with an urgency so great
it nearly sent him reeling. It was a great idea, he thought, so great in fact
that he found himself grinning like a loon all the way down Byres Road
(people round here were used to his curious ways, so no one really paid him
much attention). Oh yeah, this was a good one. This was going to work like
a dream. He couldn't wait to see the group and tell them all about it.

He'd forgotten all about the girl in the song by the time he got home, of
course. But that didn't matter. There would be other girls.

And with a final prayer for the night and day ahead, the curious boy set-
tled down to dream.

OFFICIAL RELEASES

ALBUMS

Tigermilk

U.K. release date: original vinyl LP release by Electric Honey Records on 06/06/96. Limited to 1,000 copies. Remastered and rereleased on CD by Jeepster Recordings on 06/12/99. Highest U.K. chart position: 13 (reissue). Catalogue numbers: original—EHRLP005/rerelease—CD—JPRCD007/LP—JPRLP007/cassette—JP RMC007.

The State I Am In
Expectations
She's Losing It
You're Just a Baby
Electronic Renaissance
I Could Be Dreaming
We Rule the School
My Wandering Days Are Over
I Don't Love Anyone
We Rule the School

Sleeve notes:
Sebastian met Isabelle outside the Hillhead Underground Station, in Glasgow. Belle harassed Sebastian, but it was lucky for him that she did. She was very nice and funny, and sang very sweetly. Sebastian was not to know this, however. Sebastian was melancholy.

He had placed an advert in the local supermarket. He was looking for musicians. Belle saw him do it. That's why she wanted to meet him. She marched straight up to him unannounced and said, "Hey you!" She asked him to teach her to play the guitar. Sebastian doubted he could teach her anything, but he admired her energy, so he said "Yes."

It was strange. Sebastian had just decided to become a one-man band. It is always when you least expect it that something happens. Sebastian had befriended a fox because he didn't expect to have any new friends for a while. He still loved the fox, although he had a new distraction. Suddenly he was writing many new songs. Sebastian wrote all of his best songs in 1995. In fact, most of his best songs have the words "Nineteen Ninety-five" in them. It bothered him a little. What will happen in 1996?

They worked on the songs in Belle's house. Belle lived with her parents, and they were rich enough to have a piano. It was in a room by itself at the back of the house, overlooking the garden. This was where Belle taught Sebastian to put on mascara. If Belle's mum had known this, she would not have been happy. She was paying for the guitar lessons. The lessons gave Sebastian's life some structure. He went to the barber's to get a haircut.

Belle and Sebastian are not snogging. Sometimes they hold hands, but that is only a display of public solidarity. Sebastian thinks Belle "kicks with the other foot." Sebastian is wrong, but then Sebastian can never see further than the next tragic ballad. It is lucky that Belle has a popular taste in music. She is the cheese to his dill pickle.

Belle and Sebastian do not care much for material goods. But then neither Belle nor Sebastian has ever had to worry about where the next meal is coming from. Belle's most recent song is called "Rag Day." Sebastian's is called "The Fox in the Snow." They once stayed in their favorite café for three solid days to recruit a band. Have you ever seen *The Magnificent Seven*? It was like that, only more tedious. They gained a lot of weight, and made a few enemies of waitresses.

Belle is sitting highers in college. She didn't listen the first time round. Sebastian is older than he looks. He is odder than he looks too. But he has a good heart. And he looks out for Belle, although she doesn't need it. If he didn't play music, he would be a bus driver or be unemployed. Probably unemployed. Belle could do anything. Good looks will always open doors for a girl.

* Stuart later wished he had simply called the album Belle and Sebastian. *He was also responsible for the sketch on the back cover. Cover stars are Joanne Kenney and Tigger.*

If You're Feeling Sinister

U.K. release date: 12/18/96. Didn't chart. Catalogue numbers: CD—JPRCD001/LP—JPRLP001/Cassette—JPRMC001.

The Stars of Track and Field
Seeing Other People
Me and the Major
Like Dylan in the Movies
The Fox in the Snow
Get Me Away from Here, I'm Dying
If You're Feeling Sinister
Mayfly

The Boy Done Wrong Again
Judy and the Dream of Horses

Sleeve notes:

Work is the curse of Stevie Thomas Jackson and Christopher Thomas Geddes. Stuart David, visionary and poet, cursed it before trying it, and would only lift a finger to pick his nose or write a book. *The Idle Thoughts of a Daydreamer,* Volumes 1 to 10. Ten in ten years. Like Felt records flowing freely from an uncluttered mind.

Before his idea occurred to him, Stuart David fished the Leven for seven years. Before he thought about drums, Richard practiced snooker day and night for seven years. Stevie Jackson, however, was already absorbed with rock 'n' roll. He was listening to The Beatles and was taking a beating for it before most of us had reached puberty.

Happy to have found the tool of his trade, he played the guitar where he could and worked so that he could play. He serenaded diners, then washed up after them. Stevie was a rock myth in his own post code. He changed his middle name to "Reverb" at an early age. He played his Telecaster, and the veins on his arms would stick out like a Rock Family Tree.

Belle and Sebastian were the product of botched capitalism. It would be nice to say they were the children of socialism, but it would be a fib. They rolled together as loose change is bound to. Change in the pocket of some fat cat civil servant. Who thought up Youth Training to make his boss look good. Who slept with a prostitute for credibility. We take our hats off to them all.

Chain ganged by employment training, Stevie sang Negro Spirituals as he built footbridges over the Dunbartonshire marshes. Stuart David heard his sweet voice coming over the reeds as he was fishing. Richard heard his voice as he was trying to get a position on the black. When they heard Stevie sing, they laid down their rod and staff and were comforted.

Meanwhile, Chris worked in a canteen serving coffee and food. He took whatever work the agency gave him. He liked where he was working just then, because the dishwashing machine was the best he had ever used.

The canteen was in a building that broadcast radio programs to the whole nation. The feeling amongst staff was that radio was the medium of the future. That didn't mean much to Chris. All he knew was that as long as they used and maintained a Hobart Elite, they must be doing something right.

But then Chris made it on the radio. I was thinking—Ah, wee Chris. The casuals tried to do you in when you were at school, but they're all listening now. They're sitting round with their bairns and they're sweeping up in the Burger King. And they'll be thinking, "Jesus! That's Chris Geddes from Dalry!" And Chris is sitting there, cool as a cat behind a Steinway Grand on national radio. Still Monday morning and it's back to the sink for you, boy.

Isobel's thinking of giving up her college. But Isobel, who's going to support us when our dreams crash against the rocks? We're looking to you. And Sarah. Your art degrees may not be worth the paper they're written on, but you could always temp for a while. Or teach . . .

I was on trial for the corporation, driving buses in the town. I think they were sad to lose me. I had a way with the customers. A great rapport! They thought I was scum, I drove past their stop. They gave me abuse, I gave them shaves. But it was hard to smile. The crossword was my only relief. Abuse was from punters and bosses. I was glad to get back on the dole. At least you know where you are. Rock bottom. I'll wait a while, then go back on employment training. Train to be a black-smith or window-dresser. Then go back on the buses.

* *Belle and Sebastian's first album for Jeepster Recordings and the first to feature Sarah Martin. Stuart toyed with calling the album either* Falling Sentry Blades *or—yes—* Cock Fun. *Cover star is Ciara MacLaverty.*

The Boy with the Arab Strap
U.K. release date: 09/07/98. Highest U.K. chart position: 12. Catalogue numbers: CD—JPRCD003/LP—JPRLP003/Cassette—JPRMC003.

It Could Have Been a Brilliant Career
Sleep the Clock Around
Is It Wicked Not to Care?
Ease Your Feet in the Sea
A Summer Wasting
Seymour Stein
A Space Boy Dream
Dirty Dream Number Two
The Boy with the Arab Strap
Chickfactor
Simple Things
The Rollercoaster Ride

* *Neil Robertson played bass on "A Space Boy Dream." The string section on "A Space Boy Dream" and "Dirty Dream Number Two" is Gail Anderson, Claire Campbell, Eilidh Campbell, Euan Forrester, David D. Mackay and Sarah Wilson. The bagpiper on "Sleep the Clock Around" is Ian MacKay. This was the first album to feature Mick Cooke as a full-time member. Cover star is Chris Geddes.*

Fold Your Hands Child, You Walk Like a Peasant

U.K. release date: 06/06/00. Highest U.K. chart position: 10. Highest U.S. chart position: 80. Catalogue numbers: CD—JPRCD010/LP—JPRLP010/MD—JPRMD010.

I Fought in a War
The Model
Beyond the Sunrise
Waiting for the Moon to Rise
Don't Leave the Light On, Baby
The Wrong Girl
The Chalet Lines
Nice Day for a Sulk
Women's Realm
Family Tree
There's Too Much Love

Sleeve notes:

Do you want to know what a hipster in Glasgow talks about?

The hipsters in Glasgow stay up until all hours discussing biblical matters. That is how they greet the dawn in spring. But they still get up four hours later to see how their private world is affected by commerce and necessity.

The hipsters in Hillhead stay up to talk about Jesus, and how he felt about hipsters. All conjecture, you must understand, because the straights that wrote the Bible pretty much passed over it.

But Jesus thought about them because he thought about all things. If all he said and did was written, then there would be no volume large enough to contain all the detail.

So they ponder in dialect. And the dawn creeps up on them, reminding them to go to sleep for a few hours. Hopefully, the feeling they had on shutting their eyes is the feeling that will persist until nine. For it is then that their youthful ideals will be put to the test. When they come up against the commercial world and the awakening activity of everyday life.

The hipsters will stay up to talk about things that concern them. When they wake up, they will weave their path through people shopping, signing on, visiting hospitals, and cutting back grass. Though really it is not fair to call them hipsters, because that is still a slur.

With fondness, I think about the hipsters beavering away in coolness. Because I'm looking upon a framed picture of where they live. It's one of my favorite pictures, and the change of season doesn't change the overall effect too much. The leaves are not on the trees, but the color of the sandstone is pretty enough. It seems gray and quiet in the picture, but I know for a fact there are a thousand Saturday meals being made and a thousand Saturday plans being hatched to drink and be senseless. Till the gentle tug of the working week brings sense to bear.

The first album to feature an extended string section throughout, including Greg Lawson (violin), Cheryl Crockett (violin), Alistair Savage (violin), Elin Edwards (violin), Liza Webb (violin), Murray Ferguson (violin), Clare McKeown (violin), Lorna Leitch (violin), Dervilagh Cooper (violin), Helen McSherry (cello), and Peter Nicholson (cello). These musicians joined the band for their 2001 live shows, and continue to accompany them in varying forms to this day. Also featured are Gary Grochla (double bass), with Paul Fox (flute), Ronan Breslin (trombone), and Jenny Divers (saxophone), plus Frances MacDonald from BMX Bandits, Jonny Quinn from Snow Patrol, and Mick's brother Alistair Cooke on percussion. Cover stars are Gyda and Kristin Valtysdottir from the Icleandic band Mum.

Storytelling

U.K. release date: 06/03/02. Highest U.K. chart position: 26. Highest U.S. chart position: 150. Catalogue numbers: CD—JPRCD014/LP—JPRLP014.

Fiction
Freak
Conan, Early Letterman
Fuck This Shit
Night Walk
Jersey's Where It's At
Black and White Unite
Consuelo
Toby
Storytelling
Class Rank
I Don't Want to Play Football
Consuelo Leaving
Wandering Alone
Mandingo Cliche
Fiction Reprise
Big John Shaft

Sleeve notes:
This record features music written for the Todd Solondz movie *Storytelling*. As some of the group admired Mr. Solondz's work in the past, when he expressed the desire

for us to write some music for his new film we immediately made our way to New York City armed with high hopes, dreams of artistic endeavor, and a copy of the *Pat Garrett & Billy the Kid* soundtrack.

However, once ensconced in the process of film scoring not only our fate but our true nature seemed to emerge. Soon we were behaving like veteran hacks composing seventies style sitcom jingles on demand and churning out songs with lyrics referring to the action of the plot, a bit like the Colonel's staff songwriters in the Sixties who hacked out all those appalling Elvis Presley soundtracks (although to be fair every one of those contained a classic e.g. "Rock a Hula Baby" on *Blue Hawaii* but this is hardly the place for a critique of the King).

So there we were, yoked up to the TV monitor with them big American Movie people cracking the whip. But to be honest this was no bad thing and working within the framework of a collaborative endeavor is incredibly satisfying even if the pleasure is sometimes garnished with the occasional disappointment e.g. the movie consisted of two halves and originally we were commissioned to write the second half of the movie, then at some point we were asked to do the whole thing (whoopee) but then later on still we found ourselves back to just the second half. Oh well, too many tunes and not enough celluloid time. Fair enough in my opinion; the Director has got to get his vision down after all. Anyway, as a result, not everything got used.

"Fiction" and its variations including "Freak" were written for the first half of the movie and are included in extended form for your listening pleasure. We had three goes at writing a song for the finishing credits, each one focusing on a different character in the film. These were "Wandering Alone," which refers to aspects of Consuelo's imagined family history, "Big John Shaft," which was written as an ode to Todd himself (guess which one he picked?).

"Black and White Unite" is not so much representative of the movie but more that bittersweet, slightly decaying summer feeling in the air when we were putting this record together (the tune however is based on the leftover theme from the film). "I Don't Want to Play Football" comes from the second half although the scene was deleted in the final cut. All the other tunes are featured in some form and are adapted here for the LP format.

And that's that. The film has been released, the reviews have been written, and Todd has moved on to pastures new. This record contains parts and fragments of the story he came to tell but if there is a story on this record, it should be regarded primarily as our own. I suppose it's time for the group to be moving on also, although in leaving I have to be honest in saying that in my view *Storytelling* is a great film and that this is a cracking record, maybe the best one we've made in a while but look . . . it's just my opinion and . . . what do I know?

Stevie, FEB 2002

In February 2001, we flew to New York to record some music for the Todd Solondz film *Storytelling*. We had already recorded some ideas in Glasgow before we went across. Todd kept saying, "I love it all, but it's not right for the movie." We just didn't know what was right for the movie.

Figuring out what is right can be a long, but enjoyable, process. Todd told us that the music he wanted to link some scenes should be the audio representation of a housewife stroking her favorite soap flakes box.

What ended up being right for the movie amounted to six minutes of music. What wasn't right we developed, and all of it is on this LP.

Mick, DEC 2001

* Recorded at Water Music, New Jersey, and Magic Studios, New York. Finished off at Ca Va Studios, Glasgow. Aside from the string section, Storytelling *also features Roy Hunter (double bass), Andrea Kuypers (flute), Kenneth Broom (saxophone), and Catriona MacKay (harp). Cover stars are Sarah and Liz Liew and the feet of Mark Jones.*

Dear Catastrophe Waitress

U.K. release date: 10/06/2003. Highest U.K. chart position: 21. Highest U.S. chart position: 84. Catalogue numbers: CD—RTRADECD080/LP—RTRADELP080.

Step into My Office, Baby
Dear Catastrophe Waitress
If She Wants Me
Piazza, New York Catcher
Asleep on a Sunbeam
I'm a Cuckoo
You Don't Send Me
Wrapped Up in Books
Lord Anthony
If You Find Yourself Caught in Love
Roy Walker
Stay Loose

Sleeve notes:

THE WAY OF THE EGG

A fine day in Glasgow. Feels like it's all kicking off. I don't think I've ever been so busy with band stuff, but then maybe I'm just kidding myself. The stuff that I'm busy with is stuff that I just make up and then feel a compulsion to do. My overall project just now is akin to Chicken Licken in the nursery story. You remember

Chicken Licken? He got a fright or had a small accident or something, and he decided the sky was going to fall on his head, so he went off to find the king. He was a major panic merchant. He alerted the whole countryside to his lunatic raving. But everyone he met was as daft as he was. And, crucially, they all had nutty rhyming couplet names like Licken did, only according to their species. So we had Henny Penny, Cocky Locky, Turkey Lurkey, Goosey Loosey, etc. And each one of them as mad as the little Chicken fellow. They went for his story in a big way, and dropped everything to join the lunatic band.

Ok, my analogy has gone a little far. Now that I got into the story of Chicken Licken I realize that. But there's a couple of things about the Chicken I like. I like the fact that he's trying to keep the momentum up. He's trying to keep the party going. You don't see his friends complaining much, do you? Fact is, it's probably the most excitement they've seen around the farmyard for quite some time. They're totally into it. They're getting a day trip out of it and it's costing them nothing.

I've been taking pictures and knocking about on my bike bumping into one person after the next and drinking tea and trying to get things going. Feeling a little like Chicken Licken, specifically. But one has to be careful. In the end the chicken gets eaten by a fox. I wonder if I'll reach a foxy end?

Actually, I don't care because I've been having a lot of fun. Glaswegians are nuts to want to leave this town at this time of year, when the city is reaching its most sublime point, where the sandstone and vegetation combine to create one big indie playground. That's how I found myself describing it to a friend the other night. She admitted to being "geeky" about the town as well. I don't know why I used "indie" as an adjective here, but then as I mentioned elsewhere, there are moves to keep changing the meaning of that word until it either doesn't mean anything or it means all things to all people!

And that reminds me, one of the "lunatic band" I bumped into during photographic adventures last week was Jason from V-Twin. Actually I bumped into him a couple of times, once in the caff with V-Twin Donald and Michael, and once when he was walking Fawcett, admittedly the cutest little indie raver of the lot. (Fawcett is a West Highland terrier.) We got talking about our favorite words. I can't remember the context, but Jason's was "obsequious" or "meticulous" or one of those "ouses." (Shit, sorry Jason, I can't remember which one exactly.) Whatever, you can bet the conversation did nothing to contribute to the GNP of the Glasgow area. There was nothing economy bolstering about that hour and a half. We were just shooting the breeze over expensive coffees just like we'd been doing since '93 when I first knew Jason. I don't see him around so much anymore since he switched cafés.

There is a boring stereotype going around that says that guys don't talk about stuff. If you get the right combination of people though, you can have a good old chat. It just takes a couple in a group to get it going. And I like Jason because he likes to pull the barriers down anytime anywhere. It can be nine fifteen in the morning at a rainy bus stop and he will be grinning from under his parka hood, talking about girl trouble, band trouble, dog trouble!

Justin Currie from Del Amitri was knocking about the caff. Different era from us lot. It's funny that we still sit about chattering about people like kids. I should grow up a little. I can't imagine having a coffee with Justin Currie. Not in this present situation. Well I could, of course. But I'd have to behave myself a little and not talk rubbish. I put him in with the Lloyd Cole brigade, with Edwyn, Horne, Bluebell, Kirk. It's a different generation! It'd take being drunk at a wedding to really break the ice.

Anyway, Jason said a funny thing. "Del Amitri are really underrated. They really had their moments. 'Always the Last to Know.' It's a great song." Then he proceeded to quote the lyric, like John Gielgud on Radio 4 or something. What was equally disturbing is that Donald was quietly but steadfastly backing him up. I just don't know where I stand! I had "Sense Sickness" which was like early Orange Juice. That's about it. What was funny was that Jason said "I mean, you've got to hand it to him, he's a big fucking handsome dude! If I was a girl, I'd bang him!" Ha ha!

My favorite word . . . actually I have two just now, but one of them would give away my present unhealthy obsession. My favorite word has a Gielgud connection. (Two in one diary!) He used to read the Bible on Radio 4. I mean, right from the start. They had him on for ten minutes every day reading from Genesis onwards. I like the word "creepeth." It's one that you would have trouble fitting into everyday conversation. But he just used to roll the "r," and it was good. Back in Genesis, everything and everyone was always creepething around when everything was dark and lush and overhanging, and the snakes talked and you strucketh your brother for the smallest of reasons, and the smallest of smotes would almost always kill! I'll try and fit that word into the next few diaries. And because you've read this you will be in the know. Everyone else will probably think I've just lost my head for a minute.

Like I was meant to say something at the John Peel Christmas Party thing that was meant to be a secret signal to my friend Marisa. She gave me a list of words that I had to use so she would know I was signaling her. But I didn't manage it. I can't remember the words right now but I remember we did have quite a funny time devising them. It would have been just too unlikely. I would have been wheeled away!

It's absolutely pouring down outside. "Here comes the juice!" the punters cry. Typical Glasgow Fair Monday. It always rains.

So, like I was saying, my major thing in the last few days was taking pictures. I had the shoot for the front cover of the LP on Friday there, and for the single, on the Tuesday before. And the whole week I was toying with the idea of buying a new camera. Now this was quite a big deal to me. I knew the advantages of having this camera, but to be honest I didn't know how to work the frigging thing, and even going into the shop to buy the thing was proving an ordeal. I mean, the first time I went into the shop the guy did everything in his power to not sell me the camera. He didn't even get it out the case! And all the time I'm standing there sweating like a pedophile in a creche! Like I was going to be found out as the non-photographer I so clearly am. What the hell would I want with a Hasselblad?

I think I went in there about four times before I actually got the thing. And each time I took a different person to chum me. It must be said, the underground artsy camera set in Glasgow rallied to the cause last week. Stand up Martin, Roxanne, Tris, and Ian at the lab. And Marisa of course, though she's in Boston.

Marisa's pretty much the perfect subject. She hands you the camera, primed and ready to shoot. Then she strips off and poses meticulously. It was she that opened my eyes to the possiblity of the medium format. Usually I would imagine profes-sionals are sniffy about lending equipment or handing over their tools. But Marisa must just be comfortable in the knowledge that she can do it either side of the lens. And she can, she's a talented girl. Sorry, I know I'm being a bit cartoonish here, but being able to pose is a definite skill, and one that I admire all the more because I can't do it. I'm lucky to be around such photogenic people.

The day I actually bought the thing I was meant to meet an acquaintance of an acquaintance, the aforementioned Tris, so he could give the camera the once over, and talk knowledgable bollocks to take the heat off me. But he stood me up! Later on, his friend Roxanne told me that his aquarium had broken, which is a hot one! I'm going to use that the next time I can't make it to something. Though I'd never be able to not giggle. It was true though, his aquarium had broken, threatening both flat and guppy. He came along to the shoot on Friday to make up for it, and for a bit of moral and technical support. As it turns out, everyone that I had spoken to the previous week turned up, so there was an embarrassing surfeit of the knowledgable and the artsy. Thank God we got some beers in. I felt a little self-conscious as I ponced about on top of a table, ordering the group around. They were very, very good.

Trouble with Glasgow at this time of year is that you never know how many lay-ers to put on when you leave the house. Now, I've had to become a layer expert over the years on account of my eskimo blood. And in Glasgow the sun can go in and the wind can blow up in minutes. And you can go from one to four layers accordingly. At least I can. Why can I already anticipate my own kids taking the piss out of me? Imagine I raise a real bruiser who has just no sympathy whatsoever? I would have nowhere to hide.

Well this particular sensitivity has even put the strain on that most tolerable of friendships, that between a boy and his best friend. Even Ciara feigned to lose pa-tience with me this one particular incident. I had gone into town, it had been a little overcast. But the sun came out and showed no sign of going back in and I felt a little ripped off that I should have to lug my jacket around all day while I did my indie errands. So I went to the post office and bought a sheet of brown paper and posted my jacket home. That was a few years ago now though, and I was less robust than you thankfully find me today.

It was a beautiful three-button jacket of my dad's that I posted. I subsequently lost that jacket, and of all the things over the years I have lost it is the one I have come to miss the most. Such a perfect item, I've never seen its like since, though I have searched. And all the more annoying that it should have been my dad's. I left it in a football changing room. It disappeared instantly. It's definitely in my Top 5 items of clothing of all time. Now even I might hesitate to list that list in this diary as that would surely put a strain on your readership. Maybe we can swap Top 5's and the stories they contain? That way I wouldn't feel so bad about talking about something which can't possibly have any interest to anyone but me. Ok, tell you what, send me your Top 5's and a few lines on each if you are so moved.

I just came back to the house to have a little lunch and there's a package here from Bob, who's making a little film that I'm helping with. He's sent me a Felt DVD called *A Declaration*. This to me is very interesting. It's almost too much to take. Lawrence looks so good, it's too much, it's like a dream. I can't believe this band ever existed. They're so perfect. Fuck the Smiths, fuck Orange Juice, Felt, FELT, FELT!! I have to stop watching. I feel like I'm going to have a heart attack today. They just take me to a different place. "I wasn't fooling when I said. All the people I like are those that are dead." The DVD's shit quality by the way, so don't go there unless you can join the dots for yourself.

Larkin, Cohen, Lawrence, and Moz. The rest of you boys can leave your quills in your tunics.

Oh, no, I'm in the park and I'm being checked out by a baldy headed guy. I must be in the pickup zone. Serves me right for saying how beautiful Lawrence is. C'mon, you know what I meant. I'm a bit nervous actually. What if he tries to wrench the laptop from me? Why do I never get propositioned by women? I suppose it's a law of nature. It would make life too easy, huh? Like, what is the point of feedback? Why can't we just make everything louder without the squeals? Like, what is the point of depth of field? Why can't the lens just capture everything flat, no matter how dark it is? But then we wouldn't strive. Digital has made a lot of things easy, but then without having to strive, the art has become worse. Apart from the art that is digital to the core. Like computer games and such. Am I wrong?

So I rambled on to the steps to Park Circus, and on the way I bump into Allen, our drum tech, and his two mates, Robin and Edgy. They are in exactly the same spot as I saw them in the last time I was in the park a few days ago. They realize this and are a bit bashful as I approach.

"You are the Three Coins in the Fountain."

They laugh. They are perched on the edge of the fountain. They had just been to the transport museum, but they were disappointed the man wouldn't let them get in the cars and blow the horns. The subject moves round to *The Two Towers*.

"I mean, what were the Two Towers anyway? In the film it makes out they were Saruman's bit and Sauron's bit. I always thought it was meant to be Minas Tirith and Minas Morgul."

I kind of agree with him. That would make the most poetic sense. There are four towers to choose from though. Orthanc, Morgul, Tirith, and Barad-Dur.

"I'm surprised Tolkien didn't give the Hobbits a tower as well."

Well they had a sort of mound.

There are twelve ways you can pick two towers from four, right? Pick one from four then one from three remaining. Three times four is twelve . . . I got to get out more. But I am out! Maybe I've got to stay in.

Allen is one of the gang I was talking about earlier. He was helping me with both the pictures. We were in the same spot last Tuesday, the bandstand, where the baldy guy was trying to pick me up. Me and Allen, and Katrina, Roxanne, Hannah, and Bob, who were all modeling. Bob was wandering about in a straw hat smoking a rollie. Allen motioned towards him, and says to me:

"Look at Bob, man. He just walks this land!"

And it's true. He just walks this land. Which reminds me, I was going to try and talk a bit about the other dudes in the group for a while, but I'm going to go and make dinner for a friend, so it will have to wait.

I may be a lousy cook, but at least I've learned the way of the egg.

Stuart,

21st July '03

* *Produced by Trevor Horn at Sarm West Studios and Sarm Hook End, England. The band eschewed their usual orchestra section on this record in favor of Gavyn Wright (leader), Perry Montague-Mason (leader of second violins), David Woodcock, Chris Tombling, Warren Zielinski, Jackie Shave, Patrick Kiernan, Boguslaw Kostecki, Julian Leaper, Kathy Shave, Benedict Cruft, Everton Nelson (violins), Peter Lale, Robert Smissen, Bruce White, Gustav Clarkson (viola), Anthony Pleeth, David Daniels, Martin Loveday (cello), Mary Scully (double bass), Helen Keen (flute), Kathleen Stevenson (flute/piccolo), Chris Cowie (oboe), Sue Bohling (cor Anglais), Mike Lovatt, Noel Langley, Derek Watkins, John Barclay (trumpet), Chris Dean, Jeremy Price, Barnaby Dickinson (tenor trombone), Richard Edwards (bass trombone), Jamie Talbot, Stan Sulzman, Philip Todd, Chris Davis, Jeff Daly, Billy Rumfitt, Julian Nicholas (tenor/bass/alto saxophone), Nigel Black, Richard Berry (French horn), Frank Ricotti (percussion). Cover stars are Shantha Roberts and the band, appearing together on an album cover for the*

first time. The album was nominated for the prestigious Mercury Music Prize in 2004, but lost out to their friends Franz Ferdinand.

SINGLES/EPs

Dog on Wheels EP

U.K. release date: 05/12/97. Highest U.K. chart position: 58. Catalogue numbers: CD—JPRCDS001/12"—JPR12001/7"—JPR7001.

> Dog on Wheels
> The State I Am In
> String Bean Jean
> Belle and Sebastian

* *The* Dog on Wheels EP *does not feature Belle and Sebastian, and is instead recordings made at Beatbox by Stuart Murdoch and Stuart David, plus Mick Cooke on "Dog on Wheels" itself. Also featured are Gerry Campbell, David Campbell, Mark McWhirter, Brian Nugent, Michael Angus, Steve Mackenzie. Not released in the U.S. until included as part of the* Lazy Line Painter Jane *collection in 2000. The cover stars are Joanne Kenney and Patch.*

Lazy Line Painter Jane EP

U.K. release date: 07/28/97. Highest U.K. chart position: 41. Catalogue numbers: CD—JPRCDS002/12"—JPR12002/7"—JPR7002.

> Lazy Line Painter Jane * *featuring Monica Queen*
> You Made Me Forget My Dreams
> Photo Jenny
> A Century of Elvis

Sleeve notes:

Lazy Line Painter Jane prayed for an inspiration that would lift her above the mundanity of midday on a Thursday. She was in a hole, sat with egg and chips, watching buses through the plate glass and easy radio of some old café. She was too bashful to pray outright in the café, so she pretended to read her fortune at the bottom of her tea cup, and she got what she wanted that way.

The inspiration came along quite soon. It was lucky for her. It had seemed impossible, for her to feel OK, considering the trouble she was in. It seemed impossible, considering the gloominess of that lunchtime.

Jane had never managed to build Thursday into the weekend like some other people did. She didn't look forward to the weekend anyway. The only good thing about the weekend was that it ushered in the following week. She was a slave to the working week. But she was unemployed.

She was doubtful whether she even deserved her Thursday gift. She had done a lot of swearing and shouting during her period. She almost felt guilty to take up the baton and run. But run she did. Straight to the cathedral graveyard. She took her idea straight through the cathedral graves and out, over the wall at the other end. She found herself in the East End of the city.

She took the inspiration and ran. It filled her like a playground balloon. Now she wasn't treading on any toes. Jane's agenda was clear. She just felt like running. To forget her joblessness and her hopelessness. Stripped of her present care, her skin was translucent, and she traveled fast and light over grass and stone precincts. She ran past lines of traffic into quiet streets where her breath and fast steps were the only sound she could hear. Stripped of her present care. And her guilt at being lazy.

Jane pretended she was making indie-rock videos as she tore through the East End. She thought herself quite magnificent, and caused only two minor disturbances as she went. She stopped running when she reached the river.

That was lovely. Reaching the river. A sudden wilderness of wasteland and trees. She may have been a bit worried if it wasn't for the oxygen pumping in her head, acting like a drug. There was a path, dancing with industrial mayflys, constructed with an air of municipal grants. She followed it, ducking under flyovers, flying over travelers' caravans. She ran past long curves of ash and alder. She ran until she flopped down in a bus shelter. The rain came on. She had run out of rock video fodder.

She waited in the bus shelter for a while. She had reached the main street of a town that was not part of the city at all. She had reached the provinces, and as such, the youth of the town flirted and taunted with an unaffected provincial air. Casuals drank QC. They put on a show for her, but they never challenged her directly. She was grateful they didn't pick on her strangeness. Her inspiration had flagged, and she didn't know how she could handle them by herself.

They went away, to be replaced by the town's thinking girl's talent. He smoked a regal cigarette, and paced around a little. Jane couldn't decide if he was waiting for a bus, or if he had just come out because the rain had stopped. But she liked the sound his segs made on the wet pavement. And she admired him for his quiff. It was the biggest quiff that small town beatings would allow for. He sat down in the shelter. He obliged her by staring at her boots, and rubbing his forehead feverishly. He sat for the length of his cigarette and then went off, leaving Painter Jane alone.

She drank up the peace because she knew that she would be back in her house by fall of night. In the city, a dozen things would be vying for her attention simultaneously. She thought it was around six, but in fact it was nearer nine. She pulled her knees close to her chest. Her jogging bottoms smelled of pollen. She waited for the bus to take her back to the city. As she waited, she thought about how she had got her name, and what she was going to do about it.

* All sleeve notes, unless otherwise specified, are written by Stuart Murdoch.

3 ... 6 ... 9 ... Seconds of Light EP

U.K. release date: 10/13/97. Highest U.K. chart position: 32, Catalogue numbers: CD—JPRCDS003/12"—JPR12003/7"—JPR7003.

A Century of Fakers
Le Pastie de la Bourgeoisie
Beautiful
Put the Book Back on the Shelf
Songs for Children * *bonus track*

Sleeve notes:

It was a day like today, really warm, when everybody is out of doors, happy to be lying around. Jim had something going. A little project that involved making posters for concerts that would never happen, and record sleeves for records that never existed. He had got up at around six A.M. Sprung out of bed as if the thought of sleep scared him. The sun was coming directly against the wall just beside his bed. There was a picture of Echo and the Bunnymen. It was very quiet apart from that.

He didn't wonder what would happen today. He was going to make things happen. He felt like his enthusiasm would rip his heart out of his chest. He worked himself up into a state of excitement. The possibilities of the day were endless. He was nineteen and limber, and the sun sparkled through his tea as it splashed into the cup.

He lined up his various papers and packed them into his bag. He sat at his desk at the window and arrayed his athletes' breakfast in front of him. He listened to Radio Four for a bit, and then he set to work with his blunted pencil and rub down transfers. He kept what he was trying to say in a straight line by using the edge forged Matriculation Card. As far as the University authorities knew, his name was Arthur Cooke.

Pretty soon, with all pressing matters blissfully set aside, he fell into a reverie the type of which could go on all day if you let it. He gladly let it because it echoed a dream he had once had, and dreams were as close as he ever got to matters spiritual. He had known a girl once who had a tent. They talked about going camping into the country one summer. He was fond of the girl and he was fond of her friend both. Her friend was nice and though studied architecture in another city was around often enough to be in on their plan. When they were around Jim often looked straight at his boots and wondered at the gifts the girls had for their various brainy pursuits. He was a bit ashamed. He was older than them, but was a bit of a flop in the brain department. His reverie involved the tent, the dusk, the smell of hot trainers, and not much else. He never managed to the country with them.

Jim woke up again, his plan for the day lying in tatters, he thought. It was a quarter past twelve. He had fallen asleep in a pool of sunlight and he had been woken by a ring at his neighbor's door. He was drowsy and his head full of false literature of dreams and failed schedules. He dressed with not much care. When he flicked on the radio a song was playing that he found unexpected pleasure in. This was very, very lucky. His bag was packed for a quick getaway, which was lucky too. So out and over the hill to the busy arcade where he did his photocopying. He was lucky on a day like today that he lived in an area of schools, tenants, and flowering cherries. In the winter it was dour, but his one room flat was OK as long as he had outside to step into. He stepped along the street and noticed the heat off the pavement through his black plimsoll boots. He wondered, if he painted them with hot tire rubber if they would last him till his housing check came through.

Jim came to the steps of the arcade. It was cooler for a second or two, but the hotness was replaced by the dry heat of photocopy fans. He waited in the queue of students and small business women, and he felt endless sympathy for the men that worked the machines.

Photocopying was all the rage that year so there was quite a queue of young trendies and h-------s. A man with the forward slanting mother of all pudding bowl haircuts struggled to see what he was doing. His machine was throwing out endless prints of psychedelic swirls. Chatty undergraduate girls warmed to the new craze. Jim wished slightly that he could have beaten the rush. But at least he recognized another boy at the copy shop. He watched in a trance as the boy's illustration of a cat banging a drum got bigger and bigger.

Soon it was his turn to get on a machine. He was there to make a picture for his room. He had a tiny photograph that he kept in a key-ring. He had found it in an art college when he was working as a cleaner. It was only a test for a real photograph, he thought. He didn't think they would miss it.

It was a picture of a boy and a girl on a beach. Jim took the picture and put it in the machine. He booted the enlarge up to as far as it would go. He pressed print and the light flashed across the picture. He wondered if it would come out at all but it looked pretty good, about the size of a bank card. He did the same thing twice over. He was pretty excited. The picture was terrific, burnt out and grainy, he thought it didn't look like real people at all. He felt much better now. He started to look around the little copy shop.

He noticed a paper lying underneath one of the machines. He stooped down to pick it up. It had stuff written on it. He picked it up and started to read.

Claire and I decided to devise a music workshop for a group of 20 children around the age of five. It could be carried out in a school or in a community center. Children of this age are still very uninhibited and energetic, which potentially provides teachers or workshop leaders with a vast and unlimited musical scope. The idea of our workshop is to introduce some very simple movements (such as hand-clapping and marching) that will effectively relax and improve the children's overall coordination and concentration. Alongside rhythm, melody, and movement, we would also like to draw the children's attention to musical dynamics and tempo. To demonstrate, we will get the children to perform their warm-up and song at varying speeds and volumes. The workshop will finish with a performance of the song.

To introduce the workshop we will begin with a warm-up, lasting about seven minutes. The children should be instructed to form a spacious circle. We will then demonstrate marching and clapping along to a basic 4/4 rhythm. This game can be a lot of fun. Whilst maintaining the clapping and marching along to a beat, individuals take it in turn to create any sound, at any pitch, of any length, with any words. The only restriction to the game being that they can only make their sound when it is their turn, and it must always be the same. They have to remember their own personal sound.

The report reminded Jim of the time when he was an administrator of the sick and young. He wanted to think about that for a while. He took his thoughts to the café nearby.

It was busy with people eating and talking in booths. He got some coffee and watched a man and a girl in the next booth. He thought they had been there for quite a while. There was books and paper scattered on the table, along with debris from cup after cup of coffee. They weren't aware of him watching. They weren't aware of anything as the girl was writing, while the boy read a magazine.

At another table, a girl stared solemnly into her cup. Jim wished he could've taken her picture. But then he was afraid that he might steal the moment away from her. . . .

* *Cover stars are Stuart Murdoch and Victoria Morton. Picture taken on a timer on a beach near Ayr, Scotland. After Joanne Kenney, Martin is the second of Stuart Murdoch's girlfriends to appear on a Belle and Sebastian cover.*

This Is Just a Modern Rock Song EP

U.K. release date: 12/07/98. Highest U.K. chart position: ineligible. Catalogue numbers: CD—JPRCDS009/12"—JPR12009.

This Is Just a Modern Rock Song
I Know Where the Summer Goes
The Gate
Slow Graffiti

* This Is Just a Modern Rock Song *contravened the CIN's new rules about how many songs could appear on a single and EP, and was therefore ineligible for the charts. "Slow Graffiti" also appeared on the soundtrack to the Irvine Welsh movie adaptation* The Acid House. *Additional musicians on "Slow Graffiti" are Ronin Breslin (trombone), Louise Bennie (saxophone), and Judi Mitchell (oboe). Laura Molloy features on percussion on the title track. Molloy's artwork would later adorn the sleeve of* Fold Your Hands Child, You Walk Like a Peasant. *Cover star is Alan Horne, founder of Postcard Records.*

Legal Man

U.K. release date: 05/22/2000. Highest U.K. chart position: 15. Catalogue numbers: CD—JPRCDS018/12"—JPR12018/7"—JPR7018.

Legal Man
Judy Is a Dick Slap * *instrumental*
Winter Wooskie

Press release:
A few words about our next release—"Legal Man." Something of an innovation for the group, this is an ensemble piece written by us one day while trying out an Electric Sitar. There's nothing very profound about the song I have to say, it's just a love story about a boy and a girl and the boy happens to be a member of the legal profession.

"Judy Is a Dick Slap" is our first instrumental to be released. Hard to know what to say about this, except I love it and play it all the time.

"Winter Wooskie" was assembled from a demo Stuart David cut in the studio. The rest of the group lovingly brought the song to life in true "Free As a Bird" fashion, dubbing on our parts while using the latest technology to enhance the original recording to an aesthetic conclusion we feel he would have been proud of.

And that's it, except to say that this record has been designed for the Pop Singles Market and every care has been taken at the mastering stage to ensure it sounds good on the radio.

Another innovation! No, not at all. With the exception of "This Is Just a Modern Rock Song" all our EPs have been designed for the Pop Charts, have all been chart eligible, and indeed have all charted, as high as 32 on one occasion! I read in a magazine this morning that this record is our first chart-eligible single and our first attempt at mainstream success. Nonsense. If this is an attempt at mainstream chart success, then it is no more so than any of our other releases. All our EPs were considered by us to have hit song potential and were released in the hope that they would be play-listed and become hits. Should anyone be surprised! Why ask questions!

THIS IS THE PROFESSION WE HAVE CHOSEN. We are supposed to be a Pop Group after all.

Anyway I hope you like the record.

Love, Stevie.

"Legal Man" features Johnny Quinn from Snow Patrol on congas and Rozanne Suarez on additional vocals. A different version of "Judy Is a Dick Slap" appeared on the twelve-inch. Cover stars are Suarez, Adrienne Payne, Isobel Campbell, and Stevie Jackson. Back cover stars are Katrina House and, in the picture frame, Robert White, the band's real-life legal man.

Belle and Sebastian Sing Jonathan David EP

U.K. release date: 06/18/01. Highest U.K. chart position: 31. Catalogue numbers: CD—JPRCDS022/12"—JPR12022/7"—JPR7022.

Jonathan David
Take Your Carriage Clock and Shove It
The Loneliness of a Middle Distance Runner

Sleeve notes:

The deal with the sleeve, because you're probably scratching your head, is of course a play on the David and Goliath story. There they are on the back cover slogging it out. Here they are sitting down to a nice cup of tea in between shots.

The front cover shows what happens after David beats Goliath. Everybody loves him. He becomes King, and because he's such a hotshot, he gets all the girls. The front cover also depicts his best pal. Jonathan and David swore brotherly allegiance to each other at an early age, pledging their love. But Jonathan never really moved on like David did. Never seemed to be able to get past his loyalty to his mate.

For further reading check out 1 Samuel 17 in the Old Testament.

Additional musicians on "Take Your Carriage Clock and Shove It" are Murray Ferguson (violin), Willie Gamble (pedal steel), Gary Grochla (double bass), and Mary Ward (viola). Cover stars are Bobby Kildea, Mick Cooke, and his girlfriend Gill Dodds. Back cover stars are Mick and Roy Hunter.

I'm Waking Up to Us EP

U.K. release date: 11/26/01. Highest U.K. chart position: 39. Catalogue numbers: CD—JPRCDS023/12"—JPR12023/7"—JPR7023.

I'm Waking Up to Us * *originally known as* The Season Has Arrived
I Love My Car
Marx and Engels

* *With this release Belle and Sebastian worked with an outside producer for the first time in the shape of Mike Hurst, whose credits include Petula Clark's "Downtown" among many others. Additional musicians on "I'm Waking Up to Us" are Cheryl Crockett, Murray Fergusson, Dervilagh Cooper, Elin Edwards, Clare McKeown, Dougie Lawrence, Liza Webb, Carole Howat, Fiona Steven, Gill Reecey, and Isla Robertson (violins), Joel Hunter, George Cuthbertson, and Jacqui Penfold (violas), Alison Geen (bassoon), Rona Pollard (oboe), Andrea Kuypers (flute), and, on acoustic guitars, John Hogarty and Francis MacDonald of the BMX Bandits, and Bobby Kildea making his first contribution to the group. He would become a fulltime member shortly after this recording session. The band were joined by Dixieland jazz combo The Uptown Shufflers for "I Love My Car," a tribute to Stuart's car, Max, which features in the artwork alongside Sarah, Richard, Isobel, and a whole host of cute pooches.*

Step Into My Office, Baby
U.K. release date: 11/17/03. Highest U.K. chart position: 32. Catalogue numbers: CD—RTRADESCD128/12"—RTRADES128/DVD—RTRADEDV128.

Step into My Office, Baby
Love on the March
Desperation Made a Fool of Me

* *Additional backing vocals on "Step Into My Office, Baby" by Trevor Horn and, on "Love on the March," from Rozanne Suarez. This was the first Rough Trade release from Belle and Sebastian and their first to be released concurrently on DVD. Cover stars are Bobby Kildea, Roxanne Clifford, and Hannah Robinson.*

I'm a Cuckoo
U.K. release date: 02/16/04. Highest U.K. chart position: 14. Catalogue numbers: CD—RTRADESCD157/12"—RTRADES157/DVD—RTRADEDV157.

I'm a Cuckoo * *single edit*
Stop, Look and Listen
I'm a Cuckoo * *remixed by The Avalanches*
(I Believe in) Travellin' Light

* *"(I Believe in) Travellin' Light" was produced by Trevor Horn for* Dear Catastrophe Waitress *but eventually left off the album. Cover star is Shantha Roberts. Mick and Stevie are pictured in the inside sleeve, live at the Usher Hall, Edinburgh.*

Books EP

U.K. release date: 06/21/04. Highest U.K. chart position: 20. Catalogue numbers: CD—RTRADESCD180/12"—RTRADES180/DVD—RTRADEDV180.

> Your Cover's Blown
> Wrapped Up in Books
> Your Secrets
> Cover (Version) * *remixed by Chris*

* *Vrnda Daktor supplies the spoken word passage at the beginning of "Your Cover's Blown." Cover star is Alexandra Klobouk.*

UNRELEASED SONGS

Rhoda *performed live a few times in the early days.*

Tigermilk * *a Velvets-esque instrumental performed on a few of their 1998 dates. The song ends with a clang of white noise and an ear-shredding scream from Neil, who would perform his part from the mixing desk.*

Landslide * *an Isobel song performed live at the Bowlie Weekender by Isobel and The Maisonettes. It was planned as a single—a duet with '60s soul singer Evie Sands—but remains unreleased. The band performed the song with Sands when she played at Hyndland Parish Church hall in early 1999.*

Paper Boats * *written by Stuart David and performed live on a few of the 1998 dates and at the Bowlie Weekender.*

Shoot the Sexual Athlete * *rather atypical post-punk semi-spoken-word experiment recorded for the band's 2001 John Peel session on Radio One, but never officially released.*

Magic of a Kind Word * *Stuart has claimed that this catchy hip-shaking '60s-style tune is about John Phillips from The Mamas and the Papas. Peformed live throughout 2001 and on BBC 2's* Later . . . with Jools Holland *show.*

Nothing in the Silence * *duet between Isobel and Sarah also recorded for the 2001 Peel session.*

(My Girl's Got) Miraculous Technique * *performed live on virtually every date throughout 2001. Makes reference to the John Peel session they recorded this for in 2001.*

Portland, Oregon * *a Stevie composition performed by the man himself at the Roseland Theater, Portland, September 11, 2001.*

I Took Some Time for Christmas * *jaunty bluegrass tune written by Stuart for Christmas service at Hyndland Parish Church in 2001, and recorded by Belle and Sebastian for the John Peel Christmas special in 2002.*

Ransomed by Tuesday * *delightful early Beatles/Everly Brothers–style fancy from Stevie. Recorded in 2003.*

What follows is a list of all the songs written by Stuart prior to the formation of the group:

1992 (on the piano)
1. There's No Holding Her Back
2. Special K
3. Vitamin Phil
4. Let Orange Juice into Your Life
5. Trick Photography
6. Something in an Envelope

1993 (on the guitar)
1. First Communion
2. Jean Seberg
3. Hurley's Dreaming
4. Quiet Riot Girl
5. Soccer in the New World
6. Safety Valve
7. Powder Blue
8. The Agony Aunt
9. Song for Swinging Teenagers

1994
10. American Schlock
11. T.C.P.

12. Paula and the Passion Play
13. The Olympian Boy
14. Little Hipster Wannabes
15. Domestic Chore
16. I'll Keep It Inside
17. Puch Picnic
18. Learning to Fly
19. Colette and the Mystery Girl
20. I Hope That You Get What You Want
21. Le Pastie de la Bourgeoisie
22. Melanie Voodoo
23. Desperation Made a Fool of Me
24. A Siren for a Boy Beguiled
25. Perfection As a Hipster
26. Lisa Helps the Blind
27. Dear Catastrophe Waitress
28. A Summer Wasting
29. The Disenchanted Pony

1995

30. Your Secrets
31. Puppy Fat
32. Give the Boy a Hand
33. London Has Let Me Down
34. Action Upon Circumstance
35. Should They Teach Dylan in Schools?
36. Dog on Wheels
37. Pocketbook Angels
38. The State I Am In
39. Is She the Ringing in Your Ears?
40. Lord Anthony
41. Belle and Sebastian
42. String Bean Jean
43. I Keep Seeing You Round
44. And It's Sister Song
45. Photo Jenny
46. Stop, Look and Listen
47. Beautiful
48. She's Losing It
49. Put the Book Back on the Shelf

50. Expectations
51. Family Tree
52. Evangelical
53. When the Cynics Stare Back from the Wall
54. Sleep the Clock Around
55. Mary Jo
56. If She Wants Me
57. Your Idea of Fun
58. Rhoda
59. I Don't Love Anyone
60. All Day I Dream About Disco
61. You're Just a Baby
62. We Rule the School
63. Electronic Renaissance
64. I Could Be Dreaming
65. There's a Place I Want to Be

Unfinished
1. The Slow Rocker
2. Heroin Skincare
3. Punk Rock Easy Listener
4. You May As Well Be Dead

As Stuart explains: "Quite a few were recorded or just played into tape, by my-self, or with friends. Names for early projects were such as The Bhangra Girls, Lisa Helps the Blind, and Rhode Island. I started using the name Belle and Sebastian on demos around spring/summer of 1995, I think in time for it to be B&S for the first demo broadcast on radio. ("Le Pastie de la Bourgeoisie" on Peter Easton's *Beat Patrol*, Radio Scotland)

LIVE COVER VERSIONS

A Day in the Life—The Beatles
What Goes On—The Velvet Underground
I'll Be Your Mirror—The Velvet Underground
Reel Around the Fountain—The Smiths
Rowboat—Beck * *sung by Richard*
You Trip Me Up—The Jesus and Mary Chain * *sung by Sarah*
I've Got Something on My Mind—The Left Banke
It's Hard to Be a Jew on Christmas—South Park

More Than a Feeling—Boston * *performed in—yes—Boston, in 1998.*

Poupée De Ceree, Poupée De Son—France Gall/Serge Gainsbourg * *performed several times live by Isobel*

* *NB: The following four songs were performed with Chip Taylor and Evie Sands at Hyndland Parish Church hall on February 3, 1999*

Wild Thing—Chip Taylor/The Troggs * *wild bass solo from Stuart*

Any Way That You Want Me—Chip Taylor/The Troggs

Angel of the Morning—Evie Sands/PP Arnold

I Can't Let Go—Evie Sands

Some Candy Talking—The Jesus and Mary Chain

You Must Believe Me—The Impressions

The Kids Are Alright—The Who

Sympathy for the Devil—The Rolling Stones

Pretty Vacant—The Sex Pistols

The Pink Panther Theme—Henry Mancini

Smooth Operator—Sade

Suspicious Minds—Elvis Presley

Time of the Season—The Zombies

The Sun Has Got His Hat On—Traditional * *sung by Stevie in the style of Elvis Costello*

Love at First Sight—Chick Robertson * *a song written by Neil Robertson's father, no less*

The Boy with the Thorn in His Side—The Smiths

Groovin' With Mr. Bloe—Mr. Bloe

Do Ya Think I'm Sexy?—Rod Stewart

Letter from America—The Proclaimers

BBC Snooker Theme

Dead Flowers—The Rolling Stones

Final Countdown—Europe

No Matter What—Badfinger

Je T'aime . . . Moi Non Plus—Serge Gainsbourg and Jane Birkin

Heroes—David Bowie

Alone Again Or—Love

Don't Stop Me Now—Queen * *performed at the Regent Theatre, Ipswich, July 5, 2001, with Stuart dressed as Freddie Mercury*

Gordon Is a Moron—Jilted John * *performed at the Regent Theatre, Ipswich, July 5, 2001, with Jilted John aka Graham Fellows aka mordant comedy songsmith Brian Appleton, who supported the band on their 2001 English tour*

Oliver's Army—Elvis Costello

Take Me for a Little While—Evie Sands * *performed with Sands at the Wiltern Theater, Los Angeles, September 5, 2001*

Creque Alley—The Mamas and the Papas

Leader of the Pack—The Shangri-Las * *opening song at the Warfield Theater, San Francisco, September 8, 2001, with Stuart entering from the wings on a motorbike*

San Francisco (Be Sure to Wear Flowers in Your Hair)—Scott McKenzie

Billie Jean—Michael Jackson

Turn! Turn! Turn!—The Byrds * *performed on a few occasions, including as the opening song at the Roseland Theater, Portland, September 11, 2001*

Everyday People—Sly and the Family Stone

Crosstown Traffic—Jimi Hendrix

Something on My Mind—The Left Banke

Don't Fear the Reaper—The Blue Oyster Cult

Fool's Gold—The Stone Roses

Baby—Caetano Veloso * *sung by Sarah at the São Paulo Festival, São Paulo, Brazil, October 26, 2001*

She's My Shoo Shoo (A Minhe Menina)—Jorge Ben Jor/Os Mutantes * *sung by Stevie and Stuart on the* Programa do Jô *talk show on Brazilian TV as well as at the São Paulo Festival, October 26, 2001*

Goin' Back—The Byrds/Dusty Springfield

Orangutan—Serge Gainsbourg and Jane Birkin

I Feel Fine—The Beatles

In a Nutshell—Orange Juice

Here Comes the Sun—The Beatles * *performed as a tribute to the recently deceased George Harrison at the COLD charity show at the Queen Margaret Union, Glasgow, December 20, 2001*

Space Oddity—David Bowie

Merry Xmas (War Is Over)—John Lennon

The Boys Are Back in Town—Thin Lizzy

Cool for Cats—Squeeze * *sung by Richard while reading a porn mag at Queen's University, Belfast, December 21, 2001*

I'm Waiting for the Man—The Velvet Underground * *performed with audience member—Barry—at Queen's University, Belfast, December 21, 2001*

Dancing Queen—Abba

Jesus Don't Want Me for a Sunbeam—Traditional * *performed at Vega, Copenhagen, Denmark, March 17, 2002 with support act Eugene Kelly of The Vaselines, whose version of this traditional song was recorded by Nirvana for* MTV Unplugged *in 1994*

You Think You're a Man—The Vaselines/Divine * *performed with Eugene Kelly*

Auld Lang Syne—Robert Burns * *performed with audience member at Cirkus, Stockholm, Sweden, March 19, 2002*

Bohemian Rhapsody—Queen

Another Girl, Another Planet—The Only Ones

Brown-Eyed Girl—Van Morrison

I Am the Resurrection—The Stone Roses * *played as part of a segue with "Legal Man," at the Apollo Theatre, Manchester, April 2, 2002*

Summertime—George Gershwin * *sung by audience member with Bill Wells on piano in Brussels, April 7, 2002*

Sunday Morning—The Velvet Underground

Harley Davidson—Serge Gainsbourg/Brigitte Bardot

Watermelon Man—Herbie Hancock

Canteloupe Island—Herbie Hancock

Happy Birthday—Stevie Wonder

(I Can't Get No) Satisfaction—The Rolling Stones

Green Onions—Booker T. and the MG's

Darlin'—The Beach Boys * *sung by Stevie at the Coachella Festival, California in 2002*

Texarkana Baby—Bob Wills and the Texas Playboys

So You Want to Be a Rock 'n' Roll Star?—The Byrds

The Theme from *Rocky*—Bill Conti * *performed in Rocky's hometown, Philadelphia, in 2002, with a shirtless Stuart sparring with a roadie on stage*

Freak Scene—Dinosaur Jr.

Gigantic—Pixies * *sung with audience member in Boston, May 4, 2002*

Stayin' Alive—The Bee Gees

Touched by Your Presence, Dear—Blondie

Hey, That's No Way to Say Goodbye—Leonard Cohen

Baby Love—The Supremes

Sweet Home Alabama—Lynyrd Skynyrd

The Model—Kraftwerk

Straight A's in Love—Johnny Cash

Lucifer Sam—Pink Floyd

September Gurls—Big Star * *performed live with members of Teenage Fanclub*

Running Away—Sly and the Family Stone

My Little Red Book—Love

Video Killed the Radio Star—Buggles * *performed live in L.A. in 2003 with Trevor "Buggles" Horn*

This Guy's in Love with You—Burt Bacharach/Herb Alpert * *performed by Mick*

Darlin' Be Home Soon—The Lovin' Spoonful

Tighten Up—Archie Bell and the Drells

All Blues—Miles Davis
Cecilia—Simon and Garfunkel
I Want You Back—The Jackson Five
New England—Billy Bragg/Kirsty MacColl
Don't You Want Me—The Human League
California Dreamin'—The Mamas and the Papas
Train from Kansas City—The Shangri-Las *performed in Lawrence, Kansas, November 4, 2003*
Maggie Mae—Rod Stewart
Theme from *Get Carter*—Roy Budd
We Can Work It Out—The Beatles
Vision On/Tony Hart 'Gallery' Theme—Wayne Hill
Like a Prayer—Madonna
Comment Te Dire Adieu—Serge Gainsbourg
Rivers of Babylon—Boney M/The Melodians
Some Other Guy—Ritchie Barrett
Live Forever—Oasis
Sound and Vision—David Bowie
Rock Your Baby—George McCrae
Problem Child—AC/DC
Embarrassment—Madness
Blue Suede Shoes—Carl Perkins/Elvis Presley
Waterloo Sunset—The Kinks
Taxman—The Beatles
Under My Thumb—The Rolling Stones
Linus and Lucy—Vince Guaraldi
Wichita Lineman—Glen Campbell
Sweet Caroline—Neil Diamond

RADIO SESSIONS

Radio I 07/11/1996 for Mark Radcliffe

Judy and the Dream of Horses
Like Dylan in the Movies
The State I Am In
The Stars of Track and Field

* *Show hosted by Radcliffe's holiday stand-in Mark Lamaar.*

297

Radio I 12/02/1996 for Mark Radcliffe

I Could Be Dreaming
Seeing Other People * *slower version*
We Rule the School
This Is Just a Modern Rock Song

Radio I 02/08/1997 for the Evening Session

Seymour Stein
Lazy Line Painter Jane * *without Monica Queen*
Sleep the Clock Around
Slow Graffiti

Black Sessions 10/05/1998 recorded at Studio Charles Trenet, Paris

The Boy Done Wrong Again
Dog on Wheels
Paper Boat
Seeing Other People
A Century of Fakers
I Know Where the Summer Goes
Mayfly
The Wrong Girl
Dirty Dream Number Two
Poupée De Cire, Poupée De Son * *France Gall/Serge Gainsbourg cover sung by Isobel*
Slow Graffiti
I Don't Love Anyone
Sleep the Clock Around

*Also broadcast in part on French TV.

Radio I 2001 for John Peel

Shoot the Sexual Athlete
Magic of a Kind Word
Nothing in the Silence
(My Girl's Got) Miraculous Technique

Radio I 07/25/2002 recorded at Peel Acres for John Peel

You Don't Send Me
Roy Walker
Love on the March

Asleep on a Sunbeam
Desperation Made a Fool of Me

* Recorded at Peel's home, with Chris stationed in the bathroom and Mick on the stairs. All assembled sing "Happy Birthday" to Richard. Because it was his birthday.

Radio 1 12/18/2002 for John Peel

O Come All Ye Faithful
Christmas Time Is Here—Vince Guaraldi
Santa Claus—The Sonics
Step into My Office, Baby
Jonathan David
Santa Claus, Go Straight to the Ghetto—James Brown * *sung by Chris*
Photo Jenny
Silent Night
O Little Town of Bethlehem— **jazz version*
Santa Bring My Baby Back to Me—Elvis Presley **sung by Stevie*
If You Find Yourself Caught in Love
The Boy with the Arab Strap
O Come, O Come Emmanuel * *with Tracyanne Campbell from Camera Obscura*
Get Me Away from Here, I'm Dying
I Took Some Time for Christmas
The Twelve Days of Christmas

* The group were joined on the traditional material by a enthusiastically lusty choir. The quiet, almost a capella section at the end of "The Boy with the Arab Strap" is botched by someone—Stuart? Chris?—accidentally turning on a keyboard backing track, and Richard parlays some disconcertingly convincing bird noises during a manic take on "The Twelve Days of Christmas."

KCRW 08/26/2003 for the *Morning Becomes Eclectic* show

There's Too Much Love
Step into My Office, Baby
Scooby Driver * *noticeably rearranged version*
I Believe in Travelling Light
The State I Am In * *Stuart falters at start, sings "Sears and Roebuck" instead of "Marks and Spencers" and "L.A. buses" instead of "city buses"*
Judy and the Dream of Horses * *extended Velvets-like outro*
Expectations

* Stevie painstakingly introduces the group and string section by name after Stuart backs out of the task. "Sorry, I'm just not quite awake yet," he yawns. "One of the things that has remained constant is the sound of the band," states the host Nic Harcourt. "Maybe from your perspective," replies Stuart, bridling somewhat. Shaky handheld footage of this session exists on the Web if you care to search for it.

XFM 12/2003 for Zoe Ball
Step into My Office, Baby
Stay Loose

* Hosted by Ball's stand-in Lauren Laverne.

Japanese radio session 2004
Piazza, New York Catcher
I'm a Cuckoo ** first verse sung in Japanese, this version appearing on the Japanese edition of the* Books *EP*

* Just Stuart, Stevie, and Bob. Stuart claims to be in the middle of an Internet chess game during the interview.

Virgin Radio 02/14/2004 for The Edge Session
Ransomed by Tuesday
I'm a Cuckoo

Virgin Radio 02/15/2004 for Razor Cuts
Your Secrets

Virgin Radio 02/17/2004 for Claire Sturgess
Step into My Office, Baby
I'm a Cuckoo
Stay Loose

* The versions of "Step into My Office, Baby" and "Stay Loose" were repeated from the December 2003 Zoe Ball XFM session. The version of "I'm a Cuckoo" was recorded that day at Ca Va.

Radio 2 02/17/2004 for Janice Long
Stop, Look and Listen
(I Believe in) Travellin' Light
I'm a Cuckoo

Radio 2 02/26/2004 for Stuart Maconie

Step into My Office, Baby

Get Me Away from Here, I'm Dying

Acoustic set featuring just Stuart, Stevie, Sarah, and Bobby.

KEXP 05/05/2004 for Stevie Zoom

If She Wants Me

Step into My Office, Baby

Teenage Kicks * *impromptu version*

Get Me Away from Here, I'm Dying

Acoustic set featuring whole band sans Bobby who, according to Stuart, is absent because he got his "thumb caught in a bra-strap." When asked what their plans are, Stuart replies, "To continue our unassailable rise to the top." Richard also claims he's hankering after a Tommy Lee–style revolving drum cage.

Radio 2 06/19/2004 for Jonathan Ross

I'm a Cuckoo

3PBS FM

Step into My Office, Baby

I'm a Cuckoo

Like Dylan in the Movies

Problem Child—AC/DC

Radio I John Peel Tribute 12/16/2004 hosted by Steve Lamacq

I Took a Long Hard Look

Frog in My Throat

Meat and Potatoes

TELEVISION APPEARANCES

Don't Look Down, **short STV documentary broadcast 1997**

As featured on the Fans Only *DVD, although sans Stevie's segment, which had to be removed following copyright problems with the Nilsson song used in the background.*

Sessions at West Fifty-fourth in 1998 [unbroadcast]

* A live session for New York television remained unbroadcast as the network deemed the performance "unsatisfactory." Stuart read most of the lyrics from a vinyl copy of If You're Feeling Sinister supplied by a member of the audience. Version of "Like Dylan in the Movies" (mostly dubbed by the studio version) appears on the Fans Only DVD.

The Story of Belle and Sebastian documentary broadcast 02/02/1999 for BBC2

* This half-hour documentary was directed by Duglas T. Stewart of The BMX Bandits and features interview with Richard Colburn, Mick Cooke, Stuart David, Chris Geddes, Mark Radcliffe, and Alan Rankine.

The Apocalypse Tube broadcast 11/1999 for Sky TV
The Loneliness of a Middle Distance Runner

Top of the Pops 06/01/2000 for BBC 1
Legal Man * *mimed*

Later... with Jools Holland 11/30/2002 for BBC 2
Magic of a Kind Word
I'm Waking Up to Us
The Boy with the Arab Strap

* The band were extremely unhappy with the sound recording, having trusted themselves to the BBC engineers rather than their usual crew. Isobel orates a brief spoken word passage in the middle of "I'm Waking Up to Us," which doesn't appear on the recorded version.

Late Night with Conan O'Brien 04/26/2002 for NBC
I'm Waking Up to Us

* There is a dialogue clip on Storytelling, which references O'Brien.

Programa do Jô 10/24/2002 for TV Globo
Wandering Alone

* The host, Jô Soares, forced Mick to play his trumpet during the interview, a clip cut from the version found on the Fans Only DVD.

Artworks Scotland—Alasdair Gray documentary 11/14/2004 for BBC 1

* A tribute to the great Scottish writer, painter, and political activist featuring contributions from Stuart.

John Peel Tribute 11/06/2004 for BBC 2

* Stuart is interviewed reminiscing about Peel.

MUSIC VIDEOS

Dog on Wheels directed by Karn David

* Filmed mainly on Byres Road Glasgow, including shots in Stephen Pastel's now defunct bookshop. Also features V-Twin graffiti and Stuart spraying "Le Pastie de la Bourgeoisie" on a wall. The naughty scamp.

Lazy Line Painter Jane directed by Karn David

* Starring Stuart David's sister, Karla Black. Features group performing song in church hall with Monica Queen.

A Century of Fakers directed by Stuart Murdoch, assisted by Karn David

* Features shot of band mooching outside the Halt Bar.

Is It Wicked Not to Care? directed by Isobel Campbell, filmed by Karn David

* Isobel is seen reading The Lion, the Witch, and the Wardrobe *by Stuart's favorite author C. S. Lewis.*

Dirty Dream Number Two directed by Lance Bangs

* Filmed around the Portland area and starring a multitude of Belle and Sebastian fans, many from the Sinister *mailing list.*

This Is Just a Modern Rock Song directed by Sarah Martin

* Starring Rozanne Suarez and Sara Mansoori. Suarez was part of the short-lived Maisonettes concept along with Sarah and Isobel, and features on the cover of the Legal Man *single as well as in the* Wrong Girl *video as Stevie's Dylan-loving paramour. She also appeared with the band performing "Legal Man" on* Top of the Pops.

The Wrong Girl directed by Stevie Jackson and Lance Bangs

* As well as Stevie, the video features brief cameos from Stuart and Katrina House, along with Sarah and Norman Blake from Teenage Fanclub as Stevie's parents, plus Tracyanne Campbell and John Henderson from Camera Obscura. Stevie's then girlfriend Adrienne Payne plays "The Nurse" and also features on the cover of Legal Man.

Legal Man directed by Isobel Campbell

* Filmed on location at Glasgow University student union. Neil can be glimpsed frugging in the crowd.

Jonathan David directed by Gavin Gordon-Rogers

* The girl at the apex of Stuart and Stevie's love triangle is played by one Carmen Pieraccini.

Step into My Office, Baby directed by Graham Linehan

* Linehan is one of the cowriters of the famous U.K. sitcom and Belle and Sebastian fave, Father Ted.

I'm a Cuckoo directed by Stuart Murdoch and Blair Young

* Apart from Stuart and a brief appearance from the group, the video also stars Shantha Roberts, cover star of both Dear Catastrophe Waitress *and the* I'm a Cuckoo *EP. It also features a brief cameo from Stuart David's brother and fellow Looper, Ronnie Black. Codirector Blair Young was also responsible for compiling the* Fans Only *DVD. Video available on the first of the* I'm a Cuckoo *multi-pack singles.*

Stop, Look and Listen directed by Stuart Murdoch

* A photo gallery/video hybrid featuring appearances from Neil and Katrina and Ciara MacLaverty.

Wrapped Up in Books directed by Stuart Murdoch and Blair Young

* *Filmed in Caledonian Books, Glasgow, and starring the group alongside Alexandra Klobouk (who appears on the EP cover) and Gisela Hans.*

DVD

Fans Only

* *Compiled and directed by Blair Young,* Fans Only *is an exhaustive, beautifully detailed, and entertaining gift featuring virtually all of the footage detailed above and more. Undoubtedly one of the very best music DVDs currently on the market.*

ABOUT THE AUTHOR

Paul Whitelaw is a music/arts writer based in Glasgow, Scotland. Since 2001 he has worked as the music editior at *Metro,* one of the United Kingdom's most popular newsapers. His work has also appeared in *The Scotsman, Scotland on Sunday, Melody Maker,* and *NME.*